Structural Injustice and Workers' Rights

OXFORD LABOUR LAW

Series Editors: Professor Alan Bogg (University of Bristol Law School), Professor Anne Davies (University of Oxford, Faculty of Law), Professor Keith Ewing (School of Law, King's College London), and Mark Freedland (University of Oxford, Faculty of Law).

The *Oxford Labour Law* series (formerly known as the *Oxford Monographs on Labour Law* series) has come to represent a significant contribution to the literature of British, European, and international labour law. The series recognizes the arrival not only of a renewed interest in labour law generally, but also the need for fresh approaches to the study of labour law following a period of momentous change in the UK and Europe. The series is concerned with all aspects of collective labour law and individual employment law, including the growing role of human rights and discrimination in employment. It is concerned also with the influence of politics and economics in shaping labour law, as well as the importance of legal theory and international labour standards. Recent titles address developments in multiple jurisdictions.

ALSO AVAILABLE IN THE SERIES

Reforming Age Discrimination Law
Beyond Individual Enforcement
Alysia Blackham

Putting Human Rights to Work
Labour Law, The ECHR, and The Employment Relation
Philippa Collins

Strike Ballots, Democracy, and Law
Breen Creighton, Catrina Denvir,
Richard Johnstone, Shae McCrystal,
Alice Orchiston

Living Wage
Regulatory Solutions to Informal and
Precarious Work in Global Supply Chains
Shelley Marshall

A Purposive Approach to Labour Law
Guy Davidov

Structural Injustice and Workers' Rights

VIRGINIA MANTOUVALOU

OXFORD
UNIVERSITY PRESS

OXFORD
UNIVERSITY PRESS

Great Clarendon Street, Oxford, OX2 6DP,
United Kingdom

Oxford University Press is a department of the University of Oxford.
It furthers the University's objective of excellence in research, scholarship,
and education by publishing worldwide. Oxford is a registered trade mark of
Oxford University Press in the UK and in certain other countries

First Edition published in 2023

Published in the United States of America by Oxford University Press
198 Madison Avenue, New York, NY 10016, United States of America

British Library Cataloguing in Publication Data

Data available

Library of Congress Control Number: 2023931428

ISBN 978–0–19–285715–6

DOI: 10.1093/oso/9780192857156.001.0001

Printed and bound in the UK by
CPI Group (UK) Ltd, Croydon, CR0 4YY

General Editors' Preface

There is an enduring view of the conceptual framework of labour law. It is based upon recognition of inequality of bargaining power between employers and workers. The function of labour law is to ameliorate that inequality through facilitating collective bargaining and enforcing labour standards. The employer is the bearer of duties, and the employee is the bearer of rights. The state stands ready to intervene where those rights are violated, but otherwise it must hold the ring and defer to the parties' private ordering. Diffidence about the state was unusually strong in the British tradition, given the influence of Otto Kahn-Freund's theory of collective laissez-faire. In different ways, over the last four decades a rich body of scholarship repositioned the state back at the centre of labour law theory and practice.

In this important work, Professor Mantouvalou contributes to this genre of scholarship and presents a new theoretical challenge to diffidence about the state's role in British labour law. Drawing upon theories of structural injustice in political philosophy, she identifies the myriad ways in which the state, through its creation of the background legal rules across many legal fields, underwrites the conditions of vulnerability for workers. In so doing, the state is deeply implicated in practices of exploitation. Drawing upon a rich set of examples from migrant workers, labour in penal detention, workfare regimes, and non-standard precarious work, she further suggests that the state occupies a morally ambiguous space. Often, it provides the *ex ante* legal tools to employers to engage in very serious forms of exploitation, perpetrated against the most precarious and disadvantaged in society. At the same time, it half-heartedly provides *ex post* mechanisms to workers and trade unions to challenge the injustice that it has itself enabled through legal rules. The structural injustice perspective exposes the moral duplicity of the state. It also highlights the inadequacy of legal techniques that enforce duties against an employer in a bilateral relation to an employee. Unless the laws that enable and empower exploiters are challenged, labour law serves to conceal the root causes of exploitation.

The monograph offers a bold and emancipatory vision of labour law. Professor Mantouvalou brings her deep expertise of human rights law to bear on developing progressive legal responses to structural injustice. The promise of human rights law, and in particular the role of positive duties, is to engage governments and other public agencies in reform of the wider legal framework. It stands in a line of scholarship which, like the 'law of the labour market', challenges labour lawyers to look beyond labour law to other compartments of the law. It also provides a compelling and elegant theoretical underpinning to 'labour rights as human rights'. The editors are delighted to welcome this important work to the series.

Acknowledgements

I would not have been able to complete this book without a British Academy Mid-Career Fellowship, and I am deeply grateful for this support.

I have had opportunities to present drafts to many audiences at different stages of the development of this project, including the University of Birkbeck Criminology Seminar Series; the Law and Philosophy Colloquium at Pompeu Fabra University in Barcelona; the Toronto Legal Theory Workshop; the University of Glasgow Human Rights Network; a University of Haifa conference on prison labour; the University of Southampton Annual Lecture of the Stefan Cross Centre for Women, Equality and Law; the London Labour Law Discussion Group; a Queen's University Canada conference on the foundations of labour law; a labour law seminar at the Hebrew University; a panel discussion of the Democratizing Work project; a Université Libre de Bruxelles workshop on zero-hours contracts; a seminar on labour and welfare law and a TraffLab panel at Tel Aviv University; and a MANCEPT conference in political theory. Many thanks are due to colleagues who invited me to present and commented on drafts, and particularly Einat Albin, Kevin Banks, Adelle Blackett, Guy Davidov, Elise Dermine, Isabelle Ferreras, Iñigo González Ricoy, Lord Hendy, Yingru Li, Amy Ludlow, Amaury Mechelynck, Faina Milman-Sivan, Guy Mundlak, Amir Paz-Fuchs, Megan Pearson, Jahel Queralt, Yair Sagy, Hila Shamir, Jacki Silbermann, Malcolm Thorburn, Sabine Tsuruda, Sappho Xenakis, and many others who participated and engaged in this context. My time as Visiting Professor at the Université Libre de Bruxelles was also very beneficial. I also gained a lot from participating in a workshop on 'Structural Injustice', convened by Jude Browne and Maeve McKeown at the University of Cambridge, and from discussions with Sally Haslanger and Robin West.

In addition to his ongoing friendship, Hugh Collins read early drafts and a full final draft. I am especially grateful for that and for the many times he has listened to me, raised questions, and encouraged me. Harry Arthurs has been a constructive and critical reader of aspects of my work for many years now, and I owe a lot to him too. I am also deeply thankful to Alan Bogg, Elaine Genders, Marija Jovanovic, Hadassa Noorda, Natalie Sedacca, Dean Spielmann, Jonathan Wolff, and Lea Ypi for detailed and insightful comments on draft chapters. Many other friends have discussed with me the ideas and encouraged me, each in different ways. Special mention should be made of Nicos Alivizatos, Joe Atkinson, Jackie Brown, Nicola Countouris, Hitesh Dhorajiwala, Michael Ford, Eleni Frantziou, Nicholas Hatzis, Devika Hovell, Ronan McCrea, Colm O'Cinneide, Konstantinos Papageorgiou, Tom Poole, Philip Rawlings, and Inga Thiemann. Danielle Worden was an excellent editorial assistant during the final stages of the project.

I have been very fortunate to work at UCL. I am grateful to the Law Faculty Deans and Dean's teams who have supported my work with generosity and in countless ways over the years. Presenting drafts at UCL staff seminars provided real intellectual stimulation, as did endless discussions with colleagues, doctoral researchers, postgraduate and undergraduate students, and colleagues at the Institute for Law, Politics and Philosophy. I also benefited enormously from discussions at a conference supported by the UCL Faculty of Laws, on 'Structural Injustice and the Law', which I co-organised with Jonathan Wolff. An outline of the ideas was also presented at my Inaugural Lecture at UCL in December 2019, and was subsequently published in my article 'Structural Injustice and the Human Rights of Workers' (2020) 73 Current Legal Problems 59. Moreover, parts of Chapter 5 draw on my article 'Welfare-to-Work, Structural Injustice, and Human Rights', which was published in (2020) 83 Modern Law Review 929, and parts of Chapter 6 on my paper 'Welfare-to-Work, Zero-Hours Contracts and Human Rights', which was published in a special issue on zero-hours contracts in (2022) 13 European Labour Law Journal 431. I am grateful to the journal editors and anonymous referees for comments on these papers. While working on this book, I also published blog posts illustrating some of the issues that I identified along the way. Thanks are due to the editors of the *Beyond Slavery and Trafficking Blog*, the *LSE Politics and Policy Blog*, the *Verfassungsblog*, my co-editors of the *UK Labour Law Blog*, as well as the *Made at UCL* podcast. Over the years I have learned a lot in my capacity as Trustee of Kalayaan, the main UK NGO working on the rights of migrant domestic workers, and I am thankful for that, as well as many discussions with Kate Roberts of Focus on Labour Exploitation.

The OUP Series Editors Alan Bogg, Anne Davies, Keith Ewing, and Mark Freedland have been enthusiastic about this project from the beginning, and I also greatly benefited from comments by three anonymous referees on my proposal and draft papers.

I would not have been able to write this book without George Letsas who has been there for me over many years in more ways than I can enumerate here, and the love and support of Yiannis Mantouvalos (1947–2017), Mary and Katerina Mantouvalou, Ross, and Nina.

Contents

Table of Cases

UNITED KINGDOM

EUROPEAN UNION

GERMANY

ISRAEL

SOUTH AFRICA

UNITED STATES

INTERNATIONAL JUDGMENTS

European Court of Human Rights

European Committee of Social Rights

Inter-American Court of Human Rights

United Nations Human Rights Committee

Table of Legislation

List of Abbreviations

ACHR	American Convention on Human Rights
ACLU	American Civil Liberties Union
CESCR	Committee on Economic, Social and Cultural Rights
CJEU	Court of Justice of the European Union
ECHR	Convention for the Protection of Human Rights and Fundamental Freedoms
ECSR	European Committee of Social Rights
ECtHR	European Court of Human Rights
ERA 1996	Employment Rights Act 1996
ESC	European Social Charter
EU	European Union
EUCFR	Charter of Fundamental Rights of the European Union
FLEX	Focus on Labour Exploitation
FLSA	Federal Labor Standards Act (US)
GRETA	Group of Experts Against Trafficking in Human Beings
HRC	UN Human Rights Committee
ICCPR	International Covenant on Civil and Political Rights
ICESCR	International Covenant on Economic, Social and Cultural Rights
ILO	International Labour Organization
IPEC	International Programme on the Elimination of Child Labour
JRF	Joseph Rowntree Foundation
NGO	non-governmental organisation
ODW	Overseas Domestic Worker
Rev ESC	European Social Charter (revised)
SAP FL	ILO Special Action Programme to Combat Forced Labour
TULCRA	Trade Union and Labour Relations (Consolidation) Act 1992
UK	United Kingdom
UNESCO	United Nations Educational, Scientific and Cultural Organization

PART I

WHAT IS STRUCTURAL INJUSTICE?

1
Introduction
Structural Injustice and Workers' Rights

What is the role of the law in relation to the treatment of the most vulnerable workers in society? How does it affect those who are often in a position of disadvantage for reasons such as race, gender, or poverty, and who may sometimes also not be unionised or otherwise represented in politics or in the workplace? Many will think that there are two main responses to these questions. On the one hand, there are general rules of private law, such as property and contract law. These are grounded on a particular conception of private property and contractual freedom. They constitute market relations and regulate interpersonal transactions. They do not protect individuals against social injustices such as workplace exploitation. Instead, people who are advantaged because of their wealth and education can continue to gain further advantages from these rules, whereas the least advantaged cannot easily escape patterns of disadvantage. These rules permit or help to construct structures of injustice.

On the other hand, areas of law such as labour law and social security law intervene to protect workers and others from market powers and reduce their disadvantage. Labour law achieves this by providing for entitlements and protections such as a minimum wage, protection of working time, and trade union rights. Its fundamental purpose is to help address inequality at work and set limits to the power of the employer to exploit workers. Social security law, in turn, creates a framework that aims to provide a social safety net for people when they are in need and cannot provide for themselves.

Yet, what we observe upon closer inspection is that, at times, particular provisions in these and other areas of law that regulate labour establish the background conditions for vulnerable people to be exploited. Instead of strengthening the rights of workers, these laws create opportunities for those who have advantages to exploit those who are in a position of disadvantage by making them more vulnerable than they might otherwise be. In this way, structures of injustice are created, maintained, and increased. As these patterns

Structural Injustice and Workers' Rights. Virginia Mantouvalou, Oxford University Press. © Virginia Mantouvalou 2023.
DOI: 10.1093/oso/9780192857156.003.0001

multiply, workers find it all the more difficult to escape them for there are fewer opportunities to obtain work of good quality.

I will illustrate this with Toni's story. Toni was raised in social housing, and had few education and employment opportunities. She took on low-paid temporary jobs in the caring industry through an employment agency. Even though she was paid the minimum wage for her work, the hours were patchy and travel time between jobs was not paid. She also found some of her client interactions upsetting and discriminatory. Agency workers are entitled to the national minimum wage in the United Kingdom, but legal rules exclude them from discrimination law and other labour rights while at work because they are viewed as being in a contractual relationship only with the agency, rather than the end user.[1]

Independently of the employment agency, Toni decided to find better work as she wanted a more stable income. While looking for work, she had to claim social benefits in order to pay her rent but was informed that to be eligible for social support, she had to apply for a number of jobs per month. If she did not, her benefits would be cut. The vacancies for which she was asked to apply included agency work. Toni explained that she did not want to work through an agency because of her past experience, but she was told that she had to apply because this work was suitable for her. Toni could not sustain herself without work or social support. She therefore started over again by applying for agency and other non-standard work. Toni's status was already precarious because of her gender, race, and background of poverty, and she found herself in a pattern of disadvantage from which she could not escape. Not only did rules of employment, discrimination, and welfare law not protect her, but some of these rules explicitly excluded agency workers like her from their scope, compounding her disadvantage.

In this book I examine legal rules regulating labour which set up the conditions for disadvantaged people like Toni to be exploited at work. I consider laws that affect migrant workers who work in challenging sectors such as domestic work and agriculture, under restrictive visa conditions; undocumented workers who are denied protection because they work under an illegal employment contract; working prisoners and other offenders as well as immigration detainees who are not viewed as working under an employment contract; rules on those working through social security schemes on welfare-to-work who may face serious sanctions if they do not accept exploitative work; and other

[1] See *James v Greenwich Borough Council* [2008] EWCA Civ 35. This issue is discussed further in Chapter 6.

rules affecting workers in non-standard employment relations, such as agency workers and workers in zero-hours contracts.

These rules may have an appearance of legitimacy. They cannot be viewed typically as intentionally harmful. The authorities tend to put forward justifications that are not immoral or illegal. What emerges when inspecting the rules and their effects more closely, though, is that instead of helping strengthen workers' bargaining power and addressing the inequality that is inherent in the employment relation, they increase workers' vulnerability. Disadvantaged workers find it harder to obtain better jobs, for they face pressures through these legal rules, while the number of precarious jobs is increasing. These rules contribute to the clustering of disadvantage.[2] Structures of exploitation are created and sustained, and the law has a major role to play.

Can legal rules also help destabilise these structures by challenging state action that places precarious workers in this situation? To address this question, I examine the role of workers' rights. When I refer to workers' rights, I do not mean rights that are protected in ordinary legislation: we saw that ordinary legislation sometimes excludes these workers who are also often not unionised or represented politically. My focus instead is on workers' rights as protected in human rights law.[3] Human rights law usually operates on a higher level than ordinary legislation and can be used to challenge the exclusion of disadvantaged workers from protection. My aim is to assess the extent to which courts and other bodies that monitor compliance with human rights obligations can hold state authorities accountable for their role in increasing the vulnerability of workers, making them particularly prone to exploitation at work.

Human rights law was traditionally developed to address state responsibility. For this reason, it may serve a useful role when attempting to hold the state accountable for the structures of injustice that increase workers' vulnerability to workplace exploitation and that are the subject of this study. As human rights law encapsulates abstract principles, it can develop to address changing social conditions, including the legal rules that constitute sources of exploitation. The rights that are at stake include the right to private life; the right to work; the prohibition of slavery, servitude, forced, and compulsory labour; the prohibition of discrimination; and the right to a subsistence minimum. These protections

[2] Jonathan Wolff and Avner de-Shalit, *Disadvantage* (OUP 2007).

[3] Literature on workers' rights as human rights includes Philip Alston (ed), *Labour Rights as Human Rights* (OUP 2005); Colin Fenwick and Tonia Novitz, *Human Rights at Work* (Hart 2010); Virginia Leary, 'The Paradox of Workers' Rights as Human Rights' in Lance Compa and Stephen Diamond (eds), *Human Rights, Labour Rights and International Trade* (University of Pennsylvania Press 2003) 22; Virginia Mantouvalou, 'Are Labour Rights Human Rights?' (2012) 3 European Labour Law Journal 151.

are found in legal documents at both national and international level,[4] and are monitored by a variety of mechanisms, primarily courts, but also expert committees, commissioners, rapporteurs, and so on.[5]

By considering the role of human rights law in addressing the structures of injustice that affect these disadvantaged workers, I do not claim that this is the only way in which the problem can be addressed. I also do not argue that human rights law can tackle all instances of workplace exploitation that I describe, as the causes of structural injustice are multiple and the power of human rights monitoring bodies has limits. However, I propose that human rights law can provide important tools to scrutinise state action that creates vulnerability, and may have a particularly useful role to play for workers who are not represented in politics and are not unionised. It can help challenge unjust structures by identifying problematic rules and by imposing on legislatures an urgent requirement to amend these.

Book Structure

The book is divided into three parts and is organised as follows. The first part consists of the present chapter and Chapter 2, where I introduce the problem and situate it in the theoretical framework of 'state-mediated structures of injustice'. I develop this framework on the basis of Iris Marion Young's account of structural injustice.[6] The purpose of this theoretical framework is to centre on the role of the state as a powerful actor and explain that in certain instances of injustice at work the issue is not one of 'a few bad apples', namely a few unscrupulous employers that take advantage of vulnerable workers. It is a systemic problem for which the state is responsible.[7] The wrong in question arises when state authorities enact rules which regulate labour that have an appearance of legitimacy but increase the vulnerability that already exists in the employment relation of large numbers of people. These legal rules place many workers in

[4] Legal documents that I discuss include international and regional human rights treaties, as well as some examples from national human rights documents and Constitutions.

[5] Monitoring bodies that I discuss include the European Court of Human Rights, the Inter-American Court of Human Rights, International Labour Organization monitoring bodies, the United Nations Special Rapporteur on Extreme Poverty and Human Rights, as well as courts from national legal orders.

[6] Iris Marion Young, *Responsibility for Justice* (OUP 2011).

[7] Other literature that examines structural injustice and explores the role of the state and other powerful agents in this context includes the book by Madison Powers and Ruth Faden, *Structural Injustice: Power, Advantage, and Human Rights* (OUP 2019). For an excellent discussion of recent literature on the topic, see Maeve McKeown, 'Structural Injustice' (2021) 16 Philosophy Compass 1.

a position of disadvantage, while other actors take advantage of this vulnerability and systematically benefit from this situation.

Chapters 3 to 6 constitute the second part of the book, where I examine specific categories of disadvantaged workers and demonstrate through examples how the law increases their vulnerability to exploitation by excluding them from important protections. These chapters also refer to empirical evidence that shows the effects of these rules on the workers that are excluded from protective norms. In presenting the problem, I often discuss the legal framework and evidence regarding its effects on workers' rights in the United Kingdom, but I also draw on other industrialised countries.

Chapter 3 considers the treatment of migrant workers. It is well known that certain categories of migrant workers in low-paid sectors, such as domestic work and agriculture, are exploited and ill-treated. Many blame unethical employers for this treatment but this analysis is misleading. The chapter instead examines restrictive visa schemes that make workers vulnerable, as well as legal rules applying to undocumented workers.[8] These legal rules may have an appearance of legitimacy as an acceptable exercise of state sovereignty, but we see that they constitute a source of workers' vulnerability and a major cause of workplace exploitation.

Chapter 4 turns to people working in captivity: working prisoners, those on unpaid work as a community sentence, and those in immigration detention. Legal rules exclude these workers from several protective norms. For instance, working prisoners in some countries are excluded from the right to form trade unions, from minimum wage and social security rights, and they are regularly underpaid. For many, these legal rules may appear to be justified for reasons such as the reduction of public spending on running detention facilities or the prevention of disorder in prison. Yet, we observe that they create structures of exploitation from which the state and private entities benefit by cutting costs and making a profit. Both the state and private entities, which run prisons, unpaid work as a community sentence, and detention centres all exploit the situation. There is a continuum of exploitation of those working in all these settings associated with criminal justice and immigration controls, and this is created by law.

Chapter 5 turns to welfare conditionality rules, namely schemes that impose obligations on individuals to seek and accept work on the basis that otherwise

[8] See Bridget Anderson, 'Immigration, Migration Controls, and the Fashioning of Precarious Work' (2010) 24 Work Employment and Society 300; Cathryn Costello and Mark Freedland (eds), *Migrants at Work* (OUP 2014).

they will be sanctioned by losing access to welfare support and may face homelessness and destitution. The schemes are often presented as the best route out of poverty. Nonetheless, there is evidence that legal rules enacting particularly punitive systems force those who are poor and disadvantaged into non-standard, precarious work, such as agency work and zero-hours contracts, and in conditions of in-work poverty. They turn the unemployed poor into working and exploited poor. Because schemes with strict conditionality force people to work in these conditions, further structures of exploitation are created and sustained, becoming increasingly widespread and routine.

Chapter 6 examines in more detail some of the most precarious forms of non-standard work. It considers problems created by legal rules in relation to those employed through agencies and those working under zero-hours contracts. These working arrangements are typically presented as useful for employers and workers for they are said to provide flexibility.[9] However, we observe that when looking at the employment status of these people and the legal rights that are grounded on it, legal rules exclude some workers from labour law protections, placing them in a position of vulnerability to exploitation. Workers in these jobs are regularly exploited, and labour protective norms offer little by way of protection.

When referring to workplace exploitation, governments and other actors typically deploy a rhetoric of personal responsibility. They place attention on employers who take advantage of workers, or on workers who choose these arrangements. On this account, the responsibility of the state is to address the harm inflicted by private actors, with a primary focus on the deployment of criminal law to punish the worst kinds of exploitation.[10] However, by considering these examples of disadvantaged and marginalised workers in Chapters 3 to 6, it emerges that we are often not simply faced with isolated instances of unscrupulous employers or with individual workers who opt for flexible work arrangements. Focus on individual responsibility is, therefore, insufficient when dealing with structures of exploitation for it obscures a major source of the wrong. By scrutinising legal rules that create vulnerability, we see that the state is responsible for the situation. The state also has the power to rectify these

[9] 'Good Work: Taylor Review of Modern Working Practices' (July 2017) 14, and see further the report's chapter 6. For a critique of the report, see Katie Bales, Alan Bogg, and Tonia Novitz, '"Voice" and "Choice" in Modern Working Practices: Problems with the Taylor Review' (2018) 47 Industrial Law Journal 46.

[10] See the discussion in Virginia Mantouvalou, 'The Modern Slavery Act Three Years On' (2018) 81 Modern Law Review 1017. For further critical discussion of the modern slavery agenda, see Emily Kenway, *The Truth About Modern Slavery* (Pluto Press 2021) and Genevieve LeBaron, *Combatting Modern Slavery: Why Labour Governance is Failing and What We Can Do About It* (Polity Press 2020).

legal rules and destabilise the unjust structures. It has political responsibility to do this because of the role that it has played in creating or entrenching them. It may also have legal responsibility to do so.

Can human rights law assign state responsibility for some of these legal rules? Chapters 7 and 8, which constitute the third part of the book, turn to this task by examining how human rights law can challenge their supposed justification and hold the state accountable for its treatment of disadvantaged workers. Chapter 7 introduces the role of human rights law in this context and discusses how it can challenge legal rules that regulate migrant workers and captive workers. Chapter 8 turns to those in welfare-to-work schemes and precarious work. Many human rights provisions are at stake: the legal rules that are a source of exploitation for many of these workers can be viewed as a breach of the prohibition of forced and compulsory labour, the right to fair and just working conditions, the right to private life, the right to health and safety at work, the right to form and join a trade union, and the prohibition of discrimination. When considering the role of human rights law, my attention is primarily on the Council of Europe's European Convention on Human Rights,[11] which is an established and influential regional system. I also use examples from other institutions and documents, including the European Social Charter,[12] the EU Charter of Fundamental Rights,[13] the International Labour Organization Declaration of Fundamental Principles and Rights at Work,[14] the United Nations International Covenant on Civil and Political Rights,[15] the International Covenant on Economic, Social and Cultural Rights,[16] and the Organization of American States American Convention on Human Rights,[17] as well as some national legal orders.

In these chapters, I find that human rights law can assign state responsibility for certain legal rules that are connected to the unjust treatment on which I focus, and can help address some of the problems that are the subject of this

[11] Convention for the Protection of Human Rights and Fundamental Freedoms (ETS No 005), adopted on 4 November 1950, entered into force on 3 September 1953 (hereafter ECHR).

[12] European Social Charter (revised) (ETS No 163), opened for signature 3 May 1996, entered into force on 1 July 1999 (hereafter Rev ESC). The original text of the ESC (ETS No 35) was adopted on 18/10/1961 and entered into force on 26 February 1965.

[13] Charter of Fundamental Rights of the European Union (2000/C 364/01), adopted on 18 December 2000, entered into force in December 2009 (hereafter EUCFR).

[14] International Labour Organization Declaration of Fundamental Principles and Rights at Work, adopted in 1998, amended in 2022.

[15] International Covenant on Civil and Political Rights, General Assembly Resolution 2200A (XXI), adopted on 16 December 1966, entered into force on 23 March 1976 (hereafter ICCPR).

[16] International Covenant on Economic, Social and Cultural Rights, General Assembly Resolution 2200A (XXI), adopted on 16 December 1966, entered into force on 3 January 1976 (hereafter ICESCR).

[17] American Convention on Human Rights, adopted on 22 November 1969, entered into force on 18 July 1978 (hereafter ACHR).

book. It has legal force that can require political actors to bring about change; it also has moral force that motivates a variety of actors to press for broader structural change. I argue that both the overall structures and parts of these structures may give rise to responsibility for human rights violations and that these rules must change to meet states' human rights obligations. Human rights law cannot address all aspects of workplace exploitation of course. However, it can be a powerful tool. Employing it in the context of the structures that I discuss can help identify and challenge unjust rules, and motivate legal, cultural, and structural change.

2

Structures of Injustice at Work

The contract of employment is not like other contracts.[1] The economic structure of the labour market entails that employees have weaker bargaining power than employers. The more unregulated the market is, the weaker the power of the employee. Most of the time, the harm of exploitation in these circumstances is directly caused by the employers, who are mostly private actors. They may be acting lawfully but they take advantage of the vulnerability of workers, which is caused by the capitalist economic system. Traditionally, the state tries to reduce this vulnerability of workers to exploitation by regulating working conditions and protecting workers' rights through law. Much academic scholarship has focused on general inequalities in bargaining power, failures to reform property and contract law, and the need to reform individual and collective labour law. While unquestionably important, this focus has neglected how specific pieces of legislation also actively create vulnerability, and are connected to structures of exploitation.

Building on the work of Iris Marion Young, this chapter examines what I call 'state-mediated structures of exploitation' at work, namely legal rules that increase workers' vulnerability that is then systematically exploited, primarily by private actors. My focus is on cases where the state through laws takes identifiable special measures which promote a *prima facie* legitimate aim, yet in practice increase the vulnerability of workers to exploitation by employers. The vulnerability created by these measures is systematic. We observe a pattern of exploitation that emerges as a result—a structure—and not just some occasional or isolated cases. These structures become all the more widespread, standard, and routine, as we will see in the chapters that follow.

[1] Hugh Collins, 'Is the Contract of Employment Illiberal?' in Hugh Collins, Gillian Lester, and Virginia Mantouvalou (eds), *Philosophical Foundations of Labour Law* (OUP 2018) 48; Guy Davidov, *A Purposive Approach to Labour Law* (OUP 2016) ch 1.

Structural Injustice and Workers' Rights. Virginia Mantouvalou, Oxford University Press. © Virginia Mantouvalou 2023.
DOI: 10.1093/oso/9780192857156.003.0002

Structural Injustice

Here I do not develop a theory of justice at work but focus on the role of legal rules in exacerbating and entrenching structures of injustice. When I refer to structures, I use the term to describe patterns in social relations.[2] The specific injustice that interests me is workplace exploitation, by which I mean taking unfair advantage of someone's vulnerability at work. I take the seminal work of Iris Marion Young on 'structural injustice' as a starting point.[3]

Young developed her theory on structural injustice in response to the position that people are responsible for being in poverty because of their life choices. She thought that poverty should not be analysed without examining social structures too.[4] By turning to the role of social structures, she sought to take a broad view and consider society's major social positions, and their systematic relations.[5] For Young, structural injustice is different to injustice perpetuated by individuals, by the state, or by other powerful institutions.[6] She developed the concept to describe situations where people find themselves suffering serious harm, such as exploitation and domination, which is neither through their own fault nor intentionally caused by one individual or institution. It occurs when individuals act according to normal rules and morally justifiable practices, but the preconditions and results of their actions are structural processes that produce unjust outcomes.[7] In a much-cited passage, Young said that structural injustice:

> exists when social processes put large groups of persons under systematic threat of domination or deprivation of the means to develop and exercise their capacities, at the same time that these processes enable others to dominate or to have a wide range of opportunities for developing and exercising capacities available to them. Structural injustice is a kind of moral wrong distinct from the wrongful action of an individual agent or the repressive policies of a state. Structural injustice occurs as a consequence of many individuals and

[2] Anthony Giddens, *The Constitution of Society* (Polity Press 1984) 16.

[3] Iris Marion Young, *Responsibility for Justice* (OUP 2011) (hereafter Young, *Responsibility for Justice*). See also her earlier 'Political Responsibility and Structural Injustice' (Lindley Lecture at the University of Kansas, 2003) <https://kuscholarworks.ku.edu/bitstream/handle/1808/12416/politicalresponsibilityandstructuralinjustice-2003.pdf?sequence=1> accessed 15 October 2022. For a presentation of the main themes and literature analysing Young's work, see Maeve McKeown, 'Structural Injustice' (2021) 16 Philosophy Compass.

[4] See the discussion in Young, Responsibility for Justice (n 3) ch 1. See also Tommie Shelby, *Dark Ghettos—Injustice, Dissent, and Reform* (Harvard University Press 2016) 28–29.

[5] Young, *Responsibility for Justice* (n 3) 56.

[6] ibid 45.

[7] ibid 47.

> institutions acting to pursue their particular goals and interests, for the most part within the limits of accepted rules and norms.[8]

In situations of structural injustice, there are deep power differentials between social groups, any identifiable wrongs are not traceable to specific individual or state action, and concrete agents responsible for this injustice cannot be identified: the injustice seems to be self-perpetuating.[9] A problem that follows is that assigning responsibility in this context is difficult, because it is not clear who, if anyone, is blameworthy for an injustice.

In relation to the injustice of exploitation particularly, Young argued that it 'consists in social processes that bring about a transfer of energies from one group to another to produce unequal distributions, and in the way to which social institutions enable a few to accumulate while they constrain many more'.[10] She further explained that 'the injustices of exploitation cannot be eliminated by redistribution of goods, for as long as institutionalized practices and structural relations remain unaltered, the process of transfer will re-create an unequal distribution of benefits'.[11] She adopted a structural account of exploitation, in other words, one that does not focus on opportunistic employers or other agents but examines systematic relations.[12]

The Story of Sandy

Young illustrates the problem of structural injustice with the story of Sandy, a single mother of two who was forced to move out of her apartment that was part of a city-centre apartment building which would be converted into condominiums. The building was very old and she had a long commute to work as a sales clerk in a suburban mall. Sandy decided to look for an apartment closer to her work. She realised, though, that flat rentals in the area were extremely expensive, while affordable apartments were far away. She decided to spend some money that she had saved for rent to get a car. Sandy applied for state support and was told that she had to wait for two years. She finally found

[8] ibid 52.
[9] Tamara Jugov and Lea Ypi, 'Structural Injustice, Epistemic Opacity, and the Responsibilities of the Oppressed' (2019) 50 Journal of Social Philosophy 7, 8.
[10] Iris Marion Young, *Justice and the Politics of Difference* (Princeton University Press 1990) 53.
[11] ibid.
[12] For further discussion, see Monique Deveaux and Vida Panitch, 'Introduction—Exploitation: From Practice to Theory' in Monique Deveaux and Vida Panitch (eds), *Exploitation—From Practice to Theory* (Rowman & Littlefield 2017) 1.

a small apartment that was a forty-five-minute drive from her work. Her children would have to share a bedroom and she would have to sleep in the living room. There was no washing machine or dryer in the building, nor a nearby playground, but Sandy had no other option but to take it as she would soon be evicted. However, she needed a deposit for three months' rent, according to standard landlord policy, which she could not afford because she had paid for the car. She therefore faced the prospect of homelessness.

Sandy was faced with an injustice, according to Young, because no-one should be in a position of housing insecurity, particularly in an affluent society. However, the blame for this injustice cannot be placed on a particular individual with whom she interacted, for they all acted according to the law and generally treated her with decency. In a case such as this, it is hard to assign causal responsibility, to know what can be done, and who has the power to do it.

Against this background, Young's primary aim was to show that everyone has 'political responsibility' to address unjust structures, and particularly those who are not directly responsible for causing a specific harm. People act according to their interests, and do not break the law. They do not have 'backward-looking' responsibility for the injustice, on her analysis. However, they still have 'forward-looking' responsibility to address it because they benefit from the injustice.

Young's insight is crucial because it shifts attention away from individual responsibility that was a key focal point for several scholars.[13] She does this in two ways: on the one hand, she shows that people in Sandy's position are not responsible for their predicament. On the other hand, she illustrates how those with whom Sandy interacted along the way merely complied with societal rules and practices, so they are also not necessarily responsible for having caused direct harm to her. Instead, Young places attention on broader social structures, people's social positions, and their interactions.

If Sandy herself or the other people with whom she interacted are not responsible for her situation, could it be said that the state is responsible? Young says that the state cannot be blamed for the wrong that Sandy suffered, because there is no concrete law or policy in the situation that she describes that directly harmed Sandy. To support the point, Young refers to state action where there is clear responsibility for harm and explains that Sandy's story was different to,

[13] For discussion of some of the debates, see Young, *Responsibility for Justice* (n 3) ch 1. For a critique of egalitarian theories of justice that focus on individual responsibility, see Jonathan Wolff, 'Fairness, Respect, and the Egalitarian Ethos' (1998) 27 Philosophy and Public Affairs 97.

for example, the victims of Robert Mugabe who were evicted when he razed the shantytowns where they lived, or black and Jewish people who were forbidden to buy or rent property in the United States.[14] In examples such as these, states cause injustice to groups through direct action, that is, their laws or policies, with intention to harm. This was not what the situation of Sandy exemplified, being instead an instance of structural injustice.

There is no question that some laws and policies cause direct harm to people, but in the case of Sandy no such laws were involved, on this analysis. Young acknowledged that '[s]ome laws, such as municipal zoning laws, and some policies, such as private investment policies, contribute to the structural processes that caused Sandy's plight, but none can be singled out as the major cause'.[15] Young therefore distinguishes between laws that cause harm directly, constituting a major cause of injustice, and laws that might have contributed to harm but which are not the major cause.

Young paid further attention to the role of the state in a different aspect of her analysis of structural injustice.[16] She explained that, when it is not evident who is responsible for an injustice but it is clear that someone needs to do something about this injustice, the state may have a responsibility to act. This grounds a positive obligation for state action to solve the problem of coordination in the sense that no other actor has the task of addressing the injustice.[17] The strength of focusing on the role of the state to address structural injustice is said to be based in its capacity to raise awareness and change social processes in the future.[18]

Young's conception of structural injustice aimed to capture a type of responsibility that should be distinguished from individual fault and specific unjust policies. Young viewed Sandy as embedded in a network of relations where no-one could be viewed as primarily responsible for her situation. The harm that Sandy suffered was not caused immediately and was not due to a single policy, for its sources are multiple and long-term. It was the result of many policies and the acts of thousands of individuals who acted lawfully.[19] The responsibility in

[14] Young, *Responsibility for Justice* (n 3) 47.

[15] ibid.

[16] ibid 166–69.

[17] She refers to Robert Goodin, 'The State as a Moral Agent' in *Utilitarianism as a Public Philosophy* (CUP 1995) 28.

[18] See also Serena Parekh, 'Getting to the Root of Gender Inequality: Structural Injustice and Political Responsibility' (2011) 26 Hypatia 672, 683.

[19] Young, *Responsibility for Justice* (n 3) 47–48. For insightful analysis and critique of aspects of Young's theory of responsibility, see Jeffrey Reiman, 'The Structure of Structural Injustice: Thoughts on Iris Marion Young's Responsibility for Justice' (2012) 38 Social Theory and Practice 738; and in relation to responsibility for global justice, see Martha Nussbaum, 'Iris Young's Last Thought on Responsibility for Global Justice' in Ann Ferguson and Mechthild Nagel (eds), *Dancing with Iris—The Philosophy of Iris Marion Young* (OUP 2009) 133.

which Young was interested was individual, forward-looking, and political (rather than legal).

However, probably because her focus was on forward-looking responsibility, Young did not pay sufficient attention to the powerful actors that act in a way which might appear to be legitimate, but which may in reality create or exacerbate vulnerability that is linked to structures of exploitation. For this reason, Maeve McKeown developed three different types of structural injustice—pure, avoidable, and deliberate.[20] For her, pure structural injustice exists when we cannot identify a perpetrator, as this is the result of actions of many actors who are not blameworthy, and which can only be addressed through collective action. Avoidable structural injustice exists when there are powerful agents that fail to change unjust structures, even though they are able to do so. Deliberate structural injustice is defined as a situation whereby agents are deliberately perpetuating conditions of background injustice for their benefit despite having the power to change them. McKeown's concern is that the role of powerful agents should be at the centre of analyses of responsibility for structural injustice.

My interest is specifically in the role of the state as a powerful actor and its use of the law in a manner which may increase, perpetuate, and reinforce structures of injustice at work.[21] Young may have underestimated the role that concrete laws play in creating vulnerability to exploitation. If we do identify laws that have a major role to play here, we may ground backward-looking responsibility for injustice, which can be both political and also legal, on the basis of human rights law, as I will explain later on in this book.[22] In the case of Sandy, we do not have sufficient information on the laws that affected her and put her in a position of homelessness and destitution, so it is hard to assess whether we can identify legal rules that may be to blame for her situation.

The Story of Marcell

I will now tell a different story. Marcell is a twenty-six-year-old man with a nine-year-old son and estranged partner, who live in London.[23] He had to leave

[20] McKeown (n 3).

[21] This was also discussed by Madison Powers and Ruth Faden, in their book *Structural Injustice: Power, Advantage, and Human Rights* (OUP 2019) ch 6.

[22] See Chapters 7 and 8.

[23] This testimony is a summary from the piece: Jo McBride, Andrew Smith, and Marcell Mbala, "'You End Up with Nothing": The Experience of Being a Statistic of "In-Work Poverty" in the UK' (2018) 32 Work, Employment and Society 210.

college, where he was studying health and social care, to find work to support his partner and child. He moved from London to Newcastle where life was less costly, but he initially only managed to find work for fifteen hours per week as a cleaner for an employment agency. He stayed in a hostel for a few months. While in this employment, Marcell often experienced delays in being paid because of payroll and electronic system errors. His pay in 2015 was £6.70 per hour,[24] and his monthly net pay was £420.

Marcell wanted to become a security officer, but he had to pay £220 to apply to get the Security Industry Authority Licence, which is a legal requirement for anyone working in the security industry. He could not afford this, though, because he had to use his income to cover his basic needs and support his son. Marcell tried to find more work but he could not, so he was very often in debt at the end of the month. He could only afford to pay for essentials like electricity, water, rent, and child support. At some point, he managed to survive on noodles for five months in order to save to buy a carpet. He said that it was worth the sacrifice, because he wanted to have the carpet for his son's visit. He also started using a food bank. Marcell said that he wanted to go to university, work for charity, and have a better personal and social life.

In 2016, Marcell moved to a new job as a cleaner through the same agency, working twenty-two hours a week, paid at £7.20 per hour, which amounted to about £500 per month. He also found a second, voluntary post in a community centre doing charitable work for four hours a week. He still experienced problems with being paid on time, and his hours were occasionally reduced because some of the cleaners left work early, which led the supermarket to reduce the hours and pay for everyone. He was still keen to get a licence as a security officer, but he did not manage to get financial support to obtain the certificate, even though he completed the necessary training. In the end he decided to cut down on food in order to pay for this. His social life was very limited. He went out on a date at some point, but the woman whom he dated had to pay for everything, and did not see him again. He also had few opportunities to see his son.

Marcell said that working more hours simply meant that he had to pay more rent. 'I was better off when I was doing 15 hours a week because I had help with housing benefit. So I have to pay for rent, water, broadband, transport, have some food, pay my child support and be able to save at least maybe £20 or £10 a week.'[25] However, he was usually left with nothing by the end of the month,

[24] This was compliant with the national minimum wage in the United Kingdom, which was set at £6.70 in 2015.

[25] McBride, Smith, and Mbala (n 23) 216.

because he also had to repay a loan for a mobile phone and laptop that he got when he was sixteen. Eventually, he decided that he could not go to the university, but all he wanted was to move back to London, be close to his son, and find a better job. Marcell said that his dream was to work for a charity in countries where there is real poverty. 'But for now, I'm still on the same roundabout.'[26]

The story of Marcell may seem similar to Sandy's. He is in a situation of underemployment and in-work poverty, unable to meet his basic needs, such as food and basic social contact. Here, like in the story of Sandy, there does not appear to be any direct state action that harms Marcell, and no individual—no employer, landlord, or anyone else—is breaking the law. Marcell is trapped in this situation: he wants to work longer hours, get a better job, and be able to cover his basic needs. However, he cannot afford it. Our reaction, as in the case of Sandy, is that no-one in an affluent society should be in this situation of in-work poverty and unable to cover his basic needs. At first glance, we might say that Marcell, like Sandy, is a victim of structural injustice too.

The Role of the Law

Sandy's story is fictional and presented in general terms, so we cannot scrutinise the role of the state or private actors more closely. The story of Marcell is real. Here we can attempt to take a closer look at the role of the law. Marcell is employed through an agency and is a part-time worker. In this kind of working arrangement, that is often termed precarious, it is not always clear whether there is an employer or whether the worker is self-employed, who is the employer (the employment agency or the end user), and what duties the employer owes to those who work for it (as an employee or worker). All these issues have implications for the legal rights that agency workers have, or from which they are excluded by law. Businesses, acting lawfully, often prefer to cover permanent needs through agencies so that they do not assume employer duties that they would have owed if they employed workers directly.

When we look at it more closely, then, we can see that the UK legal framework on agency work may create structures of injustice by increasing workers' vulnerability to exploitation. In a manner similar to Young, the account of exploitation that I use here is structural, in the sense that the vulnerability is created by a structural process. Through this process, some systematically benefit by accumulating power at the expense of others who are systematically

[26] ibid 217.

disadvantaged. The concept of structural exploitation on which I focus, though, concerns vulnerability of workers and injustice that is not self-perpetuating but that may be created or compounded by identifiable legal rules. My aim is to examine the fairness of the legal rules that are responsible for structures of exploitation.

In relation to Marcell, we can consider legislation and judicial decisions that involve agency workers and how these increase workers' vulnerability. Legislation that limits labour rights according to factors such as hours and place of work may mean that agency workers are not entitled to these rights. Court judgments have also played this role of excluding agency workers from protective norms by ruling that the end user is not an employer, or by taking a restrictive approach to employment status (the question whether the person employed is a worker or an independent contractor) that serves as a gateway to labour rights in legislation. I will develop this point in more detail later on.[27]

Moreover, we do not know if Marcell, like Toni in Chapter 1, has been required to work for an agency through the UK welfare conditionality scheme, which makes welfare support conditional upon applying for and accepting work. However, this is possible as he refers to his contact with a Jobcentre. Jobcentres were established in 2002 in the UK for all those who claimed benefits and were out of work. If this is the case, Marcell's work for the agency may not be freely chosen: he is required to do it under the UK Welfare Reform Act 2012, for otherwise he will lose social support. In addition, Marcell explains that when he found work for more than fifteen hours a week, he had to pay more rent as he stopped receiving a social benefit. He therefore became poorer. This is again because of the same legislation. The Act adopted a particularly punitive conditionality regime for those seeking to apply for welfare support.[28] The resulting Universal Credit system aimed to influence individual behaviour, under the assumption that individuals are primarily to blame for their unemployment. The requirement to look for work applies both to those who are unemployed and to those who are employed but do not earn enough. Under Universal Credit, those who work for over fifteen hours and earn above a set level of income lose any welfare benefits.[29]

The legal rules on agency work and welfare conditionality may not appear at first to intend to harm people directly. These have an appearance of legitimacy.

[27] See Chapter 6.
[28] See further Chapter 5.
[29] See the discussion in Kayleigh Garthwaite, *Hunger Pains—Life Inside Foodbank Britain* (Policy Press 2016) 106.

Non-standard work arrangements give opportunities for flexible working that some view as valuable. Welfare conditionality schemes allegedly encourage people to look for work and escape poverty. These rules cannot be said to constitute state action that aims to cause harm. However, the way that the rules are designed and implemented, as well as the way in which they intersect, leads to the proliferation of non-standard work, with claimants not only being forced to accept it but also being trapped in the arrangements, sometimes against the threat of very strict sanctions. They are trapped not only because precarious jobs become much more common, but also because people have very limited opportunities and resources (both material, such as funding to retrain, and non-material, such as time) to obtain better work. When looking at the legal framework somewhat more closely, then, we see that legal rules increase vulnerability and are connected to structures of exploitation.

The discussion of the laws in question here was only brief, as I will return to these in the chapters that follow. The example of Marcell and the reference to the legal framework aim to show this: when looking at certain injustices that can be described as self-perpetuating or structural, we can identify legal arrangements that have a major role to play in creating or sustaining them. The legal rules here may have an appearance of legitimacy, which is why they cannot be described as state action with intention to harm. They may appear to be justified, as the authorities can claim to have a legitimate aim: encouraging people to work and creating flexible working arrangements that some may value. However, these rules increase workers' vulnerability that is systematically exploited.

To be clear, my aim is not to question whether there is pure structural injustice in general or to criticise the use of Sandy's story, which Young employed for the different purpose of developing the concept of forward-looking political responsibility. However, it is important to appreciate that in certain cases where it appears that injustice is structural and that no agent is responsible for the injustice, it may be possible to identify backward-looking responsibility for legal rules that increase workers' vulnerability to exploitation. Having identified these rules, we can then consider responsibility for the creation of the unjust structures in question more closely,[30] and scrutinise further the role of powerful actors such as the state.[31]

[30] On the structure/agency dichotomy see Giddens, *The Constitution of Society* (n 2) 14. See also William H Sewell, Jr, 'A Theory of Structure: Duality, Agency, and Transformation' (1992) 98 American Journal of Sociology 1.

[31] Sally Haslanger, *Resisting Reality—Social Construction and Social Critique* (OUP 2012) 318.

State-Mediated Structures of Injustice

I have argued that in certain instances of injustice that are structural the state may be responsible for creating concrete rules which, despite appearing legitimate, allocate power in a way that increases and entrenches workers' vulnerability to exploitation. This should be distinguished from responsibility for direct state action that causes harm and the authorities cannot put forward a justification that is not immoral or illegal, or for omissions to act when there is harm in the private sphere, the state knows or ought to have known about it, and yet does nothing to address it.[32]

The responsibility in which I am interested is responsibility for the creation of vulnerability through law that is linked to structures of exploitation: this is why I call it *state-mediated*. It concerns responsibility for state action—the creation of vulnerability itself. However, the structures of exploitation are beneficial primarily for private employers. The state authorities know or ought to know of the vulnerability that they create, perpetuate, and increase, along with the resulting structures of exploitation. Employers act according to the law, but workers are trapped in these structures of injustice because of legal rules.

It is important to understand the examples that I discuss as state-mediated *structures* of injustice for several reasons. First, they involve rules that are connected to patterns in social relations. Because of identifiable legal rules, large numbers of people are placed in a position of vulnerability of which others take advantage systematically. The processes are set up through specific laws and policies that enable employers to exploit workers. A second reason why the concept of a structure is suitable is because it can refer to something that is erected, a construction. The structures extend beyond a single hurdle in someone's life. The example of Marcell shows how people are trapped in these structures. In addition, the idea of the structure helps us appreciate how the system may become entrenched, with aspects of it continuing to exist even when the law changes. Here it is worth clarifying that it is not only the law that creates vulnerability. The groups placed in this position of vulnerability through precarious work are often already in a position of disadvantage because of a variety of factors, such as race, poverty, or migration status.[33] This is also what the term 'clustering of disadvantage' describes: people accumulate disadvantages such as workplace exploitation, ill-health, or homelessness.[34]

[32] Young also discusses responsibility for omission and the role of the state to coordinate agencies in order to address social problems, in Young, *Responsibility for Justice* (n 3) 167.

[33] See Haslanger (n 31) 311.

[34] Jonathan Wolff and Avner de-Shalit, *Disadvantage* (OUP 2007).

By referring to vulnerability to exploitation that is increased by identifiable legal rules, I want to distinguish it from the general way in which the law affects power relations. In general, as Collins put it, 'the law respects a particular concept of private property which gives the owner of capital complete freedom to choose whether or not to put it to productive use. If the law did not respect this privilege, then the power of capital would be radically diminished.'[35] When it comes to the labour market, a system of private property places employers in a position of power, and workers in a position of dependency, as I said earlier. This is what is typically meant when people refer to power imbalance in the employment relation. It is often in this general way that some talk about injustice that is structural: the employer has the right to direct and manage employees who must follow the instructions. This is a structure of power at work that recognises an employer's ability to control the employee that is distinct from a free and equal relation.[36]

For many labour law scholars, the employment relationship is one of subordination, and the primary purpose of labour and social security law should be to reduce the vulnerability of workers through interventions.[37] However, what we observe in examples like that of Marcell is that, at times, there are identifiable special measures that do not normally harm directly but which create further vulnerability that is systematically exploited. The exploitation is not directly caused by the state: it is mostly private employers who take advantage and benefit from it. It is also not an isolated instance of exploitation: the state conduct is linked to patterns of exploitation that are all the more widespread, standard, and routine. It is important to focus attention on the responsibility of the state in relation to these structures of injustice because if the law is responsible for creating vulnerability to exploitation that is systematically exploited, a change in the law can also help remedy the injustice by removing the rules that create this vulnerability and protecting workers' rights. The state is a powerful agent. By holding it accountable for misallocating power in these situations, we can demand that power be allocated more fairly.

[35] Hugh Collins, 'Against Abstentionism in Labour Law' in John Eekelaar and John Bell (eds), *Oxford Essays in Jurisprudence* (Clarendon Press 1987) 86. Pistor examined how private law produces private wealth: Katharina Pistor, *The Code of Capital: How the Law Creates Capital and Inequality* (Princeton University Press 2019).

[36] Hugh Collins, Gillian Lester, and Virginia Mantouvalou, 'Introduction: Does Labour Law Need Philosophical Foundations?' in Hugh Collins, Gillian Lester, and Virginia Mantouvalou (eds), *Philosophical Foundations of Labour Law* (OUP 2018) 5.

[37] Hugh Collins, 'Labour Law as a Vocation' (1989) Law Quarterly Review 468, 470. See further the discussion in Davidov (n 1) chs 3 and 4 in particular.

By way of an objection to this account, it can be said that, in at least some of the structures of injustice that I call state-mediated, it is the state's intent to cause harm to some groups of people. This can be said, for instance, about welfare support recipients who are sanctioned if they do not look for work.[38] The sanctions are deliberately imposed. It can therefore be argued that the wrong in question should be placed in the same broad category of intentionally harmful state conduct as Mugabe's atrocities. However, the professed intention of the sanctions is to encourage people into work because in the long run work is said to be the best way out of poverty. This means that the declared justification is anti-poverty rather than simply causing harm.

The key point is that the laws in question have an appearance of legitimacy: the authorities can put forward a *prima facie* legitimate justification, namely a justification that cannot be described as unlawful or immoral. However, the identification of the patterns and the systematic exploitation that emerges as a result suggest that the supposed legitimacy of the action should be questioned. The role of the state here is different to its role when the authorities cause direct harm to people. We are faced with laws and policies that are not necessarily illegitimate when looked at in isolation, but which create patterns that place large numbers of people into exploitative labour relations, from which it is very hard to escape.

There is also the opposite objection to what I describe as state-mediated structures of injustice. The objection is that laws with legitimate aims can always be abused by unscrupulous employers (and others).[39] There will always be 'a few bad apples', namely individuals who identify weaknesses and gaps in the legal system. These individuals (employers very often in my examples) take advantage of the law in order to promote their own interests. The value of the rules in question should not be questioned for this reason and the state should not be held responsible for the injustice that is in reality directly caused by individual action in the private sphere.

A few things can be said in response. First, state authorities have demanding duties to treat everyone fairly. Law as an institution should be scrutinised closely because the creation of vulnerability to exploitation, even if inadvertent, is contrary to the state's duties of justice. In addition, the standard of fairness required in these cases is not impossibly high. In order for this type of state

[38] See Michael Adler, *Cruel, Inhuman or Degrading Treatment? Benefit Sanctions in the UK* (Palgrave Macmillan 2018). See also Frances Fox Piven and Richard A Cloward, *Regulating the Poor: Functions of Public Welfare* (2nd edn, Vintage 1993).

[39] I am grateful to my colleague, Charles Mitchell, for pressing me on this point.

responsibility to arise, it is important to show that the effect of the laws examined is systematic exploitation. We are not just dealing with cases where some devious employers identify gaps in the law and take advantage of them in order to exploit people. We are considering clearly identifiable legal rules, and the intersection of such rules, that compound workers' vulnerability, accompanied by widespread patterns of exploitation. It is also not the case that employers always exploit the workers in question. There will be virtuous employers who do not take advantage of vulnerabilities created by law. Nonetheless, this does not mean that there is no state responsibility for the structures of injustice in these examples, and that we should only be focusing on the responsibility of the unscrupulous individual employers alone.

By saying that we can identify state responsibility in the context of an unjust structure, I do not claim that individuals who directly exploit workers do not bear responsibility. As Haslanger put it, 'our societies are unjustly structured, and immoral people with power can and do harm others. Moreover, individual and structural issues are interdependent insofar as individuals are responsive to their social context and social structures are created, maintained, and transformed by individuals.'[40] There can be both individual and state responsibility for structural injustice. 'Structures cause injustice through *misallocation* of power; agents cause wrongful harm through the *abuse* of power (sometimes the abuse of misallocated power).'[41] I am focusing on the state because by looking at the legal framework we can propose structural reform that can be 'more sweeping and reliable'[42] than smaller changes. By identifying powerful agents that are responsible for unjust structures, and particularly by focusing on the role of the state as an especially powerful actor, we are better placed to achieve structural reform.

Neither do I claim that those who benefit from the situation of state-mediated injustice do not have political responsibility of the type that Young developed. There is moral (and sometimes legal) responsibility for the exploitation by the employer, as well as political responsibility of everyone who benefits from this situation. However, the state is also responsible for creating and sustaining the unjust structure. It is therefore crucial to examine the responsibility of the state for the additional reason that it has the power to change the unjust structures in question.

[40] Haslanger (n 31) 319.
[41] ibid 320.
[42] ibid 319.

Conclusion

The main purpose of this chapter has been to develop the concept of state-mediated structures of injustice as a mechanism that can help us diagnose certain instances of injustice and consider the responsibility of the state for these. The concept of structural injustice is important as a starting point, for it situates the issue in a framework that is not focused on individual responsibility, but also places attention on the patterns that affect people. Those affected by these patterns, as we will also see later on, are often found in a position of disadvantage for other reasons, including their race, gender, and poverty.

In the chapters that follow, I discuss concrete examples both to show more precisely examples of laws that increase vulnerability to exploitation and to explain on the basis of empirical research the evidence that these laws are linked to widespread, standard, and routine structures of exploitation of disadvantaged social groups. Often the structures that I discuss reinforce other, broader social structures such as deeply rooted poverty and disadvantage. However, to the extent that we can identify the responsibility of state authorities for an unjust structure, it is important to analyse it and press for legal change as an important step toward broader structural reform.

PART II

ILLUSTRATIONS OF STATE-MEDIATED STRUCTURAL INJUSTICE

3
Migrant Workers

Migrant workers may be in a position of disadvantage for several reasons, such as race, gender, language barriers, lack of support networks, and ignorance of their legal rights and avenues to asserting them in the host country. In addition to these factors, restrictive migration schemes increase existing vulnerabilities, and are connected to widespread structures of exploitation at work and to some of its most severe instances.[1] Moreover, the legal status of being undocumented, also constructed by immigration laws that limit entry, stay, and the right to work, generates institutionalised uncertainty and fashions precarious work.[2] Rules that are widely viewed as a legitimate exercise of state authority create structures of exploitation of migrant workers, affecting primarily those in low-paid sectors, such as domestic work and agricultural work on which I focus in this chapter.

Temporary Labour Migration

Temporary labour migration programmes are schemes whereby migrant workers arrive in a country to work, often without a route to permanent residence or citizenship. The schemes typically contain a number of restrictions, exposing the workers affected to further vulnerabilities. They generally impose limitations in terms of the length of time that the migrant worker can stay in a country, but may also contain other restrictions, such as binding the worker to a particular work sector or a particular employer, or restrictions to the right to be accompanied by family members or to form relations with locals.[3] Some

[1] See generally Cathryn Costello and Mark Freedland, 'Migrants at Work and the Division of Labour Law' in Cathryn Costello and Mark Freedland (eds), *Migrants at Work: Immigration and Vulnerability in Labour Law* (OUP 2015).

[2] See Bridget Anderson, 'Immigration, Migration Controls, and the Fashioning of Precarious Work' (2010) 24 Work Employment and Society 300.

[3] See eg Deepa Rajkumar and others, 'At the Temporary–Permanent Divide: How Canada Produces Temporariness and Makes Citizens Through its Security, Work, and Settlement Policies' (2012) 16 Citizenship Studies 483. See also Hila Shamir, 'The Paradox of "Legality": Temporary Migrant Worker Programs and Vulnerability to Trafficking' in Prabha Kotiswaran (ed), *Revisiting the Law and Governance of Trafficking, Forced Labour and Modern Slavery* (CUP 2017) 471.

Structural Injustice and Workers' Rights. Virginia Mantouvalou, Oxford University Press. © Virginia Mantouvalou 2023.
DOI: 10.1093/oso/9780192857156.003.0003

of these schemes are categorised as 'circular' migration, because workers can return regularly to the country but on a temporary basis each time. Temporary migrant workers also have no political rights.[4] Such regimes are used in many legal orders and there is no single legal definition of them.

This type of controlled migration is not new.[5] In the twentieth century, what are known also as guestworker programmes were used in many countries, including Germany, South Africa, and the United States. It is often said that the schemes constitute a 'triple win': they are beneficial for the country of nationality of the worker, the country of destination, and the workers themselves. However, the history of temporary labour migration schemes shows that they actually create 'perfect immigrants' to the particular benefit of employers and the state, rather than the migrant workers. Host states do not have to plan their integration and social support, as they are only there temporarily.[6] Employers view them as 'an unqualified good' because they constitute a 'fully flexible and temporary workforce'.[7] The workers, in turn, accept jobs in sectors with substandard working conditions that others find back-breaking or repellent, because they need to send remittances to their dependents in their home country where the incomes are much lower. Moreover, it has been argued that temporary labour migration programmes are structurally exploitative not only for migrant workers but for all workers as a class.[8] This is because they help employers increase their profit by maintaining low salaries and bad working conditions that affect both migrant workers who accept the jobs and nationals of the host country, as the schemes are the reason why these working conditions are maintained.

In reality, then, there is no 'triple win' here. The winners are only two: the host state (the national economy and the employers) and the workers' country of origin. The host state's national economy benefits from temporary migrant workers because they contribute through their work and even through being taxed without the state having to be concerned with their support, such as education or healthcare. The employers benefit from the fact that the migrant workers are temporary, and can be discarded as soon as they are no longer able or needed to do the work.[9] The workers' country of origin benefits from

[4] See the discussion in Michael Walzer, *Spheres of Justice* (Basic Books 1984) 56ff and particularly 59.

[5] See Cindy Hahamovitch, 'Creating Perfect Immigrants: Guestworkers of the World in Historical Perspective' (2003) 44 Labor History 69.

[6] ibid 73.

[7] Rita Chin, *The Guest Worker Question in Postwar Germany* (CUP 2007) 45.

[8] Lea Ypi, 'Taking Workers as a Class—The Moral Dilemmas of Guestworker Programs' in Sarah Fine and Lea Ypi (eds) *Migration in Political Theory—The Ethics of Movement and Membership* (OUP 2016) 151.

[9] Chin (n 7) 45–46.

the remittances that they send. The migrant workers, on the other hand, are trapped in structures of exploitation from which they cannot escape, for if they break their visas, they will become undocumented and even more precariously employed. When it comes to the legal regulation of the schemes, scholars have therefore observed that it has tended to privilege the interests of capital rather than the interests and rights of migrant workers.[10] In designing the schemes, states focus on the needs of businesses, and attempt to develop rules that respond primarily to those rather than the protection of workers' rights.

As states have a right to control entry of non-nationals, they generally put forward special justifications so as to allow migrant workers to be admitted under such conditions. A typical justification that governments employ to introduce temporary labour visas involves alleged labour shortages. The argument is that there are sectors where there are not enough people willing to do the necessary work, so there is a need for migrant workers in order to fulfil the tasks for which no local workers are available in the host country. The concept of labour shortages has been questioned both conceptually and empirically.[11]

The particular concern for me here, though, is that restrictive schemes that tie a worker to a work sector or a particular employer are linked to structures of exploitation. In addition to the standard inequality of power that characterises the employment relation, immigration rules create special relations of dependency on the employer and hence precarious work. This is because workers under a restrictive visa who lose their job may also lose their accommodation if they are staying at the employers' premises as well as the right to reside in the country, which may result in immigration detention and deportation. Some who may have been victims of trafficking may be vulnerable to being re-trafficked and exploited all over again. These schemes are linked to the clustering of workers who are in a very vulnerable position in specific low-paid work sectors.[12]

Temporary labour migration schemes contain a number of restrictive rules, which differ across the world.[13] One of the best-known systems for its negative effects on workers is *kafala* in Gulf countries. There are different variations of *kafala* in different countries. The main characteristics of *kafala* are as follows: a

[10] Joanna Howe and Rosemary Owens, 'Temporary Labour Migration in a Global Era: The Regulatory Challenges' in Joanna Howe and Rosemary Owens (eds), *Temporary Labour Migration in the Global Era: The Regulatory Challenges* (Hart 2016) 3, 4.

[11] See Bridget Anderson and Martin Ruhs (eds), *Who Needs Migrant Workers?* (OUP 2010).

[12] Anderson (n 2) 301.

[13] For a discussion of a few different examples, see Patti Tamara Lenard and Christine Straehle, 'Temporary Labour Migration: Exploitation, Tool of Development, or Both?' (2010) 29 Policy and Society 283.

migrant needs a visa in order to enter a country and there has to be a sponsor for the visa; permission is necessary to exit the country or change employer, whereby the sponsor declares that they do not object to the worker leaving the country or changing sponsor; and sometimes there is also a requirement for a deposit, a sum of money paid by the sponsor for costs that involve the worker.[14] The *kafala* system is regularly criticised in academic scholarship and non-governmental organisation (NGO) work for the fact that it creates structures of labour exploitation of the most severe form.[15] It has also been argued that it is connected to the institutional humiliation of racialised groups.[16]

Other countries that have or used to have particularly restrictive temporary visa schemes include Israel, Germany, Australia, and the United Kingdom. One of the best-known temporary workers' schemes was the German scheme of guestworkers, which was initiated in the 1950s in order to support the country's economic growth after the war.[17] Israel also used to have very restrictive immigration rules for migrant workers.[18] In order to work in Israel, migrant workers used to require a visa that regulated the length of their stay and the name of the employer for whom they would work. The visa bound the worker to the specific employer, who was also responsible for the departure of the worker at the expiration of the visa. It also determined the length of stay. This visa was said to be linked to patterns of exploitation and abuse of migrant workers, enabling employers to take advantage of the visa restrictions as well as other legal exclusions from protective laws,[19] and was eventually abolished after a ruling of the Supreme Court of Israel to which I will return later.[20]

In some legal orders there are temporary visa schemes for highly skilled workers too, but their conditions tend to be less restrictive than they are for workers in low-paid sectors. To illustrate further the effects of temporary visas, I discuss two sectors with restrictive schemes: domestic work and agriculture. In the final part of the chapter, I turn to undocumented workers, namely

[14] See Omar Hesham AlShehabi, 'Policing Labour in Empire: The Modern Origins of the Kafala Sponsorship System in the Gulf Arab States' (2021) 48 British Journal of Middle-Eastern Studies 291.

[15] See eg Human Rights Watch, '"Working Like a Robot": Abuse of Tanzanian Domestic Workers in Oman and the United Arab Emirates' (2017) <www.hrw.org/report/2017/11/14/working-robot/abuse-tanzanian-domestic-workers-oman-and-united-arab-emirates> accessed 15 October 2022.

[16] Bina Fernandez, 'Racialised Institutional Humiliation through the Kafala' (2021) 47 Journal of Ethnic and Migration Studies 4344.

[17] See Chin (n 7).

[18] Discussed in Einat Albin, 'The Sectoral Regulatory Regime: When Work Migration Controls and the Sectorally Differentiated Labour Market Meet' in Cathryn Costello and Mark Freedland (eds), *Migrants at Work* (OUP 2016) 134, 141. See also Maayan Niezna, 'Paper Chains: Tied Visas, Migration Policies, and Legal Coercion' (2022) 49 Journal of Law and Society 362.

[19] Albin (n 18) 142.

[20] See Chapter 7.

workers who enter a country with no visa or work permit, or workers whose work permit has expired.

Domestic Workers

An example of a very restrictive visa scheme for domestic workers in Europe is the UK Overseas Domestic Worker visa. Domestic workers are workers undertaking various household tasks, such as cleaning, cooking, and caring for children or the elderly. They are sometimes employed part-time, working for a few hours a day for different employers, and sometimes full-time, working for one employer. Some domestic workers live in the employer's household. These live-in domestic workers are mostly people who migrate to work as domestic workers and send income generated through their work back to their families.[21] This group of workers face challenges that other migrant workers may also face, such as language barriers, lack of friends and family in the destination country, and a lack of knowledge of existing networks of support and of their legal rights. Building new networks is almost impossible. An important particularity of the sector is that domestic workers have extremely few opportunities to develop social relations at work: they are isolated and they do not have a circle of co-workers with whom they would regularly interact; they interact mostly with their employer. This also creates challenges for attempts to unionise. It is hard for trade unions to reach out to workers who work in private households.

The great majority of domestic workers are women.[22] Paid domestic work is on the rise for many reasons, such as wealth inequality, the increased participation of women in the labour market outside the home in many countries, and the marketisation of care provision.[23] Without paid domestic workers, the labour force would look different today because the women who have historically

[21] Some data is available in the 2010 ILO Report, *Promoting Decent Work for Domestic Workers*, para 20. For analysis, see Bridget Anderson, *Doing the Dirty Work? The Global Politics of Domestic Labour* (Zed Books 2000). See also Bridget Anderson and Isabel Shutes (eds), *Migration and Care Labour: Theory, Policy and Politics* (Palgrave Macmillan 2014).

[22] ILO Report (n 21) para 21. For analysis, see Barbara Ehrenreich and Arlie Russell Hochschild (eds), *Global Woman* (Granta Books 2003); Helma Lutz, *The New Maids: Transnational Women and the Care Economy* (Zed Books 2011) 18.

[23] See Pierrette Hondagneu-Sotelo, *Doméstica* (University of California Press 2001) ch 1; Barbara Ehrenreich and Arlie Russell Hochschild, 'Introduction' in *Global Woman* (n 22); Isabel Shutes and Carlos Chiatti, 'Migrant Labour and the Marketisation of Care for Older People: The Employment of Migrant Care Workers by Families and Service Providers' (2012) 22 Journal of European Social Policy 392.

been in charge of household tasks, such as care work and cleaning, would not be able to work outside the home without men undertaking household tasks.

Domestic work presents challenges to feminist thought. John Stuart Mill drew an analogy between women's treatment by the law in the nineteenth century and slavery, partly because women had no right to work outside the home.[24] Today, women participate in the labour market outside the home in many countries and achieve in this way greater equality to men. But to do this they have to employ other, often migrant, women to work at home for cleaning and caring duties.[25] This is why it has been suggested that the feminist project is unfinished.[26]

Aragon and Jaggar examined migrant domestic labour as an instance of structural injustice at the global level.[27] Looking at the combination of structural factors that led to the development of the industry, they developed a powerful argument that the overall system is unjust, that everyone who benefits from it participates in the injustice and has a responsibility to resist on the basis of structural complicity: 'Because people are tainted by their participation, they have a political responsibility to work toward remedying this structurally unjust industry', they maintained.[28]

What I want to highlight further here is that the law increases the vulnerability of this category of workers that is linked to structures of exploitation.[29] This work sector is excluded from protective rules or treated differently to workers in other fields, such as through working time regulation,[30] regulation of night work,[31] and occupational health and safety protection.[32] A 2016 ILO study found that 60 million of the world's 67 million domestic workers have no access to social security.[33] All these exclusions from protective rules can be

[24] John Stuart Mill, *The Subjection of Women* (1869).

[25] Bridget Anderson shows how the employer of the domestic worker is the woman of the household. See eg Bridget Anderson, 'Why Madam Has so Many Bathrobes: Demand for Migrant Domestic Workers in the EU' (2001) 92 Journal of Economic and Social Geography 18.

[26] Barbara Ehrenreich, 'Maid to Order' in *Global Woman* (n 22) 103.

[27] Corwin Aragon and Alison M Jaggar, 'Agency, Complicity, and the Responsibility to Resist Structural Injustice' (2018) 49 Journal of Social Philosophy 439.

[28] ibid 453.

[29] On examples of legal exclusions of domestic workers from protective laws, see Virginia Mantouvalou, 'Human Rights for Precarious Workers: The Legislative Precariousness of Domestic Labor' (2012) 34 Comparative Labor Law and Policy Journal 133; see also Natalie Sedacca, 'Domestic Workers, The "Family Worker" Exemption from Minimum Wage, and Gendered Devaluation of Women's Work' (2022) Industrial Law Journal. On the role of the law in the regulation of domestic work, see Adelle Blackett, *Everyday Transgressions—Domestic Workers' Challenge to International Labor Law* (Cornell University Press 2019).

[30] ILO Report (n 21) 48–50.

[31] ibid.

[32] ibid 61ff.

[33] ILO Report, *Social Protection for Domestic Workers: Key Policy Trends and Statistics* (2016).

described as state-mediated structures of injustice. In addition, immigration rules that are my focus in this chapter further corroborate the position that the law compounds the vulnerability of precarious workers.[34] Temporary migration schemes for this kind of work that does not depend on seasonal factors create the sense that workers work for a family rather than being part of the labour market.[35]

The United Kingdom has a particularly restrictive scheme for domestic workers. The Overseas Domestic Worker (ODW) visa effectively ties domestic workers to the employer with whom they arrived in the country.[36] The recent history of the scheme shows how it was developed and maintained despite evidence of abuse and exploitation, and persistent calls for reform. Until 1998, when migrant domestic workers arrived lawfully in the country accompanying an employer, they entered under a concession that tied them to this employer. Their residency status was lawful for as long as the employer with whom they arrived employed them, with the result that the employer gained important means of controlling them.

Certain visitors coming into the United Kingdom wished to be accompanied by domestic workers due to their dependency on their labour, while domestic workers wanted to retain their job while their employers were abroad for a short period of time. In parliamentary debates, this concession from the standard immigration routes was described as a matter of national interest: 'Looking at our national interest, if wealthy investors, skilled workers and others with the potential to benefit our economy were unable to be accompanied by their domestic staff they might not come here at all but take their money and skills to other countries only too keen to welcome them.'[37] At the same time, when the concession was introduced for domestic workers from overseas, a humanitarian reason was also put forward: 'Domestic workers who were unable to accompany the household to the UK could well lose their jobs, their homes and their livelihoods.'[38] This is why provision was made for overseas domestic workers in the UK immigration system.

Since 1998, the rules have allowed domestic workers to change employers but not work sector. This was the outcome of a successful campaign by domestic workers, trade unions, and other civil society organisations that

[34] On domestic work and migration, see Maria Galliotti (2015) 'Making Domestic Work a Reality for Migrant Domestic Workers' ILO Domestic Work Policy Brief No 9.
[35] ILO Report (n 21) 10.
[36] Between 2012 and 2016 they had no right to change employer, while since 2016 they have a right to change employer only in very limited circumstances.
[37] Lord Reay, 28 November 1990, Hansard col 1052.
[38] ibid. Discussed also by Baroness Hamwee, 25 February 2015, Hansard col 1698.

supported them.[39] A domestic worker who had been employed by an employer for at least one year abroad could accompany a foreign national who entered the country for a period of six or twelve months. After five years, the worker could apply for settlement. Even though the domestic worker had entered the country with a specific employer, the worker was not tied to that employer. The worker could change employer but not work sector. The impact of this route of immigration on net migration was negligible. According to UK Border Agency data, less than 5 per cent of domestic workers who entered under an ODW visa went on to settle in the country.[40] The Draft International Labour Organisation Multilateral Framework on Labour Migration of 2005[41] and the UN Special Rapporteur on the Human Rights of Migrants cited the 1998 ODW visa as best practice.[42] In the United Kingdom, it was viewed as a safeguard against trafficking in human beings.[43]

However, in 2012 the UK government introduced a visa regime that did not permit domestic workers to change employer. This occurred against the backdrop of an outcry by domestic workers' organisations that emphasised that the rules would trap domestic workers in serious exploitation and abuse. The point was that the workers would either be fearful to leave exploitative employment relations because they would not want to become undocumented or that, if they left, their undocumented status would trap them in badly paid and exploitative work. This legal change occurred in the context of the so-called 'Points-Based-System'. Under this system, the policy was to not grant visas to low-skilled migrants, so domestic workers—typically viewed as low-skilled workers—did not fit.[44] Domestic workers' residency status was lawful only for as long as the employer with whom they entered employed them, up to a maximum of six months. The six-month period is not renewable. When the 2012 regime was introduced, the government acknowledged that 'the [overseas

[39] For further details, see Anderson, *Doing the Dirty Work?* (n 21) ch 6. See also Einat Albin and Virginia Mantouvalou, 'Active Industrial Citizenship of Domestic Workers: Lessons Learned from Unionizing Attempts in Israel and the United Kingdom' (2015) 17 Theoretical Inquiries in Law 321.

[40] In 2009, only 0.5 per cent of those awarded settlement in the United Kingdom were migrant domestic workers. See Mumtaz Lalani, *Ending the Abuse—Policies that Work to Protect Migrant Domestic Workers* (Kalayaan 2011).

[41] See Draft ILO Multilateral Framework on Labour Migration <www.ilo.org/public/english/standards/relm/gb/docs/gb295/pdf/tmmflm-1.pdf> accessed 15 October 2022, para 82.

[42] See the Report of the Special Rapporteur on the human rights of migrants, Addendum: Mission to the United Kingdom of Great Britain and Northern Ireland <www.refworld.org/cgi-bin/texis/vtx/rwmain?docid=4c0623e92> accessed 15 October 2022, paras 60–61.

[43] Home Affairs Committee, *The Trade in Human Beings: Human Trafficking in the UK*, Sixth Report of Session 2008–2009, Vol I (9 June 2011).

[44] Bridget Anderson, *Us and Them? The Dangerous Politics of Immigration Control* (OUP 2013) 175. See further discussion of the system in Martin Ruhs, *The Price of Rights—Regulating International Labor Migration* (Princeton University Press 2013) 92.

domestic worker] routes can at times result in the import of abusive employer/ employee relationships to the UK'[45] and so imposed some safeguards. These included a requirement of the existence of the employment relation for at least twelve months before arrival; written terms and conditions agreed between the employer and the worker before entry into the United Kingdom; and information given to the workers by UK authorities before they arrive on their rights and avenues for help while they are in the country. Nonetheless, these policies had been in place before 2012, and had been previously criticised for being ineffective.[46]

Kalayaan, the main UK-based NGO specialising in the labour rights of migrant domestic workers, regularly publishes information on the treatment of the workers by their employers. Two years after the new visa was put in place, the organisation's briefings showed that workers registered with the NGO who entered the United Kingdom on the 2012 visa reported significantly worse treatment than those who were not tied to their employer during the same period of time but under the previous regime. More precisely, they found that migrant domestic workers with a visa that ties them to their employers were twice as likely to report having being physically abused as those who were not so tied; that almost three-quarters of workers who were tied to the employer were not allowed to leave the house unsupervised, which is again a significantly larger number than workers under a non-tied visa; that 65 per cent of the domestic workers did not have their own rooms; and that the majority worked more than sixteen hours a day. These patterns were confirmed in subsequent years: the abuse reported by workers under the tied visa is proportionately consistently higher than the abuse reported by other workers.[47] Following a mission to the United Kingdom, the UN Special Rapporteur on Violence Against Women further highlighted the problems of the visa for domestic workers.[48]

In an empirical study that I conducted encompassing interviews with migrant domestic workers who came to the United Kingdom after 2012, the

[45] Statement by Home Secretary Theresa May, Written Ministerial Statements, 29 February 2012, col 35WS.

[46] See eg Nick Clarke and Leena Kumarappan, 'Turning a Blind Eye: The British State and Migrant Domestic Workers' Employment Rights' Working Lives Research Institute (August 2011); Kate Roberts, 'Non Priority Slaves?' Migrants Rights Network (20 December 2013).

[47] See the briefings of the NGO Kalayaan at <www.kalayaan.org.uk/>. Further reports and discussions of this issue during the first years include Human Rights Watch, 'Hidden Away', (March 2014); Centre for Social Justice Report, 'It Happens Here' (March 2013); Andrew Boff, 'Shadow City, Exposing Human Trafficking in Everyday London' GLA Conservatives (October 2013); Frank Field MP, 'Report of the Modern Slavery Evidence Review' (December 2013).

[48] UN Special Rapporteur on Violence Against Women, 15 April 2014 <www.ohchr.org/en/statements/2014/04/special-rapporteur-violence-against-women-finalizes-country-mission-united> accessed 1 July 2022.

pattern was confirmed.[49] Domestic workers under the UK ODW visa are exploited, living and working in appalling conditions, and abused. Perhaps even more importantly, the workers whom I interviewed were undocumented because they escaped abusive employers. As they had no legal right to change employer, they became trapped in this way in ongoing cycles of exploitation by employers who were aware of their legal status as undocumented workers.

The story of Ella (not her real name), one of my interviewees who is originally from the Philippines, exemplifies how the structure of exploitation is created and maintained through law. Ella migrated to work in Qatar, under a *kafala* visa, and came to the United Kingdom accompanying her employers under a UK ODW visa. While in the United Kingdom, she worked day and night as a domestic worker, cared for one of her employers who had serious health issues and the family's youngest child, and slept in the storage room. She was paid about £200 per month. The employers did not give her food and she was very hungry, so she left them after a few days in London. By leaving them she became undocumented because of her visa conditions. She had four young children back home, and she needed to continue working to support them, which is why she could not return to the Philippines. After leaving her employers in the United Kingdom, she started looking for other work as a domestic worker. She found some part-time jobs, but they were always underpaid, and often employers offered hourly pay that was below the national minimum wage: 'Sometimes if you have an interview and you tell [the prospective employers] that you don't have papers, they take advantage of you and they give you a small salary', she said to me. When the employers were away on holiday, they did not pay her. She also had some health issues but did not go to the doctor because she was undocumented.

About 20,000 ODW visas are issued each year, according to statistics provided by the Home Office. The Home Office does not provide any further information on the arrivals but produces data on the nationality of the employers. About 80 per cent of the employers under the ODW visa come from a very small number of countries in the Middle East: 4,894 from the United Arab Emirates, 3,996 from Saudi Arabia, 2,581 from Qatar, 1,005 from Kuwait, and 257 from Oman.[50]

The ODW visa became a central political issue during the passing of the UK Modern Slavery Act 2015, which codified and consolidated existing criminal

[49] See Virginia Mantouvalou, '"Am I Free Now?" Overseas Domestic Workers in Slavery' (2015) 42 Journal of Law and Society 329.

[50] Lord Bates, 25 February 2015, Hansard col 1701.

legislation, while also increasing penalties for offenders.[51] It was argued that if the government are indeed committed to tackling the worst forms of labour exploitation, they should change this visa that made workers extremely vulnerable. Despite civil society mobilisation and other forms of political pressure, there have been very limited changes to the visa. Since 2016, domestic workers have an unconditional right to change employer only during the six months of the duration of the visa.[52] This change is ineffective because it is very unlikely that someone will employ a domestic worker for a period of two or three months only, namely until the expiration of their visa.[53] In addition, domestic workers who are recognised as victims of human trafficking can change employer and stay in the United Kingdom for up to two years.[54] This change is not satisfactory either, given the fear of deportation which makes workers reluctant to contact the authorities, the challenges in being recognised as a victim of trafficking, and the fact that some will not have a right to work during lengthy periods.[55] Workers who are in the process of being recognised as victims of trafficking and whose visa expires before entering the process end up in destitution because they have no right to work. Workers who are recognised as victims of trafficking, on the other hand, may still be deported and placed at a real risk of re-trafficking, that is, a risk of being trafficked again soon after they have exited the situation.[56] In this way, their ordeal starts all over again. It is therefore clear that the legislative change of 2016

[51] I discuss this in Mantouvalou (n 49) and in Virginia Mantouvalou, 'The UK Modern Slavery Act Three Years On' (2018) 81 Modern Law Review 1017. See also Emily Kenway, *The Truth About Modern Slavery* (Pluto Press 2021) 53ff.

[52] The right to change employers is not in the Immigration Rules but is explained on the government's website 'Overseas Domestic Worker visa' Home Office, 'Immigration Rules. Appendix Overseas Domestic Worker—Updated 28 June 2022' <www.gov.uk/guidance/immigration-rules/immigration-rules-appendix-overseas-domestic-worker> accessed 1 July 2022.

[53] See the statement by Baroness Hamwee, in the discussion of the Nationality and Borders Bill, HL Deb 10 February 2022, vol 818, col 1911. See also the joint statement of Kalayaan, Immigration Law Practitioners Association, Liberty, the Voice of Domestic Workers, Joint Council for the Welfare of Immigrants and Kanlungan, 1 March 2022 <https://ilpa.org.uk/wp-content/uploads/2022/02/ILPA-JCWI-Kalayaan-and-Others-Briefing-Overseas-Domestic-Workers-Amendment-Report.pdf> accessed 1 July 2022. The piece by Robert Wright, 'Behind Closed Doors: Modern Slavery in Kensington' *Financial Times* (21 February 2020) provides further illustrations of the persisting problems.

[54] Home Office, 'Immigration Rules. Appendix Domestic Worker Who Is a Victim of Modern Slavery—Updated 28 June 2022' <www.gov.uk/guidance/immigration-rules/immigration-rules-appendix-domestic-worker-who-is-a-victim-of-modern-slavery, accessed 1 July 2022.

[55] On the right to work of domestic workers in the process of being recognised as victims of trafficking, see the 2019 Kalayaan Report by Natalie Sedacca and Avril Sharp, 'Dignity, Not Destitution—The Impact of Differential Rights of Work for Migrant Domestic Workers Referred to the National Referral Mechanism'. For a criticism of the 2016 changes, see Kalayaan, 'Overseas Domestic Workers Left in the Dark by the Immigration Act 2016' (28 June 2016).

[56] See eg Alison Jobe, 'The Causes and Consequences of Re-Trafficking' (International Organization for Migration 2010). On problems in the UK anti-trafficking system, which sometimes puts people at risk of re-trafficking, see Labour Exploitation Advisory Group, 'Detaining Victims: Human Trafficking and the UK Immigration System' (2019) 49.

does not address the structural factors that create vulnerability to exploitation. Even domestic workers who are exploited or abused will be very reluctant to leave their employer for fear of deportation. Those who leave may be trapped in exploitation and destitution, and even those who are recognised as victims of trafficking may be re-trafficked.

A further example of a restrictive visa scheme in the domestic work sector is the Live-in-Caregiver Programme in Canada. Under this scheme, which is part of Canada's Temporary Foreign Worker Programme, families in Canada can employ caregivers from overseas for care work at home, and some light household tasks. The scheme is far less restrictive than the UK ODW visa as it is linked to a route to permanent residence after a period of twenty-four months, or 3,900 hours during a period of forty-eight months. This notwithstanding, it was criticised in the past for creating vulnerability for workers. The key feature of the visa that was described as problematic was the requirement that the worker live in the employer's home. Empirical evidence showed that the live-in requirement was connected to widespread abuse, and supported the position that it should be abolished.[57] Scholars argued that the scheme exacerbates the vulnerability to exploitation of this group of workers.[58] It was particularly emphasised that domestic workers have a clear preference to live out because, when they live in the employer's household, there is an expectation of constant availability by the employer and significant restrictions on workers' autonomy, for reasons such as the fact that they cannot have a private or family life.[59] In recent years, the requirement to live in the employer's household was removed in a new programme that was introduced: the In-Home Caregiver Programme.[60]

Agricultural Workers

Another low-paid sector with a high concentration of workers under temporary labour migration schemes is agriculture. Agricultural work is

[57] Elsa Galerand, Martin Gallié, and Jeanne Ollivier-Gobeil in collaboration with PINAY and the Service aux collectivités of UQAM, 'Domestic Labour and Exploitation: The Case of the Live-In Caregiver Program in Canada' (2015) <https://www.mcgill.ca/lldrl/files/lldrl/15.01.09_rapport_en_vu1.1.13_0.pdf> accessed 15 October 2022.

[58] See eg Christine Straehle, 'Global Justice, Temporary Migration and Vulnerability' (2012) 5 Global Justice: Theory, Practice, Rhetoric 71.

[59] Blackett (n 29) 65–68.

[60] For further discussion of the live-in requirement in Canada and other legal orders, see Karin Schwiter, Kendra Strauss, and Kim England, 'At Home with the Boss: Migrant Live-in Caregivers, Social Reproduction and Constrained Agency in the UK, Canada, Austria and Switzerland' (2018) 43 Transactions of the Institute of British Geographers 462.

challenging for several reasons.[61] It is typically seasonal work, the implication being that workers do not have a guaranteed income throughout the year. Moreover, these workers may be reluctant to claim a pay rise or enforce their rights because the employer may then not want to rehire them for the following season. In addition, agricultural work is dangerous. According to estimates of the ILO, over 170,000 agricultural workers are killed each year at work around the world.[62] Many are injured in industrial accidents by the machinery used, or poisoned by pesticides. As they are temporary workers, they are more likely to be involved in accidents because they are often new to the work that they do. Working in rural areas also means that the workers are isolated: they cannot easily access legal advice or be approached by trade unions. The accommodation of agricultural workers can also constitute a challenge. It is often provided by the employer, as it can be convenient to live close to work. However, this also means that if a worker leaves their job, they will lose this accommodation. For migrant workers, the implication of this may be that they become homeless. Finally, agricultural workers are often employed through agencies, which creates further challenges because it is not always clear who is the employer: the agency or the farm business.[63]

Seasonal worker visas in agriculture exist in many countries.[64] Canada's Temporary Foreign Worker Programme has a stream for agricultural workers that allows employers to hire seasonal workers. Canada has been relying on seasonal workers in agriculture for many years now. In 2017, there were about 550,000 temporary migrant workers in Canada, and a significant percentage of them were in agriculture.[65] These workers can stay in the country for up to eight months per calendar year. They can return to Canada with a new visa every year but have no clear route to permanent residence. Similar to the Canadian

61 As highlighted in ACL Davies, 'Migrant Workers in Agriculture' in *Migrants at Work* (n 1) 79, 80–81. See also Vladimir Bogoeski, 'Harvesting Injustice: How the Legacy of Neoliberal Labour Market Regulation Helps Exclude Seasonal Migrant Workers from Social Security in Germany' (*VerfBlog*, 20 April 2021) <https://verfassungsblog.de/harvesting-injustice/> accessed 15 October 2022. For an overview on farm work in several countries, including the United States, Mexico, Brazil, and various European countries, see Philip Martin, *The Prosperity Paradox: Fewer and More Vulnerable Farm Workers* (OUP 2020).

62 ILO, 'Agriculture: A Hazardous Work' <www.ilo.org/safework/areasofwork/hazardous-work/WCMS_110188/lang--en/index.htm> accessed 15 October 2022.

63 The discussion of the challenges of the sector draws on Davies (n 61). On agency work, see ACL Davies, 'The Implementation of the Directive on Temporary Agency Work in the UK: A Missed Opportunity' (2010) 1 European Labour Law Journal 303. On legal rules on agency work, see further Chapter 6.

64 See generally Joanna Howe and Rosemary Owens (eds), *Temporary Labour Migration in the Global Era* (Hart 2016).

65 Yuqian Lu, 'The Distribution of Temporary Foreign Workers Across Industries in Canada' <www150.statcan.gc.ca/n1/en/pub/45-28-0001/2020001/article/00028-eng.pdf?st=EjyRhs1B> accessed 15 October 2022.

Live-in Caregivers scheme, the agricultural workers' scheme is regularly criticised for creating vulnerability, being connected to structures of exploitation,[66] creating health risks,[67] and keeping temporary migrants permanently at the margins of Canadian society.[68]

In Sweden, labour migration is led by employer demand and work permits are temporary. For a worker to be offered a work permit, they need to have a job offer. Writing on the topic in 2016, Olsson explained that the duration of each work permit was up to two years and renewable, but only exceptionally, for over four years.[69] After working for four years in a period of seven years, migrant workers could apply for permanent residence. The worker was tied to an employer and work sector for the first two years, but after two years they were no longer tied to an employer. Moreover, if a migrant worker wanted to change employer, they had a right to apply without leaving the country. So as to protect workers from being too reliant on a specific employer, workers had a right to stay in Sweden for three to four months to find a new job if they lost the job for which they had a permit. Even though these visa conditions were less restrictive than in other countries, workers in agriculture protested, and their treatment was even described as forced labour.[70] This underscores the challenges always faced by workers in these sectors and the reality that restrictions on their visa conditions always create severe challenges to workers' autonomy.

At European Union (EU) level, with free movement rules in place, there were relatively limited needs for workers from outside the EU.[71] All migrant workers generally face increased challenges in comparison to a country's nationals,

[66] Kerry Preibisch, 'Pick-Your-Own Labor: Migrant Workers and Flexibility in Canadian Agriculture' (2010) 44 International Migration Review 404; Vivianne Landry and others, 'The Systemized Exploitation of Temporary Migrant Agricultural Workers in Canada: Exacerbation of Health Vulnerabilities during the COVID-19 Pandemic and Recommendations for the Future' (2021) 3 Journal of Migration and Health 100035.

[67] Jenna L Hennebry and Janet McLaughlin, '"The Exception that Proves the Rule": Structural Vulnerability, Health Risks, and Consequences for Temporary Migrant Farm Workers in Canada' in Patti Tamara Lenard and Christine Straehle (eds), *Legislated Inequality: Temporary Labour Migration in Canada* (McGill-Queen's University Press 2012) 117.

[68] Lenard and Straehle (eds) (n 67).

[69] Petra Herzfeld Olsson, 'Empowering Temporary Migrant Workers in Sweden—A Call for Unequal Treatment' in Howe and Owens (eds) (n 10) 203, 207–08.

[70] Charles Woolfson, Petra Herzfeld Olsson, and Christer Thornqvist, 'Forced Labour and Migrant Berry Pickers in Sweden' (2012) 28 International Journal of Comparative Labour Law and Industrial Relations 147.

[71] There are still migrant workers from so-called third (non-EU) countries, though. See Marie-Laure Augère-Granier, 'Migrant Seasonal Workers in the European Agricultural Sector' (European Parliament, February 2021). There is a Seasonal Worker Directive: Directive 2014/36/EU of the European Parliament and of the Council of 26 February 2014 on the conditions of entry and stay of third-country nationals for the purpose of employment as seasonal workers. For critical analysis of the Directive, see Fotis Bregiannis, 'An Analysis of the EU Seasonal Workers Directive in the Light of Two Similar Regimes: Three Dimensions of Regulated Inequality' (2021) 12 European Labour Law Journal 266.

because of language barriers, lack of support networks, and other such reasons. Yet the end of free movement in the United Kingdom led to a new scheme that can serve to illustrate how restrictions on visa conditions create particularly serious problems for workers' rights.[72] The United Kingdom had a seasonal worker visa between 1945 and 2013, when it was discontinued.[73] However, from 2019, following the decision to leave the EU, it reintroduced a pilot seasonal worker visa, which it expanded in 2020 to cover the labour shortages that followed the end of free movement. The pilot involved 2,500 workers initially and was increased to 30,000 workers in 2021, while a further increase to 40,000 workers, including some on eight-week visas, was announced in 2022.[74] Early empirical evidence suggests that the workers under the pilot experience severe labour exploitation. The organisation Focus on Labour Exploitation (FLEX) produced research which showed that workers' recruitment, working conditions, and living conditions exhibit elements of compulsion and duress, and that workers cannot leave their employer.[75]

The programme is a sponsored visa which is run by certain approved intermediaries. This is another feature that creates dependency of the workers, not on the employer alone but also on the intermediaries. They are required by the scheme to make sure that workers are able to move to another employer *where possible*.[76] The fact that workers are not free to change employer, but are only permitted to change where possible, was presented by FLEX as a factor that creates vulnerability, particularly because some workers incur debts in order to travel to the United Kingdom which means that they cannot easily leave the job and return to their home country.[77] They have debts to pay back. Many workers who were interviewed by FLEX said that they were unable to change employer. For instance, one worker said:

[72] For an overview, see Melanie Gower, Sarah Coe, and Iona Stewart, 'Recruitment Support for Agricultural Workers', Commons Library Debate Pack, 24 May 2022, CDP 2022/0094.

[73] On the history of the scheme, see ACL Davies, 'Problems Continue in the Horticulture Sector: The Seasonal Workers Pilot Review 2019' (2022) 51 Industrial Law Journal 494.

[74] Answer to a parliamentary question tabled by Daniel Poulter MP, 16 June 2022 <https://questions-statements.parliament.uk/written-questions/detail/2022-06-09/15228> accessed 15 October 2022.

[75] Focus on Labour Exploitation and Fife Migrants Forum, 'Assessment of the Risks of Human Trafficking for Forced Labour on the UK Seasonal Workers Pilot' (2021) (hereafter FLEX Report). See also Work Rights Centre, 'Weed Out Exploitation', Work Rights Centre (2 March 2022); and Davies (n 73) 496ff.

[76] Home Office Guidance for sponsors on the right to change employer states:

> You must not *normally* refuse requests from participating workers to change employers. Participating workers can change employers if they wish and must normally be allowed to do so, unless there are significant reasons not to permit this (for example, their visa will imminently expire and the duration of the necessary training requirements would make such a move impractical).

See 'Workers and Temporary Workers: guidance for sponsors' (April 2022) (emphasis added).

[77] FLEX Report (n 75) 58.

> We even went to look for other farms. We found one, who wanted to accept us. There was a place, they needed workers. We wanted to go there, so we went straight there [to the employer] and we said that all wanted a transfer, she [the employer representative] said 'I can't let you go, understand us, we need workers, everything will be fine'.[78]

Workers also explained that supervisors remind them that their visa is tied to the agency and can be withdrawn at any time.[79] In this way, they create fear in order to control workers. Further restrictions faced by these workers, such as the prohibition on being accompanied by family members, are also problematic. This was accentuated following Russia's invasion of Ukraine, when Ukrainian farm workers in the United Kingdom were not permitted to bring in their family members seeking to escape war.[80]

As with domestic workers, the vulnerability of workers in agriculture is not only due to immigration rules. It is also due to other rules that exclude them from protective laws, such as social security rights,[81] as well as other factors that have to do with the nature of the work and the fact that they are migrant workers. However, the restrictive immigration regime with which these seasonal workers arrive in the host country has to be seen as a major cause of vulnerability to exploitation, and one which employers regularly exploit across the world. The complex web of immigration conditions, other legislative exclusions, and further factors, such as the workers' physical isolation and the challenges in unionising them, places these workers in a position of severe disadvantage.

Temporary migration schemes contain a range of conditions which increase workers' vulnerability to exploitation, as we have seen. The main feature of the immigration rules that exacerbates the challenges faced by migrant workers is the inability to change employer. Workers are unwilling to leave abusive and exploitative employers because they fear deportation or because they know that if they become undocumented, they are even more vulnerable to exploitation. Other visa conditions, such as the inability to change work sector and the requirement to live in the employer's household (for domestic workers) or live on the employer's farm (for workers in agriculture), also afford employers great

[78] ibid 59.
[79] Work Rights Centre (n 75) 4.
[80] Diane Taylor, '"Scandal in Plain Sight": Charities Call for Help for Ukrainian Seasonal Workers' *The Guardian* (28 March 2022. The Ukraine Extension Scheme that was announced has also been criticised for several reasons. See FLEX, 'Filling the Gaps: Preventing Increased Risks of Exploitation for Ukrainian Workers on the Seasonal Worker Visa' (8 April 2022).
[81] See eg Bogoeski (n 61).

power to exercise control over workers and seriously limit their autonomy. All the rules that contain these conditions are connected to structures of exploitation which are state-mediated.

Undocumented Workers

In 2015, forty-two Bangladeshi nationals took a case against Greece in the European Court of Human Rights.[82] The applicants were undocumented workers who worked as strawberry pickers in Manolada, in the south of Greece. They had been promised twenty-two euros for seven hours' work a day and three euros per hour for overtime, yet they had three euros per day deducted for food. In reality, they worked twelve hours a day as strawberry pickers, and were supervised by armed guards. The employers had threatened that they would only be paid if they continued working for them. The workers lived in cardboard shacks with no toilets or water. They went on strike to demand their pay but were not successful. When they complained about their ill-treatment, the workers were shot and injured by the employer's armed guards.

The situation in the Manolada region had been well-known to the Greek authorities for years before. Already in 2008, the Greek Ombudsman produced a Report on working and living conditions of undocumented workers in the area and proposed measures that needed to be taken. The issue was also covered widely in the national press and debated in Parliament. The European Court of Human Rights found a violation of the European Convention of Human Rights and awarded compensation to the applicants.[83]

The incident in Manolada is not isolated. A recent study estimated that there are about 200,000 South Asian migrants in Greece, mostly undocumented men.[84] According to in-depth interviews, many undocumented workers are exploited and constantly threatened with deportation by their employers,[85] but do not leave the country hoping that at some point their immigration status will be regularised. The employers and the overall sector, which is important for Greece's exports, benefit from their undocumented status by underpaying

[82] *Chowdury v Greece* App no 21884/15 (Judgment, 30 March 2017).
[83] See further Chapter 7.
[84] See Reena Kukreja, 'Visible Yet Invisible: The Disciplinary Mechanism of Self-Surveillance Among Undocumented South Asian Male Migrants in Rural Greece' (2021) 47 Journal of Ethnic and Migration Studies 3660.
[85] ibid.

them and keeping them in exploitative living and working conditions, and the economy benefits too.

Many other countries, such as the United States and Japan, tacitly tolerate the systematic use of undocumented workers.[86] Undocumented migrants are usually employed in precarious sectors and sectors with low union density, such as domestic labour, sex work, agriculture, construction, and manufacturing.[87] Employers often prefer to employ undocumented workers rather than documented migrants or local workers precisely because they fear deportation. Anderson and Ruhs have argued that employers perceive undocumented workers as workers with a better 'work ethic' than others, willing to accept worse working conditions than lawful residents or the country's own nationals.[88] The employer, as they explain, does not need to actually know the exact immigration status of the worker: it is the perception of this immigration status (together with the existence of this status) that makes these workers vulnerable, and makes the employers keen to employ them.[89]

Sometimes it is the same immigration rules that I described earlier as problematic, namely the restrictive visa schemes, which lead to workers becoming undocumented. Having left abusive employers, they lose the legal right to stay in the country. Employers take advantage of the status of these workers, as they believe that they are less likely than others to claim their rights, and also threaten them that they will be reported to the authorities. The legal status of illegality creates vulnerability and workers who are exploitable and regularly exploited.[90]

It is also important to underline here that, in some legal orders, being undocumented has further legal implications for workers. In some countries, undocumented workers do not have a right to join a trade union.[91] Illegality bars the judicial protection of labour rights, as the EU Fundamental Rights Agency also highlighted in a survey of EU member states,[92] and has as an effect the unjust enrichment of the employer.[93] Some legal orders place more weight on

[86] Stephen Castles, 'Guestworkers in Europe: A Resurrection?' (2006) 40 International Migration Review 741, 747.

[87] Bridget Anderson, *Us and Them? The Dangerous Politics of Immigration Control* (OUP 2013) 79ff.

[88] Bridget Anderson and Martin Ruhs, 'Migrant Workers: Who Needs Them?' in Bridget Anderson and Martin Ruhs (eds), *Who Needs Migrant Workers* (OUP 2010) 15, 30–31.

[89] ibid 31.

[90] On illegality and vulnerability, see Nicholas P De Genova, 'Migrant "Illegality" and Deportability in Everyday Life' (2002) 31 Annual Review of Anthropology 419.

[91] See Fundamental Rights Agency Report, 'Fundamental Rights of Migrants in an Irregular Situation in the European Union' (2011) 55, which refers to Cyprus, Latvia, and Lithuania.

[92] ibid. See also Nicola Countouris, 'The Legal Determinants of Precariousness in Personal Work Relations' (2012) 34 Comparative Labor Law and Policy Journal 21, 27–28.

[93] On this, see Elaine Dewhurst, 'The Right of Irregular Immigrants to Back Pay' in Costello and Freedland (eds) *Migrants at Work* (n 1). On the position in the United Kingdom, see Alan Bogg,

the preservation of the 'integrity of the legal system',[94] which on a widely held view would be undermined if undocumented workers who therefore have an illegal contract are paid for the work they do. Perhaps the worst instantiation of the role of the law for undocumented workers is when working without a work visa or other right to work documentation becomes a criminal offence. The UK Immigration Act 2016 not only criminalises 'illegal working' but also allows for workers' salaries to be seized by the authorities under the Proceeds of Crime Act 2002, a policy adopted in the context of the creation of a 'hostile environment' for undocumented migrants.[95] In this way, undocumented workers' labour is viewed as a criminal offence, for which not only are they not compensated but for which they are punished through the confiscation of their wages.

Conclusion

Migrant workers are not only vulnerable because of immigration rules. Global inequality and poverty are structural features of the world order, constituting a central reason why many people migrate and making them more vulnerable than other workers. Migrant workers in low-paid sectors are vulnerable to exploitation by employers for a number of reasons, such as background conditions of poverty in their home country; a need to support dependents; language barriers; low levels of unionisation; and working in dangerous, undervalued, and difficult jobs. We would expect legal rules to protect them from exploitation, but we find instead that immigration rules exacerbate their vulnerability and are connected to state-mediated structures of exploitation. Migrant workers are employed in substandard conditions, and the employers make a profit while national economies also benefit from the situation. These workers cannot easily change employer so as to find better conditions. Being anxious about their legal status, they are also reluctant to claim their labour rights through unionising or other avenues that are in any case difficult to access. Sometimes they are trapped in exploitative conditions because they need to pay off debts that they incurred when they travelled. The status of being an

'*Okedina v Chikale* and Contract Illegality: New Dawn or False Dawn?' (2020) 49 Industrial Law Journal 258.

[94] See the discussion in *Hounga (Appellant) v Allen (Respondent)* [2014] UKSC 47 [43]–[44].

[95] For an overview of the 'hostile environment' policies, see Melanie Griffiths and Colin Yeo, 'The UK's Hostile Environment: Deputising Immigration Control' (2021) 41 Critical Social Policy 521.

undocumented worker comes with even more fear of deportation, but also with additional legal exclusions from protective rules. Workers, trade unions, and civil society organisations that support the rights of migrant workers campaign constantly for visa rules to be liberalised in order to recognise necessary safeguards, including rights to change employer and work sector, as well as a clear path to permanent residence. However, improvements of their visa conditions have been very limited and at times ineffective, with anti-immigration sentiments being on the rise in many countries.

These structures of exploitation are not limited to substandard living and working conditions. It has been demonstrated that precarious work is a social determinant that affects workers' health.[96] Yet migrant workers in these schemes have limited social rights, such as rights to healthcare in the host country. If they are undocumented, they are even more isolated, exploited, and trapped, having greater fear and fewer avenues to claim their legal rights. Employers benefit from the vulnerability of these workers, and so do national economies. This is not a triple win: people with limited alternatives find themselves trapped in structures of exploitation, and the law has a major role to play in this situation.

[96] Joan Benach and others, 'Precarious Employment: Understanding an Emerging Social Determinant of Health' (2014) 35 Annual Review of Public Health 229.

4
Captive Workers

Prisoners, those who are sentenced to community work, and people in immigration detention are often in a position of disadvantage because of poverty or race.[1] Having work opportunities while deprived of their physical freedom can serve important purposes, such as learning new skills that can be useful for their societal reintegration after captivity. However, they are often forced to work while also being excluded from the protection of labour and social security rights. Legal rules exacerbate their vulnerability by removing fundamental protections that other workers have, and are connected to widespread structures of exploitation. In this chapter, I examine these rules and find that even though they may have an appearance of legitimacy, they increase or perpetuate people's vulnerability, thereby making them prone to exploitation, while both profit-making entities and the state systematically exploit them. There is a continuum of exploitation in all these settings which is either central to, or associated with, criminal justice and immigration controls.

Prison Work

Imprisonment is part of the criminal justice system that purports to promote a number of objectives, such as punishment of the perpetrator of a crime as well as rehabilitation.[2] In this context, legal documents that are concerned with prisoners' rights present work as 'part of an overall prison regime which aspires to the rehabilitation of criminal offenders, preparing them for eventual reintegration into life as free citizens'.[3] The European Court of Human Rights has repeatedly examined prison conditions and has recognised that rehabilitation

[1] The link between poverty and criminal justice has been discussed extensively in the literature. See eg Jeffrey Reiman, *The Rich Get Richer and the Poor Get Prison—Ideology, Class and Criminal Justice*, originally published in 1979. On poverty and race, see eg Angela Y Davis, *Are Prisons Obsolete?* (Seven Stories Press 2003); Erin Hatton, 'Working Behind Bars—Prison Labor in America' in Erin Hatton (ed), *Labor and Punishment* (University of California Press 2021).

[2] See Anthony Duff, 'Punishment and Rehabilitation—or Rehabilitation as Punishment' (2005) 60 Criminal Justice Matters 18.

[3] ILO Report of the Director General, 'A Global Alliance Against Forced Labour' (2005) 27.

Structural Injustice and Workers' Rights. Virginia Mantouvalou, Oxford University Press. © Virginia Mantouvalou 2023.
DOI: 10.1093/oso/9780192857156.003.0004

and reintegration is a central purpose of imprisonment.[4] The UN Standard Minimum Rules for the Treatment of Prisoners (Nelson Mandela Rules) provide that:

> Sentenced prisoners shall have the opportunity to work and/or to actively participate in their rehabilitation, subject to a determination of physical and mental fitness by a physician or other qualified health-care professionals.[5]

Work in prison is therefore not typically part of prisoners' punishment. It is justified, instead, on the basis of other reasons. A key reason is that prison work can promote prisoners' reintegration by teaching them new skills and improving their employability. By improving employability, it can reduce recidivism.[6] In addition to promoting prisoners' reintegration, it can provide them with income that they can use to support their dependents while in prison and make their life feel less boring and monotonous. It can give them something to do as they try to cope with lengthy and monotonous periods during which they are deprived of their freedom. For reasons such as these, opportunities to work in prison can be desirable, and fair work can be beneficial.[7] Even though work in prison is not part of punishment and should therefore be a right rather than a duty, it is often compulsory. A Council of Europe survey that looked at forty (out of its forty-seven at the time) member states found that, in twenty-five states, prisoners are required to work, at least in certain circumstances.[8] Very often, work in prison is meaningless and repetitive and is perceived by prisoners as part of their punishment rather than a route to reintegration. Those who refuse to work may be sanctioned with reduced visits from friends and

[4] *Khoroshenko v Russia* App no 41418/04 (30 June 2015) para 121. See Sonja Meinjer, 'Rehabilitation as a Positive Obligation' (2017) 25 European Journal of Crime, Criminal Law and Criminal Justice 145.

[5] United Nations Standard Minimum Rules for the Treatment of Prisoners (the Nelson Mandela Rules), Resolution adopted by the General Assembly on 17 December 2015, A/RES/70/175, Rule 96(1).

[6] On this, see Paula Smith, Lindsey M Mueller, and Ryan M Labrecque, 'Employment and Vocation Programs in Prison' in John Wooldredge and Paula Smith (eds), *The Oxford Handbook of Prisons and Imprisonment* (OUP 2017). See also Robert Sampson and John Laub, 'A Life-Course Theory of Cumulative Disadvantage and the Stability of Delinquency' (1997) 7 Advances in Criminological Theory 133; John Haggan, 'The Social Embeddedness of Crime and Unemployment' (1993) 31 Criminology 465; Christopher Uggen and Jeremy Staff, 'Work as a Turning Point for Criminal Offenders' (2001) 5 Corrections Management Quarterly 1.

[7] Richard Lippke, 'Prison Labour: Its Control, Facilitation, and Terms' (1998) 17 Law and Philosophy 533; Howard League for Penal Reform, 'Business Behind Bars: Making Real Work in Prison Work' (2011).

[8] Azerbaijan, the Czech Republic, Estonia, Finland, Georgia, Germany, Hungary, Ireland, Italy, Latvia, Lithuania, Luxembourg, Malta, the Netherlands, Norway, Poland, Montenegro, Russia, Slovakia, Spain, Sweden, Switzerland, Turkey, Ukraine, and the United Kingdom. See *Stummer v Austria* App no 37452/02 (Judgment of 7 July 2011) para 60(a).

family, reduced television or gym time, less or no income, and even solitary confinement.[9]

As early as 1932, the International Labour Organization said that:

> wherever human labour is performed in conditions of subordination, dangers arise; and with prisons, these conditions and the resulting dangers are pushed to the extreme. As a rule, the work of prisoners is performed under compulsion. Thus a penalty involving the obligation to work may easily become the cause of social evils.[10]

Incarcerated people are vulnerable because they do not have freedom of movement,[11] and are hence in a very disadvantaged position in comparison to other workers who are free to move and can change jobs subject to what work is available in the labour market. In addition, those incarcerated have no privacy as they are under constant surveillance, including when they work.[12] There are further problems with prison labour that involve the mentality of the prison authorities and their approach to prisoners, the limited number of work opportunities, and the quality of the work available.[13] All these issues impede the rehabilitative function of work in prison.

My more specific concern here, though, involves legal rules that exclude working prisoners from protection of labour and social security rights, and are connected in this way to state-mediated structures of exploitation. We can see this first of all by looking at constitutional and other human rights provisions that treat working prisoners differently to other workers. Article 4 of the European Convention on Human Rights, which prohibits slavery, servitude, and forced and compulsory labour, states: 'For the purpose of this Article the term "forced or compulsory labour" shall not include [. . .] any work required to be done in the ordinary course of detention imposed according to the provisions of Article 5 of this Convention or during release from such detention.'[14] The Thirteenth Amendment of the US Constitution states that '[n]either

9 Jenna Pandeli, Michael Marinetto, and Jean Jenkins, 'Captive in Cycles of Invisibility? Prisoners' Work for the Private Sector' (2019) 33 Work, Employment and Society 596, 604.

10 Cited in Gerard de Jonge, 'Still "Slaves of the State": Prison Labour and International Law' in Dirk Van Zyl Smit and Frieder Dunkel (eds), *Prison Labour: Salvation or Slavery? International Perspectives* (reissued by Routledge 2018, originally published in 1999) 313, 323.

11 Lippke (n 7) 553.

12 Erin Hatton, *Coerced—Work Under Threat of Punishment* (University of California Press 2020) 104–05.

13 Hatton discusses several examples of degrading treatment of prisoners by prison officers. See eg ibid 112–14. See also Pandeli and others (n 9).

14 ECHR, art 4, para 3(a).

slavery nor involuntary servitude, except as punishment for crime whereof the party shall have been duly convicted, shall exist within the United States, or any place subject to their jurisdiction'. The International Labour Organization (ILO) draws a distinction between private and public prisons in the Forced Labour Convention No 29, and places specific requirements on the regulation of private use of prisoners' labour, on the basis of a concern about the danger of exploitation of prison workers by private entities.[15] It excludes prison work from the scope of the Convention when it is performed in state prisons, but includes privately run prisons.

In comparative studies of European countries, it has been highlighted that working prisoners are often excluded from the right to form trade unions and the right to strike, from being covered by collective agreements or a social security system, and from minimum wage laws.[16] A Council of Europe survey showed that in twelve member states, prisoners are not included in a pension system,[17] while in other countries the affiliation to a social security system depends on the type of work performed, and particularly whether it is remunerated and whether it is for outside employers. In France, for instance, the Criminal Procedure Code states that the employment relations of incarcerated people are not covered by an employment contract.[18] As a result, prisoners do not have a right to form and join trade unions or a right to sick pay. They also do not have a right to have a say on working conditions, or a right to compensation for industrial accidents. Moreover, prisoners are not entitled to the minimum wage, from which they are explicitly excluded by law, as Shea explained in her study. In addition, they do not have the right to access labour courts. Similar exclusions are found in Germany, where prison work is compulsory but those working in prison have better coverage in unemployment protection than in France.[19] Rules such as these exist in many other legal orders, which either explicitly exclude them from protections or view them as outside the

[15] See Faina Milman-Sivan and Yair Sagy, 'On the International Labour Organization and Prison Labour: An Invitation to Recalibrate' (2020) 159 International Labour Review 505; Faina Milman-Sivan, 'Prisoners for Hire: Towards a Normative Justification of the ILO's Prohibition of Private Forced Prisoner Labor' (2013) 36 Fordham International Law Journal 1619; Colin Fenwick, 'Private Use of Prisoners' Labor: Paradoxes of International Human Rights Law' (2005) 27 Human Rights Quarterly 249, 273.

[16] European Prison Observatory, 'Prison in Europe: Overview and Trends' (2013) <www.prisonobservatory.org/upload/PrisoninEuropeOverviewandtrends.pdf> accessed xx xxxx 2022, 30–31. See also Evelyn Shea, 'A Comparative Study of Prison Labour in France, Germany and England' (2006) Penal Issues 11; and 'On Strike in Germany's Jails: An Interview with the Prisoners' Union' <https://rs21.org.uk/2016/01/26/on-strike-in-germanys-jails-an-interview-with-the-prisoners-union/> accessed 15 October 2022.

[17] *Stummer* (n 8) para 60I.

[18] Art 717-3 of the French Criminal Procedure Code.

[19] See generally Shea (n 16).

scope of protective laws as a result of the fact that they are not classified as employees.[20] It has therefore been said that working prisoners are used as a 'source of cheap labour or in order to undercut the wages of local workers'.[21] In other words, the exploitation of working prisoners also has effects on the wages of all workers.

In the United Kingdom, the National Minimum Wage Act 1998 explicitly excludes working prisoners by providing that a 'prisoner does not qualify for the minimum wage in respect of any work which he does in pursuance of prison rules'.[22] In a report published by the Howard League for Penal Reform in 2011, it was documented that the average pay for prison service work is £9.60 per week,[23] while it has also been reported that some prisoners work for up to sixty hours per week.[24] The Prisoners' Earnings Act 1996 applies when a prisoner is paid for 'enhanced wages work' and the person's weekly earnings exceed any prescribed amount. Enhanced wages work is work that is not directed in accordance with prison rules. In this case, the prison authorities may make deductions from the prisoner's pay. According to the Act and related rules, any earnings of prisoners over £20 per week are subject to a levy by the prison authorities to be paid for victim support. All this occurs against a background of privatisation of prison services, with the United Kingdom being described as 'the most marketized prison system in Europe'.[25]

Moreover, in a manner similar to other legal orders, even when there are no explicit exclusions, working prisoners are not covered by many legal protections because they are not viewed as working under a contract of employment.[26] For instance, looking at the question of whether the Factories Act 1937, which applies to those working in factories, also applies to prisons, it was ruled that this is not the case:

> [F]or the Factory Act to apply there must be found to exist […] the relationship of master and servant and employment for wages. There is no employment for wages in the case of prisoners. Prisons are put under the

[20] For an overview of several legal orders, see Van Zyl Smit and Dunkel (n 10).

[21] Andrew Coyle, *A Human Rights Approach to Prison Management* (International Centre for Prison Studies 2009) 92.

[22] UK National Minimum Wage Act 1998, ss 45 and 45A.

[23] Howard League (n 7) 35.

[24] Arianna Silvestri, 'Prison Conditions in the UK' (2013) European Prison Observatory 32.

[25] Kevin Albertson and Chris Fox, 'The Progress of Marketisation: The Prison and Probation Experience' in Kevin Albertson, Mary Corcoran, and Jake Phillips (eds), *Marketisation and Privatisation in Criminal Justice* (Policy Press 2020) 75, 80.

[26] *Pullin v Prison Commissioners* [1957] 1 WLR 1186; *Keatings v Secretary of State for Scotland* 1961 SLT (Sh Ct) 63 (1961).

> control of the Secretary of State, who exercises his control through the Prison Commissioners, and through visiting magistrates who visit the prisons to see that the provisions of the Prison Act 1952, are being carried out.[27]

Prison work is 'penal in the sense that the prisoners are obliged to work as a consequence of their sentence'[28] and the Factories Act cannot apply in that context. The Health and Safety at Work Act 1974 provides that the employer has duties also towards those who are not employees,[29] which suggests that the Act covers those who are not employed under a contract. However, section 52, which defines work for the purposes of the Act, requires a contract. Moreover, many of the detailed regulations, such as the Manual Handling Regulations, are restricted to employees with contracts. The question of whether there is a contract is therefore crucial, as many labour rights are dependent on it.

The issue of the employment status of working prisoners was discussed in the UK Supreme Court decision *Cox v Ministry of Justice*,[30] where a working prisoner in the prison kitchen accidentally injured the catering manager. The question was whether the prison service was vicariously liable for the act of the working prisoner. In the Court's judgment it was pointed out that the relationship of the working prisoner and the prison authorities differs from an employment relationship: prisoners do not work on the basis of contract, but rather because they have been sentenced to imprisonment, and are only paid nominally. However, these features 'rendered the relationship if anything closer than one of employment: it was founded not on mutuality but on compulsion'.[31] The Supreme Court concluded that the prison service was vicariously liable because those working in prison kitchens are integrated into the operation of the prison as their activities are essential for the running of the prison, they work in circumstances where they may commit negligent acts, and they work under the direction of prison staff.[32] The principle of *Cox* that the relationship between the prison authorities and working prisoners is even closer than an employment relation because they are compelled to work should make us question whether it is legitimate to exclude them from basic labour protections.

A purported justification for the exclusion of working prisoners from labour and social security rights is that keeping them in prison is costly and they

[27] *Pullin* (n 26) 1190.
[28] ibid.
[29] UK Health and Safety at Work Act 1974, s 3.
[30] *Cox v Ministry of Justice* [2016] UKSC 10.
[31] ibid [14]; see also [35].
[32] ibid [32].

should therefore contribute to the relevant costs of running the facilities. These reasons to exclude people from labour rights may have an appearance of legitimacy. However, what we observe when we look more closely at the laws in question and the structures that are built as a result must make us challenge the proposed justifications: prisoners and other offenders are systematically required to engage in work with very little or no pay, sometimes doing pointless, monotonous tasks which no-one else is willing to do, for the state or profit-making organisations that make financial gain. State-mediated structures of exploitation are built, and those deprived of their freedom are forced and trapped into these as they have no alternatives. Further, these structures of exploitation are connected to precarious work even after they leave the criminal justice system, as it has been observed that those who have worked in this context 'come to expect—and sometimes embrace—low-wage precarious work outside prison',[33] while they also face serious obstacles when attempting to find better work because of their criminal record.[34]

The state benefits from the exclusions as it reduces its spending on the maintenance of prisons. More crucially, private entities make profit from this underpaid or unpaid work, as we will also see is the case with unpaid work requirements and work in immigration detention. The involvement of private sector organisations in this context takes many forms.[35] Sometimes the facilities are fully privatised. At other times, there may be different forms of collaboration between the public and private, profit-making organisations: the premises may be run by the state, but some of their functions, such as detainees' work, may be outsourced to private contractors. Private entities may also buy goods that have been made by underpaid prisoners in state-run prisons. By excluding working offenders from the protection of labour rights, the law creates vulnerability to exploitation that is systematically exploited both by the state and by profit-making organisations.

Against this background, it has been documented that conditions of prison work do not in reality promote prisoners' rehabilitation.[36] Instead, empirical research has shown that private firms benefit from prisoners' labour as they cannot recruit workers for the jobs in question outside prison, but also because prisoners' labour cost is much lower thanks to their exclusion from protective

[33] Erin Hatton, 'Introduction' in Erin Hatton (ed), *Labor and Punishment—Work in and out of Prison* (University of California Press 2021) 1, 6. I discuss precarious work further in Chapter 6.

[34] See eg Dallas Augustine, 'Working Around the Law: Navigating Legal Barriers to Employment During Reentry' (2019) 44 Law & Social Inquiry 726.

[35] These are discussed in the literature in n 15.

[36] See eg Pandeli and others (n 9) 603.

laws.[37] According to the same study, most prisoners felt that they were forced to do monotonous and pointless tasks, either for the prison authorities or sometimes for private businesses that make profit, and that the skills learned would be of no use for their future employability and reintegration. The study explained that those interviewed had been either unemployed or working in low-skilled jobs before being imprisoned, but prison work gave them no new skills to use after leaving prison.

One of those working in prison who was interviewed said of the work that he was required to do while in prison:

> This job down here, I detest it, I hate it. They ... [the instructors] ... they will tell you, they will attest to this, I don't like [coming here] at all ... I'm not lazy but [these jobs] don't engage my brain, they don't make me feel like I've fulfilled something in the day ... What am I doing? Clipping wires? Smashing computers ... ? (Jermaine, aged 18, Workshop 1).[38]

Other examples of working prisoners' exclusion from protective laws come from the United States, where prison labour for private entities has been described as a 'pot of gold'[39] for this reason. There are over 1.2 million prisoners, and two out of three of them are also workers, according to an extensive study of the American Civil Liberties Union that focused on their exploitation.[40] The rate of incarceration for black Americans is much higher than for white Americans and Hispanics, a phenomenon that is often described as racialised mass incarceration. Working prisoners are not explicitly excluded from basic labour rights protections, which are found in the Fair Labour Standards Act. However, as in several other countries, courts do not view them as employees, so this has the same exclusionary effect. In *Vanskike v Peters*,[41] a court had to examine whether working prisoners who were janitors, kitchen workers, and garment workers were entitled to the minimum wage. It decided that working prisoners were not entitled to the minimum wage because they were not employed by the government: 'prisoners are essentially taken out of the national economy upon incarceration.'[42] Their work, in turn, is part of their sentence

[37] ibid 603–04.
[38] ibid 607.
[39] Linda Evans and Eve Goldberg, 'The Prison Industrial Complex and the Global Economy' (Prison Activist Resource Center 1997) cited in Davis (n 1) 84.
[40] American Civil Liberties Union Report, 'Captive Labor: Exploitation of Incarcerated Workers' (June 2022).
[41] *Vanskike v Peters* 974 F 2d 806 (7th Cir 1992).
[42] ibid.

of imprisonment. As a result, it has been documented that prisoners are paid minimal or no wages at all for prison maintenance work, which is the vast majority of prison work in the United States.[43] The principle that prisoners are not part of the economy has been reiterated in a line of cases examining whether prisoners who work are employees entitled to labour rights.[44]

In addition, *Jones v North Carolina Prisoners' Labor Union* limited rights to free speech and assembly of prisoners and circumscribed in this way their right to organise unions. A prisoners' labour union brought a case to court because the prison authorities banned prisoners from soliciting others to become union members, holding union meetings, and sending bulk mail of the union. The Supreme Court ruled that this ban does not violate free speech and associational rights under the First Amendment. The Court found that it was a reasonable measure adopted by prison authorities that should be left to their discretion as adequate alternatives existed for prisoners, while a prison labour union was fraught with threats to order and security. The majority found that curtailment of constitutional rights, such as the right to association, is justified in prison. Mr Justice Marshall (joined by Mr Justice Brennan) dissented:

> There was a time, not so very long ago, when prisoners were regarded as 'slave[s] of the State,' having 'not only forfeited [their] liberty, but all [their] personal rights....' *Ruffin v. Commonwealth,* 62 Va. 790, 796 (1871). In recent years, however, the courts increasingly have rejected this view, and with it the corollary which holds that courts should keep their 'hands off' penal institutions. [...] Today, however, the Court, in apparent fear of a prison reform organization that has the temerity to call itself a 'union,' takes a giant step backwards toward that discredited conception of prisoners' rights and the role of the courts. I decline to join in what I hope will prove to be a temporary retreat.

Sadly, the ruling in *Jones* has not been overturned. The majority decision accepted in this way a legal structure that makes incarcerated workers vulnerable to exploitation by excluding them from rights to unionise that are of central importance.[45] This is particularly problematic as it affects a group of workers

[43] Hatton (n 1) 21.

[44] Noah Zatz, 'Working at the Boundaries of Markets: Prison Labor and the Economic Dimension of Employment Relationships' (2007) 61 Vanderbilt Law Review 857, 868ff.

[45] Jones v North Carolina Prisoners' Labor Union, Inc., 433 U.S. 119 (1977). See the discussion in Kara Goad, 'Columbia University and Incarcerated Worker Labor Unions under the National Labor Relations Act' (2017) 103 Cornell Law Review 177.

who have no bargaining power because of their status as prisoners who cannot change jobs.

Moreover, there are several studies that have drawn connections between chattel slavery and prison labour in parts of the US South. It has been argued persuasively that convict labour was not only a continuation of slavery with close affinities to it, but that it was also vital for the economic development of the region.[46] The convict lease system was described as a system that 'transferred symbolically significant numbers of black people from the prison of slavery to the slavery of prison'.[47] This was beneficial for those who sought to recruit workers, as it offered to them the power, with the aid of state laws, to hire people whom they can exploit and control.[48] It was also beneficial for the state as it reduced the costs of running prisons and generated income, as Lichtenstein argued.[49]

In 2015, *The Atlantic* published a story entitled 'American Slavery, Reinvented'.[50] It accompanies a powerful documentary on Angola, a former slavery plantation now turned prison in Louisiana, United States. The inmates in that prison are forced to work under the threat of severe sanctions, such as solitary confinement. In the Louisiana Prison, many of those incarcerated are there for the most serious crimes. Some are even on death row. *The Atlantic* piece states that 'Angola's farm operations and other similar prison industries have ancestral roots in the black chattel slavery of the South'. The documentary explains that 'there is a hypocrisy in the way that we talk about these problems in America. We tend to focus on "What do the police do wrong? What do the prisons do wrong?" But the prisons and the police are doing what we and our legislators want them to do.'[51]

Those who are in prison often come from a disadvantaged background and many are imprisoned for poverty-related offences.[52] In prison they are forced into exploitative work and after that they suffer further exclusion, having not acquired skills that can help their reintegration, while also facing great hurdles to acquiring good work because of their criminal record. The state through its

[46] Alex Lichtenstein, *Twice the Work of Free Labor: The Political Economy of Convict Labor in the New South* (Verso 1996). See also Hatton, *Coerced—Work Under Threat of Punishment* (n 12) 1–2.

[47] Angela Y Davis, 'From the Prison of Slavery to the Slavery of Prison: Frederick Douglas and the Convict Lease System' in Joy James (ed), *The Angela Y Davis Reader* (Blackwell 1998) 74, 75. See also the discussion in Angela Y Davis, *Are Prisons Obsolete?* (Seven Stories Press 2003) 28ff.

[48] Lichtenstein (n 46).

[49] ibid. See also Jaron Brown, 'Rooted in Slavery: Prison Labor Exploitation' (2007) Race, Poverty and the Environment 42.

[50] Whitney Benns, 'American Slavery, Reinvented' *The Atlantic* (21 September 2015).

[51] Jeffrey Goldberg, 'Angola for Life' *The Atlantic* (21 September 2015).

[52] Victor Tadros, 'Poverty and Criminal Responsibility' (2009) 43 Journal of Value Inquiry 391.

legal rules plays a major role in the structures of exploitation in place and benefits from the situation, alongside private firms that are involved in prison labour. Even though these rules may have an appearance of legitimacy, for work in prison is said to promote reintegration and to contribute to prison costs, this is very questionable because the rules increase the vulnerability of incarcerated people and are connected to structures of exploitation.

Unpaid Work as a Community Sentence

Community service, when it consists in unpaid work as an alternative to imprisonment, constitutes another example of state-mediated structures of exploitation. Community sentences are 'sanctions and measures which maintain suspects or offenders in the community and involve some restrictions on their liberty through the imposition of conditions and/or obligations'.[53] A requirement to work as a community sentence might be viewed as legitimate in principle, especially when it is subject to conditions. The offenders are deprived of their time and are required to do work that they do not choose as payback to the community, while the main aim of the imposition of an unpaid work sentence is the offender's rehabilitation.[54] United Nations guidance states that when this sentence is imposed, it is crucial to have close supervision so that offenders are 'neither exploited nor forced to work beyond what is required or under unacceptable conditions'.[55] It is usually probation services that ensure this. Members of the community can provide work opportunities for offenders, but it is accepted that they should neither be in charge of enforcing them nor disciplining the offenders.[56]

The use of community sentences in Europe has increased in recent years,[57] while they are also widely used in the United States.[58] Community sentences could be viewed as a positive development in criminal justice because people sentenced to those do not face the grave restrictions to physical freedom

[53] Recommendation of the Committee of Ministers to Member States on the European Rules on community sanctions and measures, CM/Rec(2017)3, 22 March 2017.

[54] Gill McIvor and others, 'Community Service in Belgium, the Netherlands, Scotland and Spain: A Comparative Perspective' (2010) 2 European Journal of Probation 82, 88.

[55] United Nations Office on Drugs and Crime, *Handbook on Basic Principles and Promising Practices on Alternatives to Imprisonment* (2007) 35.

[56] ibid.

[57] See Gill McIvor and others (n 54). See also Marcelo F Aebi, Yuji Z Hashimoto, and Mélanie M Tiago, 'Probation and Prisons in Europe, 2020: Key Findings of the SPACE Reports' (Space—Council of Europe Annual Penal Statistics, June 2021).

[58] Noah Zatz, 'The Carceral State at Work—Exclusion, Coercion and Subordinated Inclusion' in Alan Bogg and others (eds), *Criminality at Work* (OUP 2020) 496, 505.

associated with incarceration. However, this would be misleading for there are specific, serious concerns and risks associated with them.[59]

It has been argued that there has been a turn towards punitive attitudes in the implementation of these sentences, rather than a focus on offenders' rehabilitation.[60] It has also been said that community sentences create a risk of 'net widening', as they may lead to increased criminalisation because of their reduced harshness.[61] They have been linked to other duties imposed by the state to work under the threat of incarceration for those who are not compliant with an obligation to work, presented in this way as an aspect of the so-called 'carceral state'.[62] This is because those who do not comply with requirements to work may be incarcerated. Indeed, in the early 2000s in the United States there were about 9,000 people in prison or jail for not complying with work requirements.[63] Community sentences may also have a humiliating element, which itself poses pressing questions about the treatment of offenders.[64] In England, for instance, those sentenced to community work are required to wear a jacket with 'community payback' written on it.[65] The aim of this can only be to humiliate and stigmatise an offender.[66]

The further issue that is central to what concerns me here is that those sentenced to community work are excluded from minimum wage and other labour rights. The work is unpaid, as it is supposed to be community payback. It is presented typically as a better alternative to incarceration, but in reality the working conditions are very similar to those in prison to the extent that there are exclusions from labour rights, while the work is not chosen: the alternative is incarceration. Similarly, the public benefit from unpaid work is questionable for sometimes the supervisory functions of the unpaid work requirements, usually exercised by the probation service, are privatised. The justification for

[59] See Andrew von Hirsch, 'The Ethics of Community Based Sanctions' (1990) 36 Crime & Delinquency 162. See also Christine Morgenstern and Dirk van Zyl Smit, 'International Human Rights Standards and Community Sanctions' in Gerben Bruinsma and David Weisburd (eds), *Encyclopedia of Criminology and Criminal Justice* (Springer 2014). On other restrictions of freedom of suspected perpetrators of crime and the effects on their autonomy, see Hadassa Noorda, 'Preventive Deprivations of Liberty: Asset Freezes and Travel Bans' (2015) 9 Criminal Law and Philosophy 521.

[60] McIvor and others (n 54).

[61] James Austin and Barry Krisberg, 'Wider, Stronger, and Different Nets: The Dialectics of Criminal Justice Reform' (1981) 18 Journal of Justice and Delinquency 165.

[62] Zatz (n 58).

[63] ibid. See also Noah Zatz, 'Get to Work or Go to Jail: State Violence and the Racialized Production of Precarious Work' (2020) 45 Law and Social Inquiry 304.

[64] See Dirk van Zyl Smit, 'Community Sanctions and European Human Rights Law' in Lucia Zedner and Julian V Roberts (eds), *Principles and Values in Criminal Law and Criminal Justice—Essays in Honour of Andrew Ashworth* (OUP 2012) 191, 203.

[65] ibid.

[66] Von Hirsch (n 59) 168.

this privatisation is that of economic efficiency, which could have an appearance of legitimacy, in a manner similar to the justification of the exclusion from protective laws of work while in prison. However, the supposed justification has to be scrutinised closely because in this way people sentenced to perform unpaid work are used by organisations that make profit. There is a continuum between the exploitation of prisoners and the exploitation of offenders in community sentences who are required to work without being paid. This can also be examined alongside other deprivations of freedom outside prison, which Noorda has described as 'exprisonment' in order to underline the similarities that they have to imprisonment.[67] Unpaid work is not in that respect a better sentence than work in prison, but very similar to it.[68]

Experience in the United Kingdom illustrates the problem of unpaid work as a sentence, which is further accentuated by privatisation. 'Unpaid work requirements' can be imposed by a court under Part 9 of the Sentencing Act 2020 (formerly under the Criminal Justice Act 2003) to those who are sentenced for a criminal offence that is punishable with imprisonment and are over 18 years old. Community sentences are given for offences such as damaging property, benefit fraud, or assault. These can range between 40 and 300 hours of work, and are also known as 'community payback'. The work is supposed to involve tasks that are beneficial to the community, including environmental conservation, decorating buildings, recycling, and working directly with local charities. According to the Justice Select Committee Report *Transforming Rehabilitation*, the purposes of using these as part of a sentence are said to be the offender's punishment, reparation to the community, increased public confidence in the criminal justice system, and reduced chances of reoffending.[69]

In the past, the unpaid work requirements were supervised by public sector Probation Trusts, the role of which was crucial: they liaised with local communities to plan the work, advised the courts on the suitability of the individual for work, and directed and supervised the work. In 2012, the UK government decided to outsource to the private sector the supervision, monitoring, and delivery of unpaid work requirements through a competitive process.[70] The only activity that was kept for the Probation Service was the provision of assistance

[67] Noorda (n 59).

[68] See further analysis in the US context in Noah Zatz, 'Better Than Jail: Social Policy in the Shadow of Racialized Mass Incarceration' (2021) 1 Journal of Law and Political Economy 212. Cf David Garland, 'Penal Controls and Social Controls: Toward a Theory of American Penal Exceptionalism' (2020) 22 Punishment & Society 321.

[69] House of Commons Justice Committee, 'Transforming Rehabilitation' Ninth Report of Session 2017–19 (22 June 2018) 57.

[70] See the Ministry of Justice Consultation Paper 'Punishment and Reform: Effective Probation Services' CP7/2012.

to courts, with the rest of the functions that were previously led by probation services to be privatised. The contract for London was initially awarded to Serco, a private company that profits from running several UK public services and has been implicated in fraud-related scandals.[71] From 2015, the running of unpaid work was privatised across the whole of England and Wales. The privatisation of probation services was the subject of a devastating report by the National Audit Office in 2019, which explained that it had failed in every respect, including the quality of probation services.[72] The government acknowledged this.[73]

In the scheme in question, there was no direct public supervision of unpaid work requirements: the work was to be controlled and supervised by Serco (and from 2015 by Community Rehabilitation Companies), and not by the Probation Trusts. It is not public authorities, in other words, but employees of private entities who exercise crucial functions such as deciding if an offender has failed to comply with an order, so as to refer them to the Probation Service that would bring them before a court. The fact that crucial public functions, such as punishment for a crime, are outsourced to private entities distorts their purpose. However, this is not my primary focus here. My primary focus is on the labour exploitation of offenders.

According to the agreement between the state and the private entity, Serco could place offenders 'at the disposal of private individuals, companies or associations' with no guarantee that work requirements would be of general interest; Serco could, in turn, profit from this work. Not only was there no effective state supervision of the scheme, but it was also placed at the disposal of private companies in the form of the third-party profit-making beneficiaries of unpaid work.[74] Examples of this work for private beneficiaries included work for general medical practitioner partnerships, private sector care homes, private sector nurseries, private sector sheltered accommodation, private cemeteries, and private landowners (via charitable intermediaries). In these examples, it was not only Serco making a profit but also other private bodies. Even though the competitive process for delivery of probation services was discontinued in 2020, the UK government emphasised that they remained committed to collaboration with the private sector in the area.[75]

[71] See eg Alice Troy Donovan, 'Serco: Rewarding Failure?' (*The Justice Gap*, 25 June 2020).
[72] National Audit Office, 'Transforming Rehabilitation: Progress Review' (1 March 2019).
[73] Ministry of Justice, 'Strengthening Probation, Building Confidence' CP 93 (May 2019) 12.
[74] Direct Request (CEACR)—adopted in 2020, published 109th ILC session (2021).
[75] Robert Buckland statement, Hansard, 11 June 2020, Volume 677, col 425–26.

The imposition of unpaid work as a sentence may have an appearance of legitimacy and may seem less restrictive than imprisonment, as discussed earlier. The privatisation of probation services may also appear legitimate, for reasons stated in UK government documentation:

> We propose to introduce a widespread programme of competition, and invite providers from the private and voluntary sectors to bid to deliver the majority of current probation services. We will award contracts to those providers who demonstrate that they can deliver efficient, high quality services and improve value for money.[76]

The authorities can claim that the privatisation in question does not aim to exploit: it aims to improve probation functions and save public money. In this way, it can be presented as legitimate.

Despite the fact that there is a professed justification with an appearance of legitimacy for the measures, the scheme creates vulnerability of offenders by forcing them to work with no pay or other labour rights, supervised by private entities and for other private entities that make profit. Through these special measures, and especially through the private running of unpaid work requirements, the state places offenders for minor offences in unpaid work relationships with profit-making organisations. That the work of offenders is not paid may appear justified as these sentences are viewed as community payback. However, it is not truly justified for it creates a body of workers who are more vulnerable to exploitation than other workers, while the aim of community payback is not met when there is heavy involvement of profit-making organisations in supervising and otherwise benefiting from the scheme.

A key purpose of unpaid work requirements is to give back to the community. A charity reported that someone who experienced the scheme said:

> I like to feel a part of my community. You know, I grew up [x] in alcohol and drugs, you know, I struggled for years and I've done bad stuff in that community if you know what I mean. And for me, [unpaid work] was like, giving something back.[77]

[76] See Ministry of Justice Consultation Paper 'Transforming Rehabilitation: A Revolution in the Way We Manage Offenders' CP1/2013.

[77] Revolving Doors Report <https://revolving-doors.org.uk/wp-content/uploads/2022/02/Revolving-Doors-Agency-MoJ-Strengthening-Probation-Building-Confidence-3.pdf> accessed 16 December 2022.

People also explained that they felt that they benefited most when they could see that they offered something to the community:

> We went to schools where there were disabled children who needed special equipment to get around and we built up their playground. And the enthusiasm of us young people in doing that, we wanted to continue to do that, it really . . . had a really positive impact.[78]

It is questionable whether this purpose is met when the measures are merely punitive and humiliating, when there is no clear and visible state involvement by way of supervision of the conditions, and when there is no protection of labour rights of those sentenced to community service. Instead, through the scheme of unpaid work requirements the state creates structures of exploitation through which private businesses and the state make a profit.

Work in Immigration Detention

Those held in immigration detention very often work while they are detained. Work is not compulsory but it can be crucial to people who are held for lengthy periods of time (months or sometimes even years).[79] Immigration detainees are deprived of their freedom because of immigration rules, not for having committed a crime. In fact, they may be victims of injustice themselves. For instance, in January 2018 a frightened 18-year-old from Vietnam went to a police station in London and reported that he had spent five years being trafficked in and out of cannabis houses by criminal gangs across the capital.[80] He explained how he travelled from Vietnam through Europe, and was then put in the back of a lorry to come to the United Kingdom and work in cannabis cultivation. The police contacted the Home Office, and the man who had been trafficked was detained and sent to an immigration centre, Brook House, where people are placed in detention before deportation.

Some detainees in immigration detention centres are asylum seekers. As a general rule, asylum seekers do not have a right to work in the United Kingdom, and have to survive on just over £5 a day, which means that they

[78] ibid.

[79] It has also been reported that refusal to work may be sanctioned in some detention centres. See Annie Hollister, 'Litigating ICE's "Voluntary Work Program"' (*On Labor*, 10 April 2020).

[80] Annie Kelly and Amelia Gentleman, 'Lorry Deaths: Police Face Trust Problem Over Appeal to Vietnamese Migrants' *The Guardian* (31 October 2019).

cannot meet their basic needs.[81] However, asylum seekers and other detainees in immigration detention centres are allowed to work while in detention, with minimal pay.[82] This was highlighted in parliamentary debates:

> My Lords, does the Minister accept the irony of providing menial, albeit voluntary, work—as she says, it is to meet detainees' recreational and intellectual needs and provide relief from boredom—when asylum seekers are not allowed to work at all? Is the rate of £1 an hour for people who have committed no crime something that as a society we can be proud of?[83]

As we see, work in immigration detention becomes part of a broader structure, together with restrictive visas and other rules, which force and trap people in exploitative labour relations.

The purpose of the institutions of immigration detention and prison is different of course. Unlike imprisonment, the aim of immigration detention is the enforcement of immigration rules by ensuring that those held do not flee to avoid deportation. Immigration detention is part of the administrative process of removal of non-nationals, not of criminal justice. What both institutions have in common is that they deprive people of their liberty, including freedom of movement, freedom to have personal relationships and privacy, but also freedom to engage in work of their choice. All those who are so extensively deprived of their liberty are vulnerable for this reason: because they can be coerced into situations for lack of options. We also observe that it is sometimes the same private firms that run prisons, unpaid work requirements, and immigration detention, and in this way it is the same entities that profit from labour in captivity.

People in immigration detention centres are held because of their immigration status. They may be undocumented because they entered a country with no legal documents in the first place, people who overstayed after their visa expired, or asylum seekers who are detained while their asylum application is pending. Some of those who are in immigration detention may be migrant workers under temporary visas who are in detention because they overstayed their visa.[84] They may even have breached their visa conditions by complying

[81] See the discussion in Melanie Gower, 'Should Asylum Seekers Have Unrestricted Rights to Work in the UK?' House of Commons Library, Briefing Paper 1908 (23 October 2019).

[82] See 'Working for a Pound an Hour: An Immigration Detainee's Perspective' (*Futures of Work Blog*, 20 September 2019) <https://futuresofwork.co.uk/2019/09/30/working-for-a-pound-an-hour-an-immigration-detainees-perspective/> accessed xx xxxx 2022.

[83] Baroness Hamwee, HL Deb 4 July 2017, col 789.

[84] On these issues, see also Chapter 3.

with employers' requirements to work longer hours or on a variety of different tasks,[85] or by escaping employers who exploited or abused them if they were on a visa that tied them to their employer.

Exact numbers of people in immigration detention around the world are not known but numbers have grown significantly the last few decades, and detention periods have become longer. According to estimates of the Global Detention Project, the United States has the most populated immigration detention centres, detaining over 50,000 people on any given day.[86] Hundreds of thousands of people are in immigration detention in the United States each year.[87] In the United Kingdom, about 30,000 people are detained every year in immigration removal centres, which are privatised, while in 1980, there were only a few dozen.[88] The fact that immigration rules have become more restrictive in recent years in the United Kingdom, combined with the government's adoption of a 'hostile environment' towards migrants as an official policy, may explain the increase in numbers of those held in immigration detention.[89]

Many immigration detention facilities either belong to or are run by private enterprises. Even when they are not fully privatised, sometimes specific services, like cleaning and catering, are outsourced to the private sector.[90] There are severe criticisms of the institution of immigration detention, which is used widely in Europe and in the United States and is described as a 'thriving business'.[91] It is regularly reported that there are suicides and attempted suicides, instances of self-harm, detainees experiencing mental health problems, and degrading treatment.[92] Immigration detention has been described as 'one of

[85] Martin Ruhs and Bridget Anderson, 'Semi-Compliance and Illegality in Migrant Labour Markets: An Analysis of Migrants, Employers and the State in the UK' (2010) 16 Population, Space and Place 195.

[86] See Global Detention Project, United States, Overview <https://www.globaldetentionproject.org/countries/americas/united-states#country-report> accessed 16 December 2022.

[87] Anita Sinha, 'Slavery by Another Name: "Voluntary" Immigrant Detainee Labor and the Thirteenth Amendment' (2015) XI Stanford Journal of Civil Rights and Civil Liberties 1.

[88] See 'Review into the Welfare in Detention of Vulnerable Persons—A Report to the Home Office by Stephen Shaw' (January 2016) 31 (hereafter cited as Shaw Report).

[89] Monish Bhatia and Victoria Canning, 'Misery as Business: How Immigration Detention Became a Cash Cow in Britain's Borders' in Kevin Albertson, Mary Corcoran, and Jake Phillips (eds), *Marketisation and Privatisation in Criminal Justice* (Policy 2020) 257, 260. On hostile environment policies more generally, see Melanie Griffiths and Colin Yeo, 'The UK's Hostile Environment: Deputising Immigration Control' (2021) 41 Critical Social Policy 521.

[90] See Lydie Arbogast, 'Migrant Detention in the European Union: A Thriving Business' (MIGREUROP, July 2016).

[91] ibid.

[92] ibid 17. See also International Rescue Committee, 'The Cruelty of Containment—The Mental Health Toll of the EU's "Hotspot" Approach on the Greek Islands' (December 2020).

the singularly most disturbing contemporary practices from the point of view of the rule of law and human rights'.[93]

My focus here is not on the justification of the institution as a whole or on the living conditions in immigration detention centres. Instead, my focus is on the working conditions of those in immigration detention centres, as another instance of what I describe as a state-mediated structure of injustice at work. Legal rules that regulate conditions in immigration detention that have an appearance of legitimacy are linked to structures of exploitation. Like working prisoners, immigration detainees who work are excluded from labour rights, such as minimum wage protection. It is questionable whether they have the protection of working time rights even if not explicitly excluded, or social security rights as they are subject to deportation. Even though immigration detention is not supposed to be punitive, immigration detainees are outside of the system of labour law protection.

In the United States, immigrant detainee labour has been described as 'a continuation of the American practice of exploiting labor through incarceration'.[94] A study explained that detainees who worked while in detention in the United States were paid $1 per day for cleaning the communal areas, cooking, and decorating the facilities. If this work were covered by minimum wage laws, it would be paid $29 to $58 per day. As a result, the entities running detention centres save at least $40 million per year.[95] The legal basis of work in immigration detention in the United States is to be found in a law passed through Congress in 1950, at a time when labour shortages were said to exist (a situation which also led to legislation for guestworkers).[96] The aim of the law in question was to reduce the costs of running immigration detention facilities.

The fact that the legislation on work in immigration detention, on the one hand, and labour shortages and guestwork, on the other, coincided chronologically suggests that immigration detainees were viewed as a source of cheap labour at a time when this was convenient. The law provided for 'payment of allowances (at such rate as may be specified from time to time in the appropriation act involved) to aliens, while held in custody under the immigration laws, for work performed'.[97] Even though the provision implies that payment rates

[93] Cathryn Costello, 'Immigration Detention: The Grounds Beneath Our Feet' (2015) 68 Current Legal Problems 143. See also Corporate Watch, 'Immigration Prisons: Brutal, Unlawful and Profitable—Yarl's Wood: A Case Study' (2011).

[94] Sinha (n 87) 23. See also Jacqueline Stevens, 'The Political Economy of Work in ICE Custody' in Hatton (ed), Labor and Punishment—Work In and Out of Prison (n 1) 86.

[95] Sinha (n 87) 23.

[96] ibid 29 fn 175.

[97] 8 US Code §1555, s 6(d).

should be reviewed regularly, Congress has not changed the minimum hourly rate since the Appropriations Act of 1978, which provides for $1 a day (and possibly an allowance of no more than $1 a day). In the case of *Guevara v INS*,[98] immigration detainees challenged the legality of their rate of pay saying that it was contrary to the Fair Labour Standards Act. The court ruled that they are not workers and are therefore not covered by the Act, the purpose of which is to protect the living standards and well-being of workers in American industry. Like those working in prisons, immigration detainees were found to be outside of this category that serves as a gateway to workers' rights, and hence excluded from important labour law protections.

The UK system of immigration detention was the first one in Europe to be privatised and is run by a small number of multinational companies.[99] It is heavily criticised on many fronts.[100] Under English law, Rule 17 of the Detention Centre Rules says that paid work 'opportunities' may be provided in detention centres. Section 59 of the Immigration, Asylum and Nationality Act 2006 excludes immigration detainees from minimum wage legislation. Detention Services Order 01/2013, in turn, provides that detainees should be paid £1 per hour for 'routine work' (eg cleaning), and £1.25 per hour for 'specified projects' (eg painting).[101] Private companies running these detention centres use detainees to perform essential work for the maintenance of the centres and pay them £1 per hour for this work, according to the Detention Order. Detainees who do not comply with rules in the immigration detention centre or with Home Office requirements to cooperate are not eligible to work.[102] In 2017, it was reported that for 887,073 hours of work while in immigration detention, the pay for detainees was £887,565.[103] In one detention centre in Scotland it was reported that sixty-four detainees worked up to thirty hours a week in cleaning, hairdressing, and gardening, namely essential work for the maintenance of the facilities. The detainees were paid £130,919 for 128,742 hours worked between 2014 and 2017. Had they been entitled to the minimum wage, they would have been paid £727,607 more. Overall, it has been said that private entities that run the centres make in this way important savings of about £3 million a year.[104]

[98] *Guevara v INS*, 902 F 2d 394, 395 (5th Cir 1990).
[99] Arbogast (n 90) 20.
[100] ibid 21.
[101] Detention Services Order 01/2013: Paid work (*Home Office*).
[102] ibid para 10.9.
[103] Bhatia and Canning (n 89) 262.
[104] Corporate Watch, 'UK Border Regime: Detention Centres Briefing' (2018).

According to research on the conditions in one of the UK immigration detention centres, Brook House, there were 116 paid work roles in the centre: '[t]hese included wing orderlies, barbers, kitchen orderlies and posts in the laundry, the garden, the chaplaincy and the food serveries.'[105] Despite performing this work, those detained cannot earn qualifications, certificates, or other forms of recognition for it.[106]

In 2016, the Shaw Report on immigration detention was published. The opening line of the report in relation to detainees' work is surprising for it asserts that the work of detainees is not used by the private contractors to increase their profits. But it continues by accepting that the rates of pay, set by the Home Office, are exploitative, and that some of the contractors would like to pay more but are restricted by the rules that set the rate of pay.[107] By contrast with the opening statement of the Shaw Report, it has been explained that immigration detention centres do make a profit. The Immigration Law Practitioners Association emphasised that:

> [t]he use of contractors ... highlights the question of profit. Details of contracts are not made public or discussed, with 'commercial confidentiality' pleaded ... The private contractor's model is dependent upon the use of their labour, for which they are paid nominal rates, far below the minimum wage. Those in immigration detention are subject to immigration detention. Not to pay them the minimum wage is to allow them to be exploited.[108]

Saving money through paying detainees far below the minimum wage for the maintenance of the detention facilities is profitable, as research by Corporate Watch has also shown.[109]

Further analysis of how work operates in immigration detention centres has shown that detainees perform a number of essential tasks, work is strictly structured through timetables and specific requirements on how to do it, and those working can be sanctioned by being removed from work if their performance does not meet the necessary standards.[110] Detainees are provided with daily schedules that explain the concrete tasks that they need to complete and

[105] Kate Lampard and Ed Marsden, 'Independent Investigation into Concerns about Brook House Immigration Removal Centre' (November 2018) para 9.45.

[106] ibid.

[107] Shaw Report (n 88) 6.145–6.146.

[108] ibid 6.143.

[109] Corporate Watch, 'Detention Centre Profits: 20% and Up for the Migration Prison Bosses' (18 July 2018).

[110] Katie Bales and Lucy Mayblin, 'Unfree Labour in Immigration Detention: Exploitation and Coercion of a Captive Immigrant Workforce' (2018) 47 Economy and Society 191, 196–97.

during which times of the day; they are given an employment job description that contains their job title, their responsibilities, hours of work, and tasks.[111] Thanks to detainees' work, private entities that run the centres do not need to hire workers who would be paid at least the minimum wage in order to do the same work. In this way, those running the immigration detention centres make significant profit, while the law is the reason why those held in immigration detention are exploited by these private entities.

John's story illustrates this.[112] John was detained in 2018 under immigration rules in Brook House, a privately run immigration detention centre, while his asylum claim was pending. He decided to work as a cleaner while in detention for a period of seven months, because he needed income to buy things such as phone credit, food, and energy drinks. The 71p per day offered by the Home Office was insufficient. Another reason why he worked was because it was challenging to be in immigration detention, where you do not know for how long you will be detained, so he needed to make use of his time doing something productive. John had qualifications in cleaning and decorating so he thought that he could contribute to the work offered to detainees in detention centres.

He started working as a cleaner in the communal areas and shower areas and rooms, having shifts of several hours throughout the day and in the evening. He took pride in the work that he did and was commended by detention officers. John never saw any external cleaners at the centre. Detainees seemed to do all the cleaning work, which was essential for the maintenance of the facilities. Despite working hard all day and following his supervisors' instructions, he was paid £4 per day and a maximum of £30 per week for 30 hours' work. Before being detained, he worked as a cleaner and decorator and was paid £9 per hour for work that was similar to the work that he did in the detention centre. The national minimum wage in the United Kingdom was just under £8 per hour at the time. However, legal rules on work in immigration detention exclude working immigration detainees from this protection, as we saw earlier.

John described the effects of this treatment as follows:

> This made me feel even more humiliated because I knew what this work was worth outside the detention walls. I felt that the Home Office were only paying me £1 an hour because they could get away with it. I felt completely exploited by this situation. I was good at my job, as many detention officers told

[111] ibid 198.

[112] This is not his real name. The story appears in 'Working for a Pound an Hour: An Immigration Detainee's Perspective' (n 82).

> me, and deserved to be paid more for the job that I did. I know how valuable that work is for the detention centre and know how much an external cleaner would have been paid to do the same job. There was no opportunity for me to get a pay rise, no matter how good my work was. I felt that this was exploitative and can only describe what I experienced as akin to slave labour.

There are other reported incidents that support the same point. The following story was reported in France, where immigration detention centres are run by the public sector but several of their functions are outsourced to private, profit-making entities: four undocumented workers were employed by a private contractor that won a contract from the French state for building works at an immigration detention centre. They were arrested by the authorities and detained in the same centre where they were working.[113] It is likely that they were paid badly as migrant workers and that they continued working while detained but with almost no pay this time. This is how the law creates structures of exploitation that employers exploit.

Conclusion

Many of those incarcerated, those on unpaid work as a community sentence, and immigration detainees are often already in a position of disadvantage for reasons such as poverty, race, and immigration status. When deprived of their freedom, they are required to work either because it is compulsory under the regime, or because they have no alternatives. The main difference with other employment relationships of course is that these workers do not have the right to quit the exploitative work and change employer. That the state excludes them from protective labour and social security laws is particularly troubling. The exclusions may appear legitimate at first: working prisoners and immigration detainees contribute to the cost of running the facilities, while offenders engaging in community work must pay back the community through their work, as this is their sentence. Yet all these legal rules increase and perpetuate existing structural unfairness: people who are often disadvantaged are excluded from the protection of labour law and are made vulnerable to exploitation by profit-making organisations that take systematic advantage of this situation.

[113] Pascal Liétout, 'Des Clandestins Arrêtés sur le Chantier d'un Centre de Rétention' (Reuters, 10 September 2010).

5

Welfare-to-Work

Welfare-to-work schemes connect welfare benefits to behavioural requirements. They impose obligations on individuals to seek and accept work on the basis that otherwise they will be sanctioned by losing access to welfare support.[1] These schemes are used across the industrialised world and have varying degrees of coerciveness. My concern in this chapter is that it has been shown that laws on schemes with strict conditionality create 'a job-ready supply of workers for the very bottom of the labour market',[2] which fit with the patterns identified in earlier chapters. There is growing evidence that schemes are becoming increasingly punitive and, in this way, they force individuals into exploitative work and in-work poverty instead of supporting them to find a route out of poverty through paid work. Welfare-to-work schemes thereby often turn the unemployed and underemployed poor into working and exploited poor. By deploying coercive conditionality, legal rules push people into precarious work and generate state-mediated structures of injustice in a manner similar to the regulation of work of offenders, immigration detainees, and migrant workers.

Welfare-to-work schemes can be viewed as having an appearance of legitimacy, as their stated purpose is to promote employment and hence social inclusion and also support people out of poverty. However, they create patterns that are very damaging for large numbers of people. The problem here is not that activation policies or non-standard work arrangements can never be legitimate. The claim is that the state creates and sustains a system that can be viewed as legitimate in its aims but problematic when it becomes particularly punitive whilst also forcing the poor into exploitative employment relations that are (mostly) lawful, making exploitation standard and routine. Even though welfare-to-work schemes and non-standard work arrangements, taken separately, might not be necessarily unjust, the overall structure that forces people into workplace exploitation is unjust. Since the state has a role to play in creating the unjust structure, it also has a duty to rectify it.

[1] For an introduction see Beth Watts and Suzanne Fitzpatrick, *Welfare Conditionality* (Routledge 2018).

[2] Jamie Peck and Nikolas Theodore, '"Work First": Workfare and the Regulation of Contingent Labour Markets' (2000) 24 Cambridge Journal of Economics 119, 135.

Structural Injustice and Workers' Rights. Virginia Mantouvalou, Oxford University Press. © Virginia Mantouvalou 2023.
DOI: 10.1093/oso/9780192857156.003.0005

Welfare-to-Work and Poverty

It is typically said that work is the best route out of poverty.[3] On this basis, through welfare-to-work schemes, welfare benefits for working-age people are usually conditional upon making an effort to obtain work. These schemes should be understood as part of the so-called activation policies, which are policies that encourage active engagement with the labour market. A standard justification of activation policies is that they 'improve economic self-reliance and societal integration via gainful employment instead of joblessness and benefit receipt'.[4] This argument that grounds activation policies in the best interests of the recipients is commonly deployed in politics.[5] In addition, it has been argued that active labour market policies can promote equality in the labour market by improving the training of people with low skills.[6]

There are a variety of schemes. In certain countries, activation policies are limited to funding vocational training programmes in order to match supply and demand needs in the market,[7] while others have a stricter conditionality approach. Welfare-to-work schemes are grounded on a promise that people will have either a job or social support that will enable them to cover their basic needs, but also a threat that if they do not make the required effort to get a job and if they do not accept job offers, they will be sanctioned. The sanctions that are imposed either involve reduction or withdrawal of benefits, or replacement of benefits with food stamps.

Even though work is an important good and people generally want to work, there are reasons of principle to question conditional systems of benefit. In 1998, Wolff questioned whether they are compatible with equality, as they require the most disadvantaged in society to reveal information about their circumstances while 'the rich do not have to explain how they got rich',[8] but

[3] See eg the UK government's Response to the Work and Pensions Committee's Nineteenth Report (2017–19) [6].

[4] Werner Eichhorst and others, 'Bringing the Jobless into Work? An Introduction to Activation Policies' in Werner Eichhorst, Otto Kaufmann, and Regina Konle-Seidl (eds), *Bringing the Jobless into Work?* (Springer 2008).

[5] Other arguments that are used to justify these policies include arguments of economic efficiency, sustainability, and justice. See Anders Molander and Gaute Torsvik, 'Getting People into Work: What (if Anything) Can Justify Mandatory Activation of Welfare Recipients?' (2015) 32 Journal of Applied Philosophy 373.

[6] This is discussed in David Rueda, 'The State of the Welfare State—Unemployment, Labor Market Policy, and Inequality in the Age of Workfare' (2015) 47 International Politics 296, 297–98.

[7] See generally Giuliano Bonoli, 'The Political Economy of Active Labor-Market Policy' (2010) 38 Politics and Society 435.

[8] Jonathan Wolff, 'Fairness, Respect and the Egalitarian Ethos' (1998) 27 Philosophy and Public Affairs 97.

also because of what he called 'shameful revelation'.[9] On this analysis, there are things that people do not want to reveal to anyone, including themselves. If someone is unemployed at a time of low unemployment, the failure to be employed is not perceived to be due to external circumstances, but due to lack of talent or aptitude for the jobs that are available. Welfare-to-work schemes in this case require that those who want welfare support prove to themselves and to state authorities that they have failed to get a job despite the fact that there are employment opportunities. They have to reveal facts that may be degrading, embarrassing, or humiliating, and in a manner that makes it impossible to think of themselves as equals in society. 'This removes any last shred of dignity from those already in a very unfortunate position.'[10] Wolff was concerned that egalitarian theories of distributive justice focus on individual responsibility for people's conditions in order to assess the fair distribution of resources, and argued that an egalitarian ethos is not only about fairness in distribution of resources, but also about respect.[11] Wolff's argument is an important normative argument involving the compatibility of these schemes with egalitarian values.[12]

From Unemployed Poor to Working Poor: Clustering Disadvantage

Even though welfare-to-work schemes and their underlying principles are not a new phenomenon, what is new is that they have become especially punitive in recent years.[13] This leads to a 'clustering of disadvantage'.[14] The underlying

[9] ibid 109.
[10] ibid 114.
[11] See also his more recent article, Jonathan Wolff, 'Fairness, Respect and the Egalitarian "Ethos" Revisited' (2010) 14 Journal of Ethics 335.
[12] There are other criticisms of social welfare programmes that target the poor in terms of how effective they are in promoting equality. See eg Walter Korpi and Joakim Palme, 'The Paradox of Redistribution and Strategies of Equality: Welfare State Institutions, Inequality, and Poverty in the Western Countries' (1998) 63 American Sociological Review 661.
[13] For a historical overview that traces the origins of welfare-to-work programmes in the English Poor Laws of the seventeenth century, see Amir Paz-Fuchs, *Welfare to Work* (OUP 2008) ch 2. See also Frances Fox Piven and Richard A Cloward, *Regulating the Poor—The Functions of Public Welfare* (2nd edn, Vintage 1993); Simon Deakin and Frank Wilkinson, *The Law of the Labour Market* (OUP 2005) ch 3; Desmond King, *Actively Seeking Work? The Politics of Unemployment and Welfare Policy in the United States and Great Britain* (University of Chicago Press 1995). For detailed analysis of the evolution of social security and welfare conditionality in the twentieth and twenty-first centuries, see Michael Adler, *Cruel, Inhuman or Degrading Treatment? Benefit Sanctions in the UK* (Palgrave Macmillan 2018) ch 2. See also Mark Freedland and others, *Public Employment Services and European Law* (OUP 2007) ch 6.
[14] I referred to the concept of clustering of disadvantage in earlier chapters. It was developed in Jonathan Wolff and Avner de-Shalit, *Disadvantage* (OUP 2007).

justification for the increased punitiveness is captured in the work of scholars like Mead, one of the main advocates of welfare conditionality in the United States and the United Kingdom, who argued that:

> [t]he poverty of today's underclass differs appreciably from poverty in the past: underclass poverty stems less from the absence of opportunity than from the inability or reluctance to take advantage of opportunity. The plight of the underclass suggests that the competence of many of the poor—their capacity to look after and take care of themselves—can no longer be taken for granted as it could in the past.[15]

On this view, the problem of the poor is that they are idle and do not therefore pursue existing work opportunities.

However, a very different picture has emerged over the years as strict welfare conditionality schemes have been developed and become more punitive than in the past in many countries. From early on, analyses of policies in the United States and United Kingdom drew connections between welfare-to-work schemes and precarious work arrangements.[16] Writing in 2000, Peck and Theodore explained how activation programmes in the United States '"trap" many of these individuals in the lower reaches of the job market, where real wages are static or failing, career ladders are truncating, and employment insecurity is a common characteristic'.[17] On the basis of evidence that existed at the time, they identified a series of 'deleterious'[18] effects: welfare claimants are directed 'into the lower reaches of the labour market',[19] they remain trapped in these jobs with no opportunities for better work, and, in addition, the programmes have a negative effect on employment standards more broadly. Exploitation at the bottom end of the labour market therefore increased.[20]

In the context of the United States and discussing the problem of the ghetto poor, Shelby explained that welfare-to-work schemes lead to a 'self-reproducing exploitative relationship' between the ghetto poor and more affluent citizens.[21] The exploitative relationships appear self-perpetuating in this context, but the laws in question have a role to play, as I explain further in this chapter. The work that the ghetto poor are required to do does not increase

[15] Lawrence Mead, 'The New Politics of the New Poverty' (1991) 103 Public Interest 3, 3.
[16] Peck and Theodore (n 2).
[17] ibid 126.
[18] ibid 131.
[19] ibid 127.
[20] ibid 128–32.
[21] Tommie Shelby, *Dark Ghettos—Injustice, Dissent, and Reform* (Harvard University Press 2016) 197.

their skills or their work opportunities but traps them in a situation where they are permanently exploited.[22] The nature of the injustice is such that Shelby argued that the ghetto poor can reject the obligation to work in order to 'affirm their self-respect'.[23]

Analyses of sanction reforms in several countries show that schemes have become more coercive than in the past.[24] Increasingly punitive systems that aim to discourage people from accessing welfare benefits while forcing them into low-paid jobs have become the norm.[25] It has been argued that the increased punitiveness of welfare-to-work schemes across industrialised countries represents a turn from a welfare state to a workfare state.[26] A significant implication of this is that strict activation policies can increase income inequality both because they push people into low-paid work and because their welfare benefits are reduced. Activation policies that are described as workfare rather than a welfare system, then, represent a pattern whereby participation in the labour market promotes inequality.[27]

Reform patterns of activation policies across Europe show that benefits are less generous than in the past, access has been restricted, the level of suitability of jobs that claimants must accept has been lowered, the monitoring of claimants has intensified, and the obligation to accept jobs has been strengthened.[28] While there has been a shift in policies across Europe, significant differences still exist between Continental Europe and the US-style model. This can be seen in the harshness of sanctions (where Germany imposes an initial reduction of 10 per cent of benefit income, the United Kingdom 100 per cent for a first breach of the conditions, and the United States 'full-family' sanctions), as well as the length of the time-period during which sanctions are imposed.[29]

Against this background, I discuss further the development of welfare conditionality in the United Kingdom since the 1990s as an example of how schemes have evolved and what effects this has had in a legal order that now has

[22] ibid.
[23] ibid 200.
[24] See Carlo Knotz, 'Why Countries "Get Tough on the Work Shy": The Role of Adverse Economic Conditions' (2019) 48 Journal of Social Policy 615.
[25] Rueda (n 6).
[26] ibid 298.
[27] ibid.
[28] Daniel Seikel and Dorothee Spannagel, 'Activation and In-Work Poverty' in Henning Lohmann and Ive Marx (eds), *Handbook on In-Work Poverty* (Edward Elgar 2018) 245, 249. See also Anja Eleveld, 'The European Pillar of Social Rights and the Instrumentalization of the Right to Adequate Minimum Income Benefits' in Tania Bazzani and Reinhard Singer (eds), *Dealing with Unemployment: Labour Market Policy Trends* (Humboldt-Universität zu Berlin 2018) 95.
[29] Watts and Fitzpatrick (n 1) 57–58.

particularly punitive policies, a very flexible labour market, and places strong emphasis on individual responsibility for poverty and workplace exploitation.

Welfare Conditionality in the United Kingdom

At the time that Peck and Theodore were writing, in 2000, there was limited evidence on the effects of welfare conditionality in the United Kingdom.[30] However, analysis of the development of the schemes in recent years confirms that there are links between strict conditionality and exploitative work.[31] The schemes represent a shift away from social security as a way to prevent hardship to a way to get people into work,[32] and have been endorsed both by Labour and Conservative governments. The way in which they have evolved helps illustrate how, over the last two decades, there has been a turn towards a particularly strict conditionality system.

In 1995, the Jobseekers Act was enacted, which involved the assessment of jobseekers' behaviour. Labour governments (1997–2010) endorsed welfare-to-work as a key element of their policy, insisting that the unemployed should access paid work as quickly as possible, otherwise there would be stepped-up sanctions, consisting in the reduction of their welfare benefits. During this same period, conditionality applied to more groups of welfare support claimants than before, including people with disabilities and single parents.

In 2002, an agency called Jobcentre Plus was established, for all those who claimed benefits and were out of work. Personal advisers were introduced who would support claimants to find work, and a weekly plan (the 'jobseeker's agreement') was put in place for everyone. The advisers would regularly monitor compliance with the agreement and refer claimants who had not met the conditions to the Department for Work and Pensions. Other tasks of the advisers were to issue a 'Jobseeker's Direction' which gave specific guidance on how to look for a job, receive training, and improve their employability. Advisers also had the power to impose sanctions if the claimants did not meet the conditions imposed. One of the key aims of the regime was to support not only jobseekers but also those with childcare responsibilities, the ill, and the disabled to find work. The Welfare Reform Act 2007 introduced, among other things, a stricter test for disabled claimants, who were assigned personal advisers and would be

30 Peck and Theodore (n 2).

31 I discuss this in Virginia Mantouvalou, 'Welfare-to-Work, Structural Injustice and Human Rights' (2020) 83 Modern Law Review 929.

32 Adler (n 13) ch 3.

sanctioned if they did not take part in the scheme. The Welfare Reform Act 2009 extended conditionality to other groups, such as single parents.

The Coalition government (2010–15) developed welfare conditionality further. This was accompanied by the rhetoric of 'alarm clock Britain', namely the idea that there are hard-working people who are concerned about their living standards and dislike those who live on welfare benefits.[33] People on benefits started being regularly presented in the press, policy, and political discourse as 'benefit cheats', a concept that also drove the welfare reform agenda.[34] The Welfare Reform Act 2012 adopted a particularly punitive conditionality regime. The resulting Universal Credit system merged six separate in-work and out-of-work benefits into one means-tested payment, and was one of the key reforms introduced through the Act. The aim was to simplify the benefits system, and the underlying idea of the system is that it can constitute a 'nudge' that will make people turn to the paid labour market, instead of being passive recipients of benefits. The purpose was to influence individual behaviour, as the assumption is that individuals are primarily to blame for their unemployment, often presented as voluntary.[35] Universal Credit claimants have to prepare a plan with their work coaches at their local Jobcentre, called a 'Claimant Commitment'. This explains what has been agreed between the two with respect to what claimants need to do to get a job.

Universal Credit also introduced for the first time conditionality for those who are already employed but are on a low income. These claimants must apply for additional work or they will face sanctions. In-work conditionality suggests that the rationale of the system was not only to get people into work, but also to get them to work harder. The government's broader purpose was 'to ensure that any type of paid work is more financially rewarding than reliance on benefits'.[36] Low-paid workers who do not meet a threshold of income face sanctions. The scheme was criticised from early on for creating a perverse incentive for people to work for less than sixteen hours a week, in order to qualify for benefits.[37] Low-paid workers were therefore also presented as undeserving poor who can

[33] See Patrick Wintour, 'Nick Clegg to Speak Up for "Alarm Clock Britain"' *The Guardian* (11 January 2011). See also Anne Daguerre, 'The Unemployed and the Moral Case for Benefit Sanctions' (2015) 22 Journal of Social Security Law 130.

[34] See Simon Duffy and Jonathan Wolff, 'No More Benefit Cheats' (2022) 91 Royal Institute of Philosophy Supplement 103.

[35] Daguerre (n 33) 133. On behavioural change in this context, see the discussion in Watts and Fitzpatrick (n 1) 82.

[36] Peter Dwyer and Sharon Wright, 'Universal Credit, Ubiquitous Conditionality and Its Implications for Social Citizenship' (2014) 22 Journal of Poverty and Social Justice 27, 30.

[37] ibid 31.

be sanctioned if they do not make the appropriate efforts to secure a higher income.[38]

Non-compliance with Universal Credit requirements incurs the second-harshest sanctions in the world:[39] the lowest ones for those who, for instance, do not attend a work interview, and the highest for those who do not apply for a job, and range from losing their benefit for 28 days the first time that this happens, to 182 days the second time, and 1,095 days the third time.[40] The number of those who were sanctioned increased from about 300,000 sanctions and disqualifications in 2001 to over 1,000,000 in 2013,[41] with empirical evidence suggesting that sanctions are imposed unfairly, when for instance someone misses an appointment because of a clashing funeral commitment about which the individual has informed the authorities.[42]

Soon after the system was introduced, Dwyer and Wright described it as:

> unprecedented in offloading the welfare responsibilities of the state and employers onto citizens who are in receipt of *in work* and *out of work* social security benefits. Unemployed and low paid citizens are now held to be solely responsible not only for a lack of paid employment, but also partial engagement with the paid labour market and the levels of remuneration that they may receive.[43]

The system was also likened to the penal system by Adler because, as he showed, the fines imposed at times exceed fines imposed by criminal courts. He argued persuasively that they are deeply problematic for disciplining and managing the poor.[44] Wright, Fletcher, and Stewart explained that sanctioning of welfare benefits claimants leads to their suffering.[45] They explained that suffering encompasses not only material deprivation but also the experience of domination and repression, as well as feelings of humiliation, anger, and so on. Empirical research further highlighted that sanctioned individuals tend to

[38] ibid.

[39] The United States has the harshest sanctions in the world. See Herwig Immervoll and Carlo Knotz (2018) 'How Demanding Are Activation Requirements for Jobseekers?', OECD Social, Employment and Migration Working Papers No 215, 12 July, 47.

[40] ibid 32.

[41] Adler (n 13) 46–47.

[42] ibid 58.

[43] Dwyer and Wright (n 36) 33 (emphasis in original).

[44] Michael Adler, 'A New Leviathan: Benefit Sanctions in the Twenty-first Century' (2016) 43 Journal of Law and Society 195. See also the discussion in his book (n 13).

[45] Sharon Wright, Del Roy Fletcher, and Alastair BR Stewart, 'Punitive Benefit Sanctions, Welfare Conditionality, and the Social Abuse of Unemployed People in Britain: Transforming Claimants into Offenders?' (2020) 54 Social Policy and Administration 278.

be disadvantaged, and often homeless.[46] It has also been shown that welfare conditionality schemes with harsh sanctions force people into non-standard, precarious work that they do not want to do.[47] In addition, it has been shown that people are sometimes punished not for refusing to take these jobs, 'but for being unable to do so because of poverty, homelessness and ill health'.[48]

In addition to the above, it is important to appreciate that there are further exclusions from protective rules that affect those who are employed under 'workfare' schemes,[49] whereby they have to undertake unpaid work with an employer in order to receive a benefit, and are sometimes excluded from protective labour legislation. Writing on workfare in the United Kingdom and the Netherlands, Paz-Fuchs and Eleveld observed that the relevant schemes exclude, albeit not always explicitly, participants from various labour law protections.[50] They explained that recipients are not classified as workers entitled to the national minimum wage; it is unclear to what extent they are covered by the Working Time Regulations 1998; they are not protected against unfair dismissal, which is a protection that only employees have; and it is unclear whether they are covered by equality law.

In-Work Poverty and Welfare Conditionality

The particular problem that this section highlights is that those under welfare-to-work schemes are often forced and trapped into exploitative work and in-work poverty.[51] There are two central questions to be considered in order to understand the phenomenon of in-work poverty: first, who is a worker, and secondly, how we define poverty. The Bureau of Labour Statistics, the European Union (EU), and the International Labour Organization (ILO) take different approaches to in-work poverty, but these do not lead to fundamental

[46] Kesia Reeve, 'Welfare Conditionality, Benefit Sanctions and Homelessness in the UK: Ending the "Something for Nothing Culture" or Punishing the Poor?' (2017) 25 Journal of Poverty and Social Justice 65.

[47] Mantouvalou (n 31).

[48] Reeve (n 46) 75.

[49] For discussion of the scheme and an empirical study in the United Kingdom, see John David Jordan, 'Welfare Grunters and Workfare Monsters? An Empirical Review of the Operation of Two UK "Work Programme" Centres' (2018) 47 Journal of Social Policy 583. Problems associated with these schemes have been covered in the press. See eg Shiv Malik, 'Tesco Under Pressure to Withdraw from Unpaid Work Experience Schemes' *The Guardian* (16 February 2012); Brian Groom, 'Tesco Agrees to Pay Work Scheme Interns' *Financial Times* (21 February 2012).

[50] Amir Paz-Fuchs and Anja Eleveld, 'Workfare Revisited' (2016) 45 Industrial Law Journal 29.

[51] The concept of 'in-work poverty' in not new. One of the first systematic studies of poverty was about the working poor. See Benjamin Seebohm Rowntree, *Poverty: A Study of Town Life* (Macmillan 1901).

differences in measurements. The definition of who is a worker is generally broad. When someone engages in paid work for at least one hour in a given period of usually one week, they are viewed as 'at work'.[52] For the ILO, someone is part of the working poor if he or she has been or is usually working for at least one hour in a week, and is in a household with a level of consumption that is lower than the threshold of poverty. According to the EU definition, people are part of the working poor if they are employed more than half of the reference year, and live in a household with a disposable income below the 60 per cent median income threshold.[53] Despite certain differences in measuring in-work poverty, there are significant similarities. Crucially, both definitions adopt a broad conceptualisation of employment.[54] In-work poverty may be due to either low wages or low working hours.[55] This generally applies to people who are employed in non-standard arrangements, such as part-time and zero-hours contracts, which are defined as personal work relations for which 'there are no fixed or guaranteed hours of remunerated work'.[56]

Against this background, Seikel and Spannagel examined the links between activation policies and in-work poverty.[57] They explained that research on activation policies often ignores employment conditions, such as whether the new job is full-time or part-time work, and the levels of remuneration. On the basis of empirical evidence from eighteen European countries, they stressed that an increase in employment does not necessarily mean less poverty: 'simply making the jobless work is no guarantee for a reduction of in-work poverty'.[58] Activation policies, as they explained, force individuals to take up any job irrespective of how much it is paid, while cuts to benefits reduce the total income of the household. They argued that 'activation can be seen as a driver of in-work poverty' and found that 'strict conditionality of welfare benefits and a high degree of commodification of labour seems to force unemployed persons to accept jobs regardless of the pay levels'.[59] They also highlighted that the stricter a welfare conditionality system is, the more likely it is that participants will become part of the working poor. Activation policies that focus on upskilling can have a positive effect on household income, while strict conditionality systems

[52] Henning Lohmann, 'The Concept and Measurement of In-work Poverty' in Lohmann and Marx (n 28) 7, 14.
[53] ibid.
[54] ibid 22.
[55] ibid 15.
[56] Mark Freedland and Nicola Kountouris, *The Legal Construction of Personal Work Relations* (OUP 2012) 318.
[57] Seikel and Spannagel (n 28) 245.
[58] ibid 251.
[59] ibid 257.

force people to accept jobs irrespective of pay, which means that some schemes often turn the unemployed poor into working poor,[60] or the partially employed poor into the even poorer 'in-work full-time' poor.

Returning to the example of the United Kingdom, the Joseph Rowntree Foundation has repeatedly documented the problem of in-work poverty. A report of 2018 found that there were four million workers in poverty, a rise of half a million in comparison to five years before.[61] Since 2004–05, the number of those in in-work poverty has been rising faster than the total number of people in employment.[62] The 2020/21 Joseph Rowntree Foundation Report on 'Poverty in the UK' explained that in-work poverty affects Black, Asian, and minority ethnic people more than white people. It also particularly affects other marginalised groups, such as single parents (typically mothers).[63] The report also highlighted that the effects of the coronavirus pandemic were greater for those in in-work poverty.[64] A specific risk that it emphasised is that recovery from the pandemic may be connected to a risk of underemployment and an increase of in-work poverty that again mostly affects certain racial groups, and even more so women in these groups.[65]

To further corroborate the claim of Seikel and Spannagel, empirical research conducted in the United Kingdom on the effects of Universal Credit suggests that claimants are routinely forced to apply for and accept jobs that are precarious. It is crucial to underline here that claimants are expected to accept zero-hours contracts, which I discuss in Chapter 6, because these are viewed as valuable flexible arrangements. For instance, in 2014, the Minister for Employment said that 'jobseekers on any benefit should do all they reasonable [sic] can to get into paid employment.... We do not consider zero-hours contracts to be—by default—unsuitable jobs.... So in Universal Credit our coaches can mandate zero-hours contracts.'[66]

[60] ibid.

[61] Joseph Rowntree Foundation Report, 'UK Poverty 2018'.

[62] ibid. In 2011–12, for the first time on record, it was documented that of those who live in poverty, the majority are in in-work poverty. See Tom MacInnes and others, 'Monitoring Poverty and Social Exclusion', Joseph Rowntree Foundation, 2013.

[63] Joseph Rowntree Foundation Report on Poverty in the UK, 2020/21, 26.

[64] ibid 31, 36–37.

[65] ibid 38.

[66] Letter from Esther McVey MP to Sheila Gilmore MP, 1 March 2014 <https://researchbriefings.files.parliament.uk/documents/SN06553/SN06553.pdf> accessed 15 November 2022.

See also the response to a question asked by Chris Stevens MP at <www.parliament.uk/business/publications/written-questions-answers-statements/written-question/Commons/2018-11-29/197460/> accessed 15 November 2022, and the exchange in Parliament between Work and Pensions Secretary Amber Rudd MP and Chris Stevens MP in December 2018 at <www.independent.co.uk/news/uk/politics/amber-rudd-zero-hour-contracts-benefit-sanctions-universal-credit-work-pensions-dwp-a8690626.html> accessed 15 November 2022.

For those who have accessed the Jobcentre, the experience of applying for many unsuitable and inappropriate jobs is reported to be 'soul destroying', in the words of a food-bank volunteer.[67] The duty to accept exploitative work accentuates the problem. One interviewee said:

> I used to work in hotels doing waiting on silver service. I've done all kinds of work, do you know what I mean, all kinds. Whatever job come up I'd take really. Mostly factory work. Just boring work really. No skills in it.
>
> [...]
>
> Any job I'd do. Any job. As long as I know it's a permanent job. Not one of these zero-hour contract things, because I don't want to take a job and not afford where I'm living now and end up back on the streets.[68]

According to the findings of Kamerade and Scullion, some people first come into contact with non-standard work through Jobcentres, where they are 'encouraged, directed or coerced to apply for low-skilled, low-paid, and precarious jobs, such as temporary agency work and zero-hours work'.[69] They used examples of someone who turned down a job with an agency because it did not cover travel expenses from Derbyshire to Manchester (a distance of about fifty miles), and was therefore sanctioned. Another man accepted a zero-hours contract, and was told that he would receive a text message if he were needed. Having not heard, he was offered the option to turn up at work at 7am but was again not offered any work. He eventually secured a few hours' temporary work, but he still had to be on Universal Credit, attend appointments, and apply for jobs. Further empirical research by Garthwaite suggested that most people working in non-standard work arrangements (agency, part-time, or zero-hours), do not do so by choice, and would like to see zero-hours contracts banned.[70] This is because under many of these arrangements people cannot meet their basic needs, such as clothing, food, or accommodation. It has been reported that people accept exploitative work, such as work paid below the national minimum wage, to avoid claiming out-of-work benefits in a system that treats them in a humiliating way.[71] Large

[67] Kayleigh Garthwaite, *Hunger Pains—Life Inside Foodbank Britain* (Policy Press 2016) 104.

[68] John Flint, 'Social Class, Urban Marginality and Narratives of the Ethics of UK Welfare Sanctions', Welfare Conditionality Project Report, 14.

[69] Daiga Kamerade and Lisa Scullion, 'Welcome to Britain: A Land where Jobs May Be Plentiful but Are More and More Precarious' *The Conversation* (21 November 2017).

[70] Garthwaite (n 67) 108.

[71] Sharon Wright and Ruth Patrick, 'Welfare Conditionality in Lived Experience: Aggregating Qualitative Longitudinal Research' (2019) 18 Social Policy and Society 597, 606.

employers, known for their exploitative labour practices, benefit from welfare conditionality.[72]

Some of these jobs lead people into food banks.[73] This has further stigma attached to it, with those using them being embarrassed to admit it. An in-work Universal Credit claimant interviewed by the Welfare Conditionality project explained the humiliating effect of the experience:

> It's a bit degrading … my adviser, she isn't too bad. She says to me most times, 'I'm quite happy with what you're doing, and obviously you want to work because you're working, and it's not as though you're not looking for jobs'. But like they're always checking up on you. They always want to know …. 'If I wasn't happy with you, we can sanction you'. Every other meeting it's kind of there, a reminder that like keep on doing what you're doing, otherwise this will happen to you.[74]

Further challenges are faced by in-work claimants whose first job is a zero-hours contract, and who are required to apply for more work. This is exemplified by an interviewee of the Welfare Conditionality project who said:

> All the first employers want you to be available at the snap of a finger for the zero-hour contracts … So when you go for a second job, if you're in retail everybody's going to want you on a Saturday, aren't they? If you go, 'Oh no, I'm at such-and-such that day' they're going to go, 'No.'[75]

A related issue that emerges from empirical studies and shows how the system in the United Kingdom leads to the proliferation of non-standard work involves those who use a combination of paid work and welfare benefits. Those who work for over fifteen hours and earn above a set level of income lose any welfare benefits. For instance, one interviewee said that she was offered a placement for three weeks and worked sixteen hours at a care home with people with dementia, but was paid for fifteen hours so that she would not lose her benefits and become unable to afford her rent.[76] Scholars analysing the system

[72] Kendra Briken and Phil Taylor, 'Fulfilling the "British way": Beyond Constrained Choice—Amazon Workers' Lived Experiences of Workfare' (2018) 49 Industrial Relations Journal 438, 449.

[73] Garthwaite (n 67) 109.

[74] Written Evidence from the Welfare Conditionality: Sanctions, Support and Behaviour Change Project, Submission to the Work and Pensions Select Committee Inquiry: Universal Credit 'In-Work Progression' (January 2016).

[75] ibid.

[76] Garthwaite (n 67) 106.

early on had predicted that Universal Credit would create this perverse incentive.[77] In this way, the scheme leads to the proliferation of non-standard work, with claimants not only being forced to accept it, but also being trapped in the arrangements. They are trapped both because these jobs become standard and routine, and because people have very limited opportunities and resources (material, such as funding to retrain, and non-material, such as time) to obtain better work.[78]

It is important to appreciate that it is also highly questionable whether the system of sanctions is effective in its stated aims.[79] The National Audit Office observed that more data and evidence are required, but early analysis suggests that even though employment rates of those formerly in receipt of unemployment benefit have increased, there is no increase in earnings. Sanctions force people to accept jobs that are badly paid, and this leads to a reduction of their long-term income.[80] This finding is in line with research on several industrialised countries discussed earlier that connects strict conditionality schemes with income inequality.[81]

Schemes with strict conditionality have several further effects on recipients. The Welfare Conditionality project in the United Kingdom produced studies that examine the effects of welfare conditionality not only on material well-being but also on the physical and mental health of those who use it; these studies produced devastating criticisms of different aspects of the scheme.[82] In addition, empirical research suggests that there is stigma associated with the benefits system, which is a reason why some people prefer not to claim benefits during periods of unemployment.[83] The main focus of this section in particular, though, is that welfare-to-work schemes with strict conditionality force people into exploitative jobs, the use of which becomes all the more widespread and routine. It leads to 'clustering of disadvantage', whereby people accumulate disadvantages such as poverty, workplace exploitation, ill-health, or homelessness.[84] It creates a system that is convenient for employers, but unsuitable for

[77] Dwyer and Wright (n 36) 31.

[78] For an illustration of how people are trapped in this situation, see the story of Marcell that I discussed in Chapter 2, based on Jo McBride, Andrew Smith, and Marcell Mbala, '"You End Up with Nothing": The Experience of Being a Statistic of "In-Work Poverty" in the UK' (2018) 32 Work, Employment and Society 210.

[79] House of Commons, Committee of Public Accounts, 'Benefit Sanctions', Forty-second Report of 2016–17 (21 February 2017).

[80] National Audit Office, Report on 'Benefit Sanctions', HC 628, Session 2016–17 (30 November 2016) [3.10].

[81] Rueda (n 6).

[82] See eg Peter Dwyer (ed), *Dealing with Welfare Conditionality* (Policy Press 2019). See also Watts and Fitzpatrick (n 1) 99.

[83] Garthwaite (n 67) 102.

[84] Wolff and de-Shalit (n 14).

the main aim that activation policies are supposed to pursue, namely encouraging the unemployed to engage with the paid labour market as a route out of poverty. The system instead stigmatises the poor and traps them in exploitative working conditions and in-work poverty.

In response to criticisms of non-standard work arrangements,[85] the UK government has regularly insisted that people are positive about part-time work or zero-hours contracts, because these give them flexibility. The Taylor Review of Modern Working Practices, for instance, said that flexibility is important for workers, and that they should not be deprived of the capacity to choose flexible working arrangements, such as zero-hours contracts.[86] Evidence on in-work poverty, though, and the fact that many in this condition are in precarious work calls this position into question. The Taylor Review argued that people should have a choice of working arrangements, and that their options should not be hindered. However, we can see that many who are employed in such contracts would rather have secure, stable, full-time work, with which they can meet their basic needs, but do not have this option. Some have been forced into these arrangements through the welfare system. As it emerges from empirical research, for many people atypical work is not necessarily freely chosen work. There are many who do not opt to work in zero-hours or agency arrangements because of the flexibility inherent in such arrangements, but because they will otherwise lose any welfare support and will be unable to meet their basic needs.[87] Yet even when they do this work, they may still be unable to meet their basic needs, and have to use food banks.[88] The story of Marcell, who was trapped in non-standard work through which he could not meet his basic needs, exemplified this.[89]

Welfare-to-Work and Structures of Injustice

I have so far explained that welfare-to-work programmes with strict conditionality force people into precarious work through which they cannot meet their basic needs, while employers benefit from this situation. This section suggests

[85] See eg Abi Adams, Mark Freedland, and Jeremias Prassl, 'The "Zero-Hours Contract": Regulating Casual Work or Legitimating Precarity?' Oxford Legal Studies Research Paper 11/2015.

[86] See the 'Good Work: Taylor Review of Modern Working Practices' (July 2017) 14. For a critique of the report, see Katie Bales, Alan Bogg, and Tonia Novitz, '"Voice" and "Choice" in Modern Working Practices: Problems with the Taylor Review' (2018) 47 Industrial Law Journal 46.

[87] Malcolm Ball and others, *Agency Workers and Zero-Hours—The Story of Hidden Exploitation* (University of Salford Research Report July 2017) 6.

[88] Garthwaite (n 67) 109.

[89] See n 78 and Chapter 2.

that the situation should be understood as an instance of a state-mediated structure of injustice, for this analysis helps us identify where the injustice lies, who is responsible for it, and how it should be addressed.

The rhetoric of personal responsibility, which is typically deployed in discussions on welfare-to-work programmes, places the blame on the undeserving poor, as was explained earlier. The aim is to exclude them from welfare support, to impose on them duties to work, and to direct this support to recipients who are said to be 'worthy'. Following a related line of thinking, when the poor are exploited and the employers have broken the law, the employers are to blame. The responsibility of the state is limited to addressing the harm inflicted by private actors. This neglects an important aspect of the role of the state in relation to this unjust structure.

The state-mediated structure of injustice that I discuss in this chapter involves the intersection of legal rules that can be analysed as follows. It is constituted by certain laws, namely welfare-to-work schemes with strict conditionality, which target those who are already in a position of disadvantage because of poverty, together with the legal framework that permits non-standard work. It is sustained by an administrative system, exemplified through the UK institution of Jobcentres with work coaches, who set up demanding and often unproductive tasks for claimants and monitor them closely. The structure ends up forcing people into in-work poverty through punitive measures. The intrusive system constrains individual choices, with claimants having to take exploitative work in order to secure income to cover their basic needs, having in reality a choice to make between either out-of-work or in-work poverty. The poor are targeted through legislation that forces them into exploitative arrangements. Laws with strict conditionality impose harsh sanctions on them for not seeking or accepting work. Jobcentres turn the meeting of people's basic needs into a bureaucratic exercise. In this way, and through laws that have an appearance of legitimacy, people are forced into exploitative work, while employers benefit from this situation.

It is well documented that zero-hours working arrangements, for instance, that constitute some of the most precarious working arrangements, often pay wages that are below the minimum wage, are insecure in the sense that there is no guaranteed minimum monthly income, and that many employed under such contracts need more hours than they are offered.[90] As Adams, Freedland, and Prassl have explained, fear of poverty, destitution, and stigmatisation along

[90] See eg Garthwaite (n 67) 109. See further Chapter 6.

with an obligation to accept such work creates 'the perfect instantiation of the self-intensifying normalisation and legitimation of Zero-Hours contracting'.[91]

The conception of state-mediated structures of injustice underlines the responsibility of the state for a situation that might not otherwise be evident if we did not examine the overall structure. It has emerged that it is misleading to focus on the individual responsibility of the poor for not taking advantage of the available work opportunities. It is also insufficient to place our attention on unscrupulous employers who may break the law and exploit workers. This position underestimates the role of the law that creates the vulnerability of workers and is linked to patterns across the industrialised world, whereby large numbers of poor people are required to take precarious work that is lawful, while the employers benefit from the situation. The increasing body of evidence on the effects of legal rules on those who are already disadvantaged supports the position that the state has a duty to correct the injustice which it has created. Identifying a series of laws and policies that are *prima facie* legitimate but that create unjust structures forms the first step, and provides the basis for a normative argument to ground moral and legal responsibility of state authorities themselves for creating and sustaining these structures.

Conclusion

Parallels have been drawn between criminal justice and the harshest aspects of welfare conditionality schemes because both fields of state policy impose harsh sanctions that affect the most disadvantaged and aim in this way to manage the poor.[92] In a line of thinking similar to Chapter 4, where I discussed the treatment of offenders and immigration detainees as workers, in this chapter I have explained that welfare-to-work schemes end up coercing those who are poor and disadvantaged into conditions of in-work poverty and exploitation through the menace and imposition of severe sanctions. The schemes are becoming increasingly harsh across the industrialised world. They are supposed to support people to enter into paid work, because work is presented as the most effective route out of poverty. However, schemes with strict conditionality create and sustain structures of exploitation that become widespread and routine. The disadvantaged are forced into exploitative conditions while employers benefit from this situation.

[91] Adams, Freedland, and Prassl (n 85) 20.

[92] Loic Wacquant, *Punishing the Poor* (Duke University Press 2009); Adler (n 44).

6
Precarious Workers

In the last chapter my focus was on welfare conditionality schemes. The discussion was motivated by growing evidence that schemes with strict conditionality force people into precarious work, such as agency and zero-hours contract work. It is often said that workers choose these arrangements, and that the flexibility they offer is valuable for both employers and workers. However, through schemes with strict conditionality, it emerged that precarious work is frequently not freely chosen, but that people are forced into and trapped in precarious jobs. Low-paid workers in the bottom segments of the labour market in particular are compelled to accept these because of the fear of sanctions that, in some circumstances, may result in destitution. We also observed that working under these arrangements may mean that people cannot meet their basic needs, for they sometimes have to use food banks or cannot afford to have a family life. It should be evident by now that in a variety of settings, legal rules make different categories of workers vulnerable, and that structures of exploitation are built and sustained by law.

This chapter examines some non-standard work arrangements in more detail so as to get a better understanding of the role of the law in exacerbating the vulnerability of workers that is systematically exploited by employers. Standard work arrangements are typically full-time and permanent. Any kind of non-standard work could be described as precarious, but here my focus is on agency work and zero-hours contracts, which can be viewed as reflecting some of the most precarious conditions. Legal rules treat these workers in a manner that sometimes excludes them from crucial labour law protections. This occurs, first, through legislation that limits worker-protective rights to certain categories of workers, rather than covering anyone in a personal work relation.[1] The effect of this legislation is that those who do not fall within the relevant categories are excluded from protection. Secondly, courts contribute to

[1] On the idea of the personal work relation, see Mark Freedland and Nicola Kountouris, *The Legal Construction of Personal Work Relations* (OUP 2011).

Structural Injustice and Workers' Rights. Virginia Mantouvalou, Oxford University Press. © Virginia Mantouvalou 2023.
DOI: 10.1093/oso/9780192857156.003.0006

this exclusion when interpreting legislation to determine whether some claimants fall under the protective scope of the law. In this process, they often apply rules of contract law that do not reflect the special nature of the employment relation. This is because the contract of employment is not like other contracts as it is grounded on the submission and subordination of the worker to the employer.[2] For this reason, rules of contract law are ill-suited when addressing questions of worker exploitation.

Problems associated with agency and zero-hours work include the lack of a guaranteed monthly income; the uncertainty regarding who is the employer that owes workers legal duties; a lack of clarity surrounding employment status, which determines entitlement to labour rights and any duties owed by the employer; and the lack of protection from unfair dismissal either because the workers may not be viewed as employees or because of the lengthy qualifying period for unfair dismissal protection.[3] It is often workers in undervalued and poorly paid sectors that find themselves in non-standard work. These workers may be vulnerable to exploitation for other reasons, such as their immigration status, gender, race, or poverty. This chapter explains how the legal framework on non-standard work sometimes exacerbates existing vulnerabilities, and how these workers are in this way systematically trapped in structures of exploitation, while the employers benefit from this situation.

Agency Workers

Agency work is not a new phenomenon but its use by employers has changed over the years. Originally the purpose and use of employment agencies was to mediate between workers and employers so as to cover specific temporary business needs. Such needs might arise, for instance, when a worker is on parental leave and the employer needs another worker as cover for a limited period of time. The agencies used to cover the temporary needs by supplying workers during that restricted period. In recent years, though, agency work has become much more common, and the agency industry has grown at an explosive rate.[4] Data collected in 2013 from countries across the EU showed that

[2] For analysis, see Hugh Collins, 'Is the Contract of Employment Illiberal?' in Hugh Collins, Gillian Lester, and Virginia Mantouvalou (eds), *Philosophical Foundations of Labour Law* (OUP 2018) 48; Guy Davidov, *A Purposive Approach to Labour Law* (OUP 2016) ch 1.

[3] On this, see UK Employment Rights Act 1996, s 108(2).

[4] Nik Theodore and Jamie Peck, 'Selling Flexibility—Temporary Staffing in a Volatile Economy' in Judy Fudge and Kendra Strauss (eds), *Temporary Work, Agencies and Unfree Labour—Insecurity in the New World of Work* (Routledge 2016) 26, 27.

agency work has grown across the board.[5] There has been similar growth of agency work arrangements in the United States, where the business 'has grown to "industrial" and indeed "infrastructural" scale'.[6] Some workers may value these arrangements because they give them flexibility, sometimes higher pay than if they were permanent employees, and an opportunity to avoid office politics. This may be the case primarily for workers in the top end of the labour market. However, it has been explained that many agency workers come from disadvantaged groups.[7]

There are several problems arising from the legal regulation of agency work. The most significant problem that makes agency workers vulnerable to exploitation is that this work constitutes a triangular arrangement between the worker, the agency, and the so-called end user. The agency enters into a contract with the worker, while the end user has an agreement with the agency. It is not immediately clear whether the agency or the end user is the employer. In addition, it is not clear what is the status of the worker (either in relation to the agency or the end user), namely whether it is an employment relationship or whether the worker is self-employed.

While in the past these kinds of questions would arise for workers who were genuinely in temporary work, over the years temporary work agencies have evolved and now cover many permanent business needs. By outsourcing these functions to agencies, end users can avoid legal obligations that are attached to the status of the employer, even if workers cover permanent needs. Workers, in turn, can be deprived of legal rights that are attached to the status of worker, such as rights to holiday or sick pay. Collective labour rights are also undermined, as the workers who are employed by the agency are not part of the bargaining unit that negotiates with the end user[8] or are not viewed as workers who have a right to collective bargaining with the employer.[9] Moreover, analysis of agency work both in the United States and the EU shows that when there is a financial crisis, the availability of temporary agency work shrinks, showing that this group of workers bears the risks of economic downturns more than

[5] Eckhard Voos and others, 'Temporary Agency Work and Transitions in the Labour Market' (Eurociett/UNI Europa Project 2013) 23 <https://weceurope.org/uploads/2019/07/2013_WECEU_Study-TAW-Role-Labour-Transitions.pdf> accessed 1 June 2022.

[6] Theodore and Peck (n 4) 42.

[7] Lindsay Judge and Daniel Tomlinson, *Secret Agents—Agency Workers in the New World of Work* (Resolution Foundation 2016) 6–8, (hereafter Resolution Foundation 2016); Lindsay Judge, *The Good, the Bad and the Ugly—The Experience of Agency Workers and the Policy Response* (Resolution Foundation 2018) 6–7 (hereafter Resolution Foundation 2018). See also Malcolm Ball and others, Agency Workers and Zero Hours—The Story of Hidden Exploitation (July 2017).

[8] Guy Davidov, 'Joint Employer Status in Triangular Employment Relationships' (2004) 42 British Journal of Industrial Relations 727, 730.

[9] *R (on the application of the IWGB) v CAC and Roofoods Ltd (T/A Deliveroo)* [2021] EWCA Civ 952.

workers in standard employment relations.[10] An additional challenge faced by agency workers is that they may not easily leave the agency with which they initially contracted, either because there is a contractual term that limits their ability to do so by restricting their rights to claim arrears if they change employer, or by imposing fees on end users.[11] There is also evidence that accident rates are higher amongst temporary agency workers as their training or knowledge of workplace hazards is limited.[12]

Writing on the outsourcing of these workers and their exclusion from labour protective legislation, Collins described the phenomenon as a 'legislative artefact'.[13] He explained that, '[b]ecause employment protection laws limit rights according to hours of work, length of service, and place of work, many employees fail to acquire rights simply by virtue of the choice of the legislature'.[14] Analysis of the interaction between market conditions and state action in the production of employment agencies in the United States has also shown that 'without the supportive framework ultimately provided by government, temporary work as we know it could not have become the staple part in the scheme of employment relations that it is in the United States today'.[15] Legal arrangements on agency work can also be examined in the context of the 'fissured workplace', a business model that relieves 'the organizations that most directly benefit from contracted work from obligations to follow standard employment and labor laws'.[16] Even though these arrangements are usually presented as an aspect of deregulation whereby state authorities do not interfere with the labour market, in reality we see that the state has an important role to play in relation to the structures in place and the resulting exploitation of workers, as I explain in more detail in what follows.

The legal regulation of agency work varies across industrialised countries.[17] In many countries, the workers are recognised as employees of the agency (rather than the end user). To address the vulnerability created by this situation,

[10] Report (n 5) 24; Theodore and Peck (n 4) 35–36.

[11] Deirdre McCann, *Regulating Flexible Work* (OUP 2008) 146.

[12] Nicola Countouris and others, *Report on Temporary Employment Agencies and Temporary Agency Work* (International Labour Office 2016) 27.

[13] Hugh Collins, 'Independent Contractors and the Challenge of Vertical Disintegration to Employment Protection Laws' (1990) 10 Oxford Journal of Legal Studies 353, 354.

[14] ibid. See also 361.

[15] George Gonos, 'The Interaction between Market Incentives and Government Action' in Kathleen Barker and Kathleen Christensen (eds), *Contingent Work: American Employment Relations in Transition* (Cornell University Press 1998) 170, 170.

[16] Tanya Goldman and David Weil, 'Who's Responsible Here? Establishing Legal Responsibility in the Fissured Workplace' (2021) 55 Berkeley Journal of Employment & Labor Law 55, 59.

[17] Resolution Foundation 2018 (n 7) 44. On the different legal responses to agency work, see Countouris and others (n 12) 39ff. See also Davidov (n 8) 731ff.

several European countries have adopted legal rules that protect agency workers by, for instance, limiting the use of agency workers to their original role of meeting temporary business needs, by protecting agency workers' labour rights, or by identifying the end user as the employer under certain conditions.[18] In the United States, case law has developed the doctrine of a single employer or joint employer as a way to address the power of the end user to avoid its legal responsibilities.[19] The Federal Labor Standards Act (FLSA), for instance, provides for a federal minimum wage for all employees. If agency workers are viewed as employees (rather than self-employed), they will be covered by the Act. In relation to the entity that owes the relevant duties to the workers, the US Supreme Court ruled that an employee can have more than one employer under the Act.[20] It was later held that 'all joint employers are responsible, both individually and jointly, for compliance with all of the applicable provisions of the [FLSA], including the overtime provisions'.[21]

Protective rules for agency workers are especially limited in the United Kingdom,[22] with the existing legal framework creating structures of injustice. Legislation that affords labour rights to certain categories of workers withholds them from others, despite the fact that they are in a personal work relation, and so do court decisions that determine who is the employer and what is someone's employment status. The effects of classification of someone as an employee, worker, or self-employed are crucial. Employees have an extensive set of statutory protections, including job security.[23] The category of 'worker', developed on the basis of the Employment Rights Act 1996,[24] constitutes an intermediate level that recognises some but not all labour rights that employees have. Workers have rights, such as the right to a minimum wage and working time, but forego certain employment rights in exchange for some supposed flexibility. Self-employed contractors who are not within the statutory concept of worker have almost no employment rights. Agency workers have certain labour rights, such as a right to a minimum wage,[25] which are explicitly protected, but face a number of challenges to which I now turn.

18 Davidov (n 8) 732–33.

19 ibid 734–35. For further discussion of US law and atypical work, including agency work, see Katherine VW Stone, 'Legal Protections for Atypical Employees: Employment Law for Workers without Workplaces and Employees without Employers' (2006) 27 Berkeley Journal of Employment & Labor Law 251.

20 *Falk v Brennan*, 414 US 190, 195 (1973).

21 *Lopez v Silverman*, 14 F Supp 2d 405, 412 (SDNY 1998).

22 See generally Deirdre McCann, *Regulating Flexible Work* (OUP 2008) 143ff.

23 Employment Rights Act 1996, s 94(1).

24 ibid s 230(3).

25 National Minimum Wage Act 1998, s 34.

A 'legal no man's land'

Judicial decisions that have examined the question of who is the employer that owes legal duties to agency workers have increased workers' vulnerability by ruling that the end user is not an employer, or by taking a restrictive approach to employment status and barring the gateway to labour rights.[26] *James v Greenwich Borough Council*[27] is a good example of the courts' approach to the issue of whether the end user is an employer. Ms James was supplied by an agency to work for Greenwich Borough Council ('the Council') and signed an agreement with the agency but not with the Council. The Council and the agency, in turn, signed an agreement with each other according to which the agency would remunerate her. After a period of three years during which Ms James worked for the Council, she fell ill and was off work. When she returned, another agency worker had replaced her and she had no job. When she brought a claim for unfair dismissal, the Court of Appeal ruled that there was no employment relation between the Council and herself, as there was no contract between them.

Crucially, they decided that no contract could be implied between the parties as there was no necessity to do so. The question of whether it was necessary to imply a contract is one that is typically used in commercial contracts and was applied in the employment contract without recognition of the particularities of the employment relation. Lord Justice Mummery accepted in *James* that:

> a significant move in the direction of the casualisation of labour and the growth of a two tier workforce, one tier enjoying significant statutory protection, the other tier in a legal no man's land being neither employed nor self employed, vulnerable, but enjoying little or no protection, may create social injustice and a festering sense of grievance which would not be satisfactory in the interests of an efficient workforce, a competitive economy, a healthy society or anything else.[28]

However, he explained that courts and tribunals develop the law but 'are not architects of economic and social policy. As they must operate within the legal architecture created by others, they cannot confer the right not to be unfairly dismissed on a worker who is without a contract of employment.'[29]

[26] *James v Greenwich Borough Council* [2008] EWCA Civ 35 [60].
[27] ibid.
[28] ibid [60].
[29] ibid [56].

On the basis of *James*, agency workers cannot bring claims against the entity for which they work, even when they work for this entity for years. The effect of this reasoning is such that agency workers may even be left outside the scope of UK anti-discrimination law. In *Muschett v HM Prison Service*,[30] an agency worker employed as a cleaner was excluded from the protection of anti-discrimination legislation as the Court found that he had no contract with the end user.

Another example of how workers employed through agencies are excluded from the protection of collective labour rights is *Smith v Carillion*.[31] Smith worked in the construction industry as an engineer and site agent. He was also an active trade union member and health and safety representative. After 2001 he was unable to obtain any work in the industry. He claimed that this was because he had been blacklisted for his lawful trade union activities. Blacklisting was a widespread practice in the UK construction industry (which may still be going on), whereby workers who were members of a trade union, and who might therefore be perceived as 'troublemakers', were included in a secret list that employers consulted. This list was created by an organisation called Consulting Association. The workers included in the list lost their jobs and were unable to find work for years or decades, with grave implications for their well-being, income, health, and personal life.[32] Both the practice and the effects of blacklisting on workers' lives are devastating.

Mowlem, which was subsequently acquired by Carillion, was one of the companies that provided information about Smith's activities to the Consulting Association. One of the questions in the case was whether there was an employment relationship between Smith and Mowlem. Smith said that he was a worker of Mowlem but the company claimed that he was not its worker, as he was employed through an agency. The reason this was important was because Smith claimed that he was victimised by Mowlem for being a trade union member, which is contrary to the Trade Union and Labour Relations (Consolidation) Act 1992 (TULCRA) (s 146), and for being a health and safety representative, which is contrary to the Employment Rights Act 1996 (ERA 1996) (s 44). At first, section 146 of TULRCA applied to employees only, but was amended in 2004 to apply to workers in response to a judgment of the European Court of

[30] [2010] EWCA Civ 25.

[31] *Smith v Carillion* [2015] EWCA Civ 209, [2015] IRLR 467.

[32] This has been documented extensively in publications of the Institute of Employment Rights. The first publication was by Keith Ewing, *Ruined Lives—Blacklisting in the UK Construction Industry* (IER 2009).

Human Rights.[33] An employee is someone who works under a contract of employment or apprenticeship according to the Act, while a worker is someone who is an employee or who works 'under any other contract whereby he undertakes to do or perform personally any work or services for another party to the contract who is not a professional client of his'.[34] A similar provision exists in the ERA 1996 for health and safety representatives but this applies only to employees, not to workers.[35] While many health and safety representatives are trade union members, not all of them are. This means that some health and safety representatives who are not employees are not protected from detriment by the employer. When the information on Smith was passed to the Consulting Association, the relevant legislation only protected employees, so this was also going to be a significant hurdle for him in court.

In relation to the question of whether there was any contractual relationship between Smith and Mowlem, the Court of Appeal relied on the test of *James*: no contract should be implied unless there is business necessity for such a move. The Court acknowledged the fact that businesses use agency arrangements to avoid worker protective laws but said that 'a contract cannot be implied merely because the court disapproves of the employer's objective'.[36] As an agency worker, Smith was not a worker or employee of Mowlem so there was no way for him to turn against it for the blacklisting and its effects on his life. This is a devastating outcome for workers' rights, with severe implications for many aspects of their private lives too.[37] Blacklisting itself is direct action by private entities with intention to harm that involves putting together blacklists of workers and consulting these to make hiring and firing decisions. However, the legislation and rules on the employment status of agency workers that determine who is entitled to protection from blacklisting exclude some workers from protective rules. Even though these rules are supposed to protect flexibility at work, they exacerbate existing vulnerabilities and create structures of injustice.

It should be clear by now that the relationship between the worker and the agency can take different forms, typically devised by the agencies themselves: they may be employees of the agencies, workers, or merely

[33] *Smith* (n 31) [13]. The European Court of Human Rights case in question is *Wilson, National Union of Journalists v UK* App nos 30668/96, 30671/96, 30678/96 (Judgment, 2 July 2002).

[34] TULRCA, s 296.

[35] ERA 1996, s 44.

[36] *Smith* (n 31) [22].

[37] I discuss it further in Virginia Mantouvalou, 'Human Rights, Labour Rights and Criminal Wrongs' in Alan Bogg and others (eds), *Criminality at Work* (OUP 2019) 210. For a critique of Smith and an alternative test for triangular relationships, Alan Bogg, 'The Common Law Constitution at Work: *R (on the application of UNISON v Lord Chancellor*' (2018) 81 Modern Law Review 509, 524.

self-employed.[38] Courts examining the relationship between the agency and the worker have tended to find that it is a contract for services, rather than an employment contract, as we also saw in *Smith*. In *Montgomery v Johnson Underwood*,[39] the claimant had been supplied by an agency to a company to work as a receptionist. After two and a half years, the company requested that the agency terminate her contract because they were not satisfied with her performance. She claimed that her dismissal was unfair, but the Court of Appeal ruled that she was not an employee and was therefore not covered by the law of unfair dismissal. It recognised that agency workers find themselves in limbo given the uncertainty of their status and stated that the government should give further consideration to their employment status.[40]

It is also important to appreciate that when there were efforts to regulate agency work at EU level, the UK government took an active role in undermining rules that protect workers' rights and supported instead the interests of industry against regulation.[41] The EU Temporary Agency Directive requires agency workers to be treated equally with other workers. Article 5(1) states: 'The basic working and employment conditions of temporary agency workers shall be, for the duration of their assignment at a user undertaking, at least those that would apply if they had been recruited directly by that undertaking to occupy the same job.' However, the Directive also permits member states to impose a qualifying period for protection.[42] On this basis, UK law contains a three-month qualifying period for the principle of equal treatment to apply.[43] This has as an effect the exclusion of more than half of agency workers from the principle of equal treatment, while it has also been observed that several posts for temporary agency workers are designed to last for eleven weeks exactly in order to avoid the legal obligations imposed by the Directive.[44] In addition, tribunals and courts consider that agency workers who are permanently placed with an end user are not covered by the Directive because they are

[38] Resolution Foundation 2018 (n 7) 15. The UK Supreme Court has ruled that the power of the employer to present the relationship as one of self-employment through the contract has limits when the reality of the relationship does not reflect the contractual terms. See *Autoclenz Ltd v Belcher* [2011] UKSC 41; Alan Bogg, 'Sham Self-Employment in the Supreme Court' (2012) 41 Industrial Law Journal 328.

[39] *Montgomery v Johnson Underwood* [2001] EWCA Civ 318.

[40] ibid [43], citing a passage of the Employment Appeal Tribunal decision.

[41] Michael Wynn, 'Power Politics and Precariousness—The Regulation of Temporary Agency Work in the European Union' in Fudge and Strauss (n 4) 48. On the problems of the Temporary Agency Work Directive, see Nicola Countouris and Rachel Horton, 'The Temporary Agency Work Directive: Another Broken Promise?' (2009) 38 Industrial Law Journal 329.

[42] Art 5(4) of the Directive.

[43] Agency Workers Regulations 2010, reg 7(2).

[44] Countouris and others (n 12) 46.

not temporary.[45] This leads to further exclusions from the principle of equal treatment in the Directive.

For all the above reasons, the treatment of agency work in UK law has been repeatedly criticised. Davidov described the approach to the question of employment status in this context as a 'formalistic contractual analysis'.[46] Albin and Prassl said that the legal framework of agency work leads to a 'complete breakdown of employment law coverage'.[47] More recently, the UK Supreme Court decision in the case of *Uber v Aslam*[48] ruled in favour of a purposive approach in the interpretation of labour law, as developed by Davidov and also analysed by Bogg and Ford.[49] According to this ruling, the question of the scope of employment legislation is to be determined by the purpose of the legislation in question, consisting in the protection of 'vulnerable workers' who are in a 'subordinate and dependent' position.[50] It remains to be seen how this development will affect the legal rights of those working through an agency.

Empirical research on the effects of the existing arrangements on workers illustrates how they experience the legal rules. Research of the Resolution Foundation found that there were about 865,000 agency workers in the United Kingdom in 2016 and that there has been a significant growth of the numbers over time.[51] This research found that there are several problems with the legal framework, such as the fact that the workers do not know under what kind of agreements they work or what employment rights they have. This has also been highlighted in the judicial decisions discussed earlier.[52]

Interviews with agency workers have also shown that they often do not choose this kind of work for the flexibility that it offers but that they are required to accept it through the UK welfare conditionality system that imposes very strict sanctions if claimants turn down work.[53] For instance, one worker said: 'I got offered a job with an agency in Manchester with no expenses for travel and so on. I said "no" and then was sanctioned for refusing work.'[54]

45 *Moran v Ideal Cleaning Services Ltd* [2013] UKEAT 0274_13_1312.

46 Davidov (n 8) 731.

47 Einat Albin and Jeremias Prassl, 'Employees, Employers and Beyond' in Mark Freedland (ed), *The Contract of Employment* (OUP 2016) 341, 354.

48 *Uber BV v Aslam* [2021] UKSC 5.

49 For analysis of the purposive interpretation, see Davidov (n 2); Alan Bogg and Michael Ford, 'Between Statute and Contract: Who is a Worker?' (2019) 135 Law Quarterly Review 347. See also Joe Atkinson and Hitesh Dhorajiwala, 'The Future of Employment: Purposive Interpretation and the Role of Contract after *Uber*' (2022) 85 Modern Law Review 787.

50 *Uber* (n 48) 71.

51 Resolution Foundation 2016 (n 7).

52 See eg *Montgomery* (n 39) [43].

53 See further the discussion of welfare conditionality and precarious work in Chapter 5.

54 Ball and others (n 7) 15.

Another worker said: 'I was sanctioned by the Benefits Agency, who had already cut my benefits for three months, so I did not have any choice. I had to come from Llanelli where six agencies were recruiting at the Job Centre and at the end of the day one took me on to start the next day at Amazon.'[55]

As already mentioned, if those working through agencies are classified as workers, they have more limited rights than employees. For instance, they may have no rights to sick, maternity, paternity, or adoption pay, or protection from unfair dismissal, depending on their employment status. It has therefore been documented that agency workers are afraid to get sick:

> If you're working for my agency the first three days you're off you don't get nothing, then you get your stat [statutory sick pay]. So basically you're scared of taking sick aren't you, you're begging 'Can I use some of my holiday pay to cover this?'[56]

Piotr Dzuga, an agency worker in agriculture, explained the challenges that he faced when he was sick:

> I had a really bad chest infection in the autumn; so that I could still work and get paid; I asked the agency if I could work indoors, so until last week I was in the salad packing factory. I did ask if there was any chance of sick pay while I got right but was told that they don't do contracts and you have to be on a contract to get sick pay. I'm not on a contract so I could ask if I can have a contract but think they will tell me that there are plenty more people who will do the job, so I don't want any trouble. You hear that when anyone complains or asks a question, there's plenty more people.[57]

Moreover, agency workers are reluctant to turn down work that is offered to them through the agency because they are concerned that if they turn down work, they will not be used again:

> I got a phone call at 11 o'clock at night as I was getting into bed. They offered me a single night shift (unloading pallets) and called it a 'work placement'.

[55] Kendra Briken and Phil Taylor, 'Fulfilling the "British way": Beyond Constrained Choice—Amazon Workers' Lived Experiences of Workfare' (2018) 49 Industrial Relations Journal 438, 449.
[56] Resolution Foundation 2018 (n 7) 41.
[57] Helen Collins, Susan Barry, and Piotr Dzuga, '"Working While Feeling Awful is Normal": One Roma's Experience of Presenteeism' (2022) 36 Work, Employment and Society 362, 367.

> I turned it down and have had no contact with the agency since. Basically you can't refuse a job.[58]

Agency workers avoid making complaints about their working conditions because they know that, if they do, the agency will not use them again.[59] The lack of protection against unfair dismissal is crucial when they exercise other rights such as refusing to work under exploitative arrangements. Fear of losing their job will deter them more than other workers from making complaints. They experience lower pay compared to workers who are directly employed by the end user,[60] and have limited knowledge and understanding of the contractual arrangements under which they are employed.[61]

Employers, including large businesses, in turn, benefit from the limited legal protections in place. It has been shown, for instance, that entities like Amazon rely on employment agencies to supply them with workers for their fulfilment services who are easily disposable, even mid-shift, without any notice.[62] The law is not violated by the employers in many of these situations but this does not mean that we cannot identify state responsibility for the structures of injustice in question. And even though we could focus on the responsibility of unscrupulous employers only, or a few bad apples like Amazon,[63] upon closer inspection it emerges that legal rules on agency work arrangements also have a major role to play in these structures of exploitation.

Zero-Hours Contracts

Another example of precarious work arrangements where legal rules exacerbate vulnerability to exploitation are zero-hours contracts. Other terms used to describe these arrangements include on-demand, intermittent, or casual work. There is some overlap between workers in agency arrangements and on zero-hours contracts.

[58] Ball and others (n 7) 18.
[59] Resolution Foundation 2018 (n 7) 27–28.
[60] ibid 34.
[61] ibid 13.
[62] Briken and Taylor (n 55) 451.
[63] On working conditions in Amazon, see James Bloodworth, *Hired—Six Months Undercover in Low-Wage Britain* (Atlantic Books 2018).

There is no generally accepted definition of the term 'zero-hours contracts'.[64] Here I use it to refer to arrangements that constitute personal work relations for which 'there are no fixed or guaranteed hours of remunerated work'.[65] Casual arrangements of this type exist in many legal orders, including Germany, the Netherlands, and Italy.[66] An overview of casual work in a small number of EU member states showed that some legal orders permit zero-hours work without restrictions, while others set requirements on minimum hours in certain types of casual arrangements.[67] For instance, in the Netherlands, there are 'on-call contracts' where if the worker accepts the work offered by the employer, the two parties sign a contract for a fixed period of time.[68] In the United Kingdom there are no similar limitations of the employer's power in zero-hours relations.[69]

Working arrangements of this kind are prevalent in sectors that are seasonal or the demand for which varies during the year, like hospitality and care.[70] Certain categories of workers are overrepresented in zero-hours contractual arrangements, including women, people with disabilities, non-white people, and migrants.[71] In a manner similar to agency work, these arrangements can be useful for some workers for the flexibility that they offer and for employers who do not have to employ people long-term, including for periods where there are fewer business needs. However, even though occasionally a zero-hours agreement may be suitable for some ad hoc work, often employers use these arrangements to cover permanent business needs. The flexibility that is valued by some is linked to insecurity for many, and particularly for those who are already in a position of disadvantage for other reasons. In addition, many people are forced into this work through systems of welfare conditionality, as welfare benefits are

[64] Abi Adams, Mark Freedland, and Jeremias Prassl, 'The "Zero-Hours Contract": Regulating Casual Work, or Legitimating Precarity?' (2015) Oxford Legal Studies Research Paper 11/2015 <https://papers.ssrn.com/sol3/Papers.cfm?abstract_id=2507693>.

[65] Mark Freedland and Nicola Kountouris, *The Legal Construction of Personal Work Relations* (OUP 2012) 318.

[66] See Elise Dermine and Amaury Mechelynk, 'Zero-Hour Contracts and Labour Law—An Antithetical Association?' (2022) European Labour Law Journal, introduction to special issue on zero-hours contracts. See also Valerio de Stefano, 'Casual Work beyond Casual Work in the EU: The Underground Casualisation of the European Workforce—and What to Do about It' (2016) 7 European Labour Law Journal 421.

[67] Eurofound, 'Casual Work: Characteristics and Implications' New Forms of Employment Series (Publications Office of the European Union 2019) 8.

[68] See further Anja Eleveld, 'Flexi-Insecurity and the Regulation of Zero-Hours Work in the Netherlands' (2022) 13 European Labour Law Journal 375.

[69] For detailed analysis and an agenda for reform, see Joe Atkinson, 'Zero-Hours Contracts and English Employment Law: Developments and Possibilities' (2022) 13 European Labour Law Journal 347.

[70] Eurofound, 'New Forms of Employment' (Publications Office of the European Union 2015) 61.

[71] Abi Adams and Jeremias Prassl, 'Zero Hours Work in the United Kingdom' (ILO 2018) 7.

conditional upon accepting the jobs in question with the threat of imposition of serious sanctions.[72]

In the United Kingdom, in 2021 there were 876,800 workers in zero-hours contracts according to research by the Trades Union Congress.[73] Others estimate that the numbers are higher, while it is beyond dispute that they have risen significantly over the years.[74] The detail of the working arrangements varies, which leads to different types of classification of the employment relationship by courts, with differing degrees of legal protection for workers.[75] Some people on zero-hours work may not be classified as employees or workers, and will in this way be denied even the most basic labour law protections.[76] Rules developed by courts on employment status, in other words, together with the legislation that excludes workers and the self-employed from protection are responsible for the structures of injustice that are created for workers in zero-hours arrangements. In this area too, it remains to be seen whether recent developments before the UK Supreme Court in the *Uber* case will have an effect on the legal protection of those under zero-hours contracts, but it has been argued that for effective regulation in this area, statutory intervention is needed.[77]

The uncertainty characterising the question of worker status means that those under zero-hours working arrangements face insecurity that has serious implications for their lives. Their income fluctuates, and hence they cannot plan their private life, support a family, pay their rent, and cover other basic needs.[78] In addition, there is evidence that workers under these arrangements are frightened to complain about their working conditions because they fear that they will not be offered any more work.[79] The implications of being on zero-hours contracts for some workers have been described as follows:

> It is not just about insecurity. It is also about no guarantee on hours, giving absolute control to the employer [. . .] There is no process; there is no access to justice. Even though on paper you may be regarded as an employee and able

[72] See the discussion in Chapter 5.

[73] This estimate excludes the self-employed and those in other precarious work, such as agency work and seasonal work. See TUC, 'Insecure Work' (July 2021) 5 <www.tuc.org.uk/sites/default/files/2021-07/insecurework2.pdf> accessed 15 October 2022.

[74] On the challenges in measuring prevalence of these arrangements, see Adams and Prassl (n 71) 7–11. On the rising numbers, see Labour Force Survey (Office for National Statistics 2019) 157.

[75] Adams, Freedland, and Prassl (n 64) 10.

[76] *Secretary of State for Justice v Windle* [2016] EWCA Civ 459. See the analysis in Atkinson (n 69) 11.

[77] Atkinson (n 69).

[78] Ball and others (n 7) 17.

[79] ibid 17.

> to access, if indeed you can afford it, the employment tribunal system, the reality is, for most zero-hour workers and short-hour workers, you are simply denied work if you raise a grievance or raise a concern with your employer.[80]

A zero-hours contract worker explained the experience of insecurity and the challenge in making life plans through the following incident:

> I went for a flat and got turned down because I'm really on a zero hours contract and have no guaranteed hours. But I don't want to house share any more—and I threw away £300 I hadn't got on all the references and everything. I didn't even know [I was on a ZHC] until the searches came back![81]

It has been documented that there are workers on zero-hours contracts who cannot cover their basic needs through their income, and may have to use food banks.[82] Analysis of the arrangements in EU member states explained that the effects of the unpredictability of work and income make workers feel 'desperate and exploited'.[83]

Care Workers

To discuss further the predicament of those under zero-hours work arrangements, I will focus on the relatively coherent category of care workers in the United Kingdom who are often employed under these contracts. This discussion also illustrates how other legal rules on precarious work, working time, and employment status interact to exacerbate existing vulnerabilities and are connected to structures of exploitation of care workers.

The category of care workers that concerns me here are people who support others in their own homes by helping them with basic daily activities, such as washing and feeding. The majority of care workers are women and many of them are migrants. Care work is a sector that is undervalued for reasons such as the fact that it was traditionally women's work, while also being characterised by a high concentration of agency and zero-hours work, which has as an implication their exclusion from protective labour rules. In 2015/16, it was found

[80] See UK Parliament, Business, Innovation and Skills Committee, 'Employment Practices at Sports Direct' (2016) para 16.
[81] Resolution Foundation 2018 (n 7) 41.
[82] Ball and others (n 7) 30.
[83] Eurofound (n 70) 66.

that 58 per cent of care workers and 57 per cent of nurses working in homecare were on zero-hours contracts.[84] The Covid-19 pandemic both further exposed the challenging working conditions for care workers and exacerbated them.[85]

Care work in the United Kingdom has been outsourced to the private sector. In the past, care workers were directly employed by local authorities. This changed with several reforms to make the system more cost-effective, and the majority of care workers are now in the private sector.[86] It has been suggested that the wide use of zero-hours contracts in the sector is due to the commissioning models employed by local councils.[87] The decisions of councils and funding provided by central government determine the operation of the sector. At the same time, it has been suggested that the private businesses that are in charge of providing care work are controlled by private equity firms that make significant profits.[88]

Care workers on zero-hours contracts do not have a guaranteed number of hours per day or per week, while their working arrangements are such that they are remunerated at rates below the minimum wage. Their allocated time slots can be very short. They work and are paid for periods of fifteen, thirty, forty-five, or sixty minutes per day for each individual in need of care. The fifteen-minute slots have been particularly criticised because they do not provide sufficient time for the worker to attend to the needs of the care receiver. A further implication of the fifteen-minute slots is that care workers are paid below the national minimum wage.[89] Even though the National Minimum Wage Regulations 2015 provide that travel time needs to be remunerated normally,[90] very few councils include this as a contractual condition with the providers. As a result, most travelling time is unpaid,[91] as well as time spent on training, assistance provided in an emergency, and time between visits. When travel time is unpaid and care workers are systematically allocated fifteen-minute care slots, they risk being paid the amount of £1.63 for fifteen minutes

[84] Skills for Care, *The State of the Adult Social Care Sector and Workforce in England*, 2016.

[85] Hugh Alderwick, Phoebe Dunn, and Jennifer Dixon, 'Editorial: England's Health Policy Response to Covid-19' (2020) British Medical Journal 369; Ian Kessler and others, 'Fair Care Work—A Post Covid-19 Agenda for Integrated Employment Relations in Health and Social Care (2020) King's Business School Covid-19 Research Impact Papers 1/2020, June, 13.

[86] See Lydia JB Hayes, 'Care and Control: Are the National Minimum Wage Entitlements of Homecare Workers at Risk under the Care Act 2014?' (2015) 44 Industrial Law Journal 492, 497–98.

[87] Unison, *Time to Care*, 2013.

[88] Kessler and others (n 85) 13.

[89] See Low Pay Commission, National Minimum Wage Report 2012.

[90] Section 20.

[91] Unison, 'Fifteen Minutes of Shame—Stories from Britain's Homecare Frontline' (2015) 20. The Court of Justice of the European Union has found that travelling time, at least for certain categories of workers, should be paid: Case C–266/14 *Federación de Servicios Privados del sindicato Comisiones obreras* [2016] 1 CMLR 22.

of crucial care work, according to an independent report on the system.[92] Studies have also shown that, in reality, care workers have to work for longer than the fifteen-minute time slots in order to attend to the needs of care receivers.[93] A care worker was reported to have said: 'When I reflect on my pay it can often work [out] that I earn £3.50 sometimes less per hour.'[94] In 2014, it was established that 220,000 homecare workers in England were earning below the minimum wage.[95]

Moreover, an effect of minimum wage rules is that care workers are excluded from important protections in relation to time that they spend at the employer's premises and being on call. This was exemplified in the UK Supreme Court case of *Royal Mencap Society v Tomlison Blake and Shannon v Rampersad (T/A Clifton House Residential Home)*.[96] The question was whether care workers who are required to stay overnight and sleep in at the employer's home are entitled to the national minimum wage for the entirety of their sleep-in shifts, namely for the hours that they were required to be at the employer's premises. The National Minimum Wage Regulations provide in regulation 32(1) that the minimum wage is due for 'hours when a worker is available, and required to be available, at or near a place of work for the purposes of working'. However, regulation 32(2) also states that this does not apply when the worker 'by arrangement sleeps at or near a place of work' in suitable facilities provided by the employer. On this basis, the Supreme Court decided that care workers are not entitled to the minimum wage for the hours that they sleep in at the employer's home.

In addition, as care workers are typically employed through agencies and not directly by the client, they are excluded from the protection of discrimination law when they experience discrimination by the client, who is an end user and not in a contractual relationship with the worker.[97] As for protection from harassment, section 40(2) of the Equality Act stated that '[t]he circumstances in which A is to be treated as harassing B under subsection (1) include those where—(a) a third-party harasses B in the course of B's employment,

[92] The Kingsmill Review, 'Taking Care—An Independent Report into Working Conditions in the Care Sector' (2014) 15.

[93] *Time to Care* (n 87) 12.

[94] ibid.

[95] Unison, 'UNISON Urges Illegal Wage Crackdown in Homecare Sector' (29 October 2014) <www.unison.org.uk/news/article/2014/10/unison-urges-illegal-wage-crackdown-in-homecare-sector/> accessed xx xxxx 2022.

[96] *Royal Mencap Society v Tomlinson Blake and Shannon v Rampersad (T/A Clifton House Residential Home)* [2021] UKSC 8. On the Court of Appeal decision, see ACL Davies, '"Sleep-in" Shifts and the National Minimum Wage: *Royal Mencap Society v Tomlinson-Blake, Shannon v Rampersad*' (2018) 47 Industrial Law Journal 553.

[97] *Muschett* (n 30).

and (b) A failed to take such steps as would have been reasonably practicable to prevent the third-party from doing so', explaining that liability is limited to situations in which the person has been harassed by a third party on at least two other occasions. However, the section was removed from the Act for being 'unworkable' and too burdensome for businesses.[98]

As mentioned earlier, the employment status of those under zero-hours contracts is unclear. However, there has been a case where care workers were ruled to be employees despite the wording of the contract. The UK Employment Appeal Tribunal had to assess contracts described as 'zero-hours agreements' that had been prepared by Carewatch, an agency providing care services.[99] The claimants provided around-the-clock care for a severely disabled person. At some point, the contract with Carewatch was terminated and transferred to a different agency, Pulse. The workers argued that they should be classified as employees of Carewatch and that they therefore had rights to be transferred to Pulse under the Transfer of Undertakings (Protection of Employment) Regulations 2002. The Tribunal ruled that the contracts signed suggesting that the work was 'zero-hours' did not reflect the reality of the relation. There were mutual obligations between the workers and the agency, and a permanent contract in place. The claimants were therefore employees entitled to the full range of employment law rights. This decision was a positive development for care workers. However, the reality remains that the status of many care workers is still unclear, and very few will be able to go to a tribunal to have the issue resolved.

In the example of care workers on zero-hours contracts, we are faced with a situation where different legal rules on casual work, employment status, and working time exacerbate their vulnerability which can be, and is, systematically exploited by private entities. This has been repeatedly highlighted in reports by government bodies, think tanks, and in academic work.[100] Studies have illustrated how care workers experience zero-hours arrangements. For instance, one worker said:

> I am on call from 7 in the morning until 10 at night. I work 6 days on 4 off. With 30 hours in the 6 days I can't do anything else in case there is extra work.

[98] See the discussion in Einat Albin, 'Customer Domination at Work: A New Paradigm for the Sexual Harassment of Employees by Customers' (2017) 24 Michigan Journal of Gender and Law 167, 194.

[99] *Pulse Healthcare Ltd v Carewatch Care Services Ltd* [2012] UKEAT 0123/12/BA [35].

[100] See reports cited earlier in this chapter. See also Lydia JB Hayes, *Stories of Care: A Labour of Law—Gender and Class at Work* (Palgrave Macmillan 2017); Laura Gardiner and Shereen Hussein, *As if we Cared—The Costs and Benefits of a Living Wage for Social Care Workers* (Resolution Foundation 2015).

> So I'm always available between these hours but we are only paid for the work we do not the standby time we have to spend by the phone.[101]

A care worker explained to Hayes that she had to sign a contract confirming that she would accept zero-hours work in order to be flexible.[102] The agency asked her to work for increasing numbers of clients every day, rushing from one person to the other throughout the day. Even though she worked very long hours, she realised that she was only being paid during the time that she was at a client's house, and not for the time that it took her to travel from one client to the other during the day. For a day that she worked for about fifteen hours, her pay was for between five and eight hours. This reality is supported by many other studies on care work.[103]

A former care worker whose travel time was not paid by the agency explained the effect of this on his life:

> I found myself in a bad situation—my bike was stolen and I had to go by bus. I didn't even earn enough to pay for my public transport and had to get a loan from the company. I was expecting a payout for my stolen bike and had to delay paying rent. So the council took me to court and I had to pay £250 court costs. I decided ENOUGH—I left my home and the job.[104]

This worker also explained that when working in the care sector, he was always in debt: 'I was caring for others but ended up in poverty.'[105]

Hayes described care workers' treatment through law as 'institutionalised humiliation',[106] while Conservative MP Richard Bacon said in a parliamentary debate:

> The best argument against zero-hours contracts is that they provide opportunities for unscrupulous employers who are determined to exploit people and who engage in practices that they would not wish to endure themselves, and that, in certain sectors such as domiciliary care, the problem amounts to systematic exploitation.[107]

[101] *Time to Care* (n 87) 17.
[102] Hayes (n 100).
[103] See eg *Time to Care* (n 87).
[104] Ball and others (n 7) 24.
[105] ibid 30.
[106] See Hayes (n 100).
[107] HC Deb 27 May 2015, vol 596, cols 152–60. See also Lord Hendy's statement in HL Deb, cols 2092–93.

The structure of injustice affecting care workers is created by the interaction of several rules including the Care Act, zero-hours contracts, and agency rules, as well as the regulation of working time and case law on worker status. These laws exacerbate the vulnerability of care workers who are systematically exploited, while both private entities and the state benefit from this situation. Care workers are a category of workers who are essential in countries with ageing populations and an underfunded welfare state. That the law is a major factor in making these workers vulnerable and creating structures of exploitation is disturbing.

Conclusion

A review of modern employment practices to which I also referred in earlier chapters described non-standard work arrangements as the 'British way' of flexible work which should be viewed as largely successful,[108] and made limited recommendations for reform. It is true that non-standard work arrangements can be viewed as having a legitimate aim, which consists in flexibility for employers and workers that may be valued by some. Yet what we observe is that the legal framework in the United Kingdom and other legal orders that maintain particularly flexible non-standard work arrangements has led to the legal construction of vulnerability and contributed in this way to the creation of large-scale structures of exploitation.

Workers who may already be vulnerable for other reasons find themselves in precarious work arrangements that have become increasingly standard and routine. This is not through the exercise of choice, but because some are forced to accept these through strict welfare conditionality schemes that I discussed in Chapter 5 or to cover their basic needs while there are no better jobs available for them. People are often exploited in these arrangements in sectors that are undervalued and badly paid, and find it hard to challenge their employers or change jobs.

In addition, workplace exploitation and poverty are not the only structures of injustice associated with these arrangements. The Marmot Review analysed the social determinants of health that are associated with health inequality, including lower life expectancy, and discussed the role of zero-hours arrangements in this context.[109] Workers who are already in a disadvantaged position

[108] See 'Good Work: Taylor Review of Modern Working Practices' (July 2017) 7.

[109] See Michael Marmot and others, *Health Equity in England: The Marmot Review Ten Years On* (Institute of Health Equity 2020).

are employed in insecure and exploitative arrangements through which they cannot meet their basic needs, and that have damaging effects on many other aspects of their lives.

The realisation that the state has a major role to play in the structures of exploitation that I discuss is important. It pushes us to think about the responsibility of the authorities for this situation. It also signifies that, in a manner similar to how these structures of exploitation have been constructed, they can also be modified and made fairer. In the chapters that follow I consider human rights principles that can guide this change, as well as the actors that can support this.

PART III

HUMAN RIGHTS

7
Human Rights I

In the previous chapters, we observed that several categories of workers who may already be in a position of disadvantage for reasons such as race, gender, or poverty are excluded from rights to receive the minimum wage, to organise, to social security, and other protection. However, employers often do not break the law by treating them in this way. It may appear that we are faced with instances of structural injustice of the kind that Iris Marion Young described, where people find themselves suffering serious harm, but we cannot assign responsibility for this because no state or individual action can be viewed as a major cause of the harm. People act according to normal rules and morally justifiable practices, but the preconditions and results of their actions are structural processes that produce unjust outcomes.[1]

Yet, we saw that at times the law may have an important role to play in unjust structures. I demonstrated that rules with an appearance of legitimacy increase workers' vulnerability to exploitation: migrant workers, offenders working in prison or doing other unpaid work and those in immigration detention, those who are required to accept precarious work under strict welfare-to-work schemes, and others who are employed in non-standard work, such as zero-hours or agency work, are systematically disadvantaged by being excluded from protections that other workers enjoy. Legal rules are connected to structures of exploitation that become all the more widespread, standard, and routine. Just as identifiable legal rules create this situation, legal reform can help destabilise the unjust structures and improve the position of the workers by removing this vulnerability.

The state has political responsibility to change legal rules that are connected to structures of exploitation, but this is not only forward-looking responsibility of the kind that Young envisaged, but also backward-looking: it is due to the fact that the law increases and compounds vulnerability. In what follows I argue that state authorities may also have legal responsibility to change some of these rules when they are in breach of workers' rights as protected in human

[1] Iris Marion Young, *Responsibility for Justice* (OUP 2011) 47.

Structural Injustice and Workers' Rights. Virginia Mantouvalou, Oxford University Press. © Virginia Mantouvalou 2023.
DOI: 10.1093/oso/9780192857156.003.0007

rights law.[2] In this chapter, I first address some preliminary issues in relation to the role of human rights law in state-mediated structures of injustice. I then turn to the examples of migrant workers and captive workers to identify legal rules affecting them that may be incompatible with states' human rights obligations. In Chapter 8, I examine legal rules concerning those under welfare conditionality schemes and precarious work so as to identify whether these may violate human rights law.

State Responsibility in Human Rights Law

In international human rights law, states typically have obligations to refrain from wronging individuals. This is enshrined in fundamental protections that we find in this body of rules that was born out of the necessity to stop the atrocities of the twentieth century by holding the authorities accountable for their conduct. In addition, international human rights law recognises positive obligations of state authorities to put in place an institutional machinery that makes rights effective, to guarantee that people have a remedy for violations of their rights, to provide goods and services to satisfy rights, and to promote rights by bringing changes to public consciousness.[3] Most human rights treaties impose obligations on state authorities (not directly on private employers) to guarantee the rights in question. On this basis, legislation that breaches workers' rights may give rise to human rights violations.

The rights that are affected by the state-mediated structures of injustice that I discuss are included in documents of the Council of Europe, including the European Convention of Human Rights (ECHR) and European Social Charter (ESC), and in the Charter of Fundamental Rights of the European Union (EUCFR). They are also protected in UN treaties, such as the International

[2] On the normative grounding of labour rights as human rights, see the discussion in Pablo Gilabert, 'Labor Human Rights and Human Dignity' (2016) 42 Philosophy and Social Criticism 171. See also Virginia Mantouvalou, 'Are Labour Rights Human Rights?' (2012) 3 European Labour Law Journal 151; Guy Mundlak, 'Human Rights and Labor Rights: Why Don't the Two Tracks Meet?' (2012) 34 Comparative Labor Law and Policy Journal 217; and for theories of rights as justifications of labour law, see Joe Atkinson, 'Human Rights as Foundations for Labour Law' in Hugh Collins, Gillian Lester, and Virginia Mantouvalou (eds), *Philosophical Foundations of Labour Law* (OUP 2018) 122; Hugh Collins, 'Theories of Rights as Justifications for Labour Law' in Brian Langille and Guy Davidov (eds), *The Idea of Labour Law* (OUP 2011).

[3] Philip Alston and Ryan Goodman, *International Human Rights* (OUP 2013) 182–85. Powers and Faden have written about structural injustice and human rights as moral principles rather than legal rules, arguing that human rights violations and structural unfairness should be viewed as intertwined. See Madison Powers and Ruth Faden, *Structural Injustice—Power, Advantage and Human Rights* (OUP 2019).

Covenant on Civil and Political Rights (ICCPR) and the International Covenant on Economic, Social and Cultural Rights (ICESCR), and by the International Labour Organization (ILO) as the specialist UN branch on labour rights, as well as documents of the Inter-American human rights system, such as the American Convention on Human Rights. Each of these has a different monitoring machinery. The European Court of Human Rights (ECtHR), for instance, hears individual and inter-state applications in relation to the ECHR against state authorities, while the European Committee of Social Rights (ECSR) examines reports and hears collective complaints on the basis of the ESC. The EUCFR imposes an obligation on institutions of the EU and member states to interpret EU law in a manner that is compliant with it. The ICCPR is monitored by the Human Rights Committee, and the ICESCR by the Committee on Economic, Social and Cultural Rights, while there are also special mechanisms, some of which have concrete mandates in the areas that I consider. These include the UN Special Rapporteur on Human Rights and Extreme Poverty, and regionally the Council of Europe Commissioner for Human Rights and the Group of Experts Against Trafficking in Human Beings (GRETA). These institutions typically produce reports on member states' human rights obligations.

Workers' rights protected in human rights law that are affected by these structures of injustice that I address are found at domestic level too. Typically in national law, human rights have higher status than other legislation. Courts and other non-judicial bodies assess compliance with human rights obligations. Certain courts may have power to require the authorities to change the laws in question if they are incompatible with human rights. By way of an example, under the UK Human Rights Act 1998 that incorporated ECHR rights in UK law, courts have a duty to interpret legislation in a way that is compatible with human rights in so far as possible, while the Act also provides for the power of courts to issue a declaration of incompatibility if legislation breaches human rights law.[4] In addition, it provides that it is unlawful for public authorities to act in a way that is incompatible with Convention rights. The term 'public authorities' also includes courts and tribunals.[5]

In what follows, I provide a critical account of some central cases and other legal materials from national and international legal orders, with a primary focus on the ECHR, but I also draw on other legal orders. This is not an exhaustive account of cases and other materials on each of the issues that

[4] UK Human Rights Act 1998, ss 3–4.
[5] ibid s 6.

I discussed in earlier chapters or of human rights provisions and case law.[6] My aim, instead, is to identify some key human rights principles that can address aspects of these unjust structures. Two questions arise at this point. First, when do state-mediated structures of injustice violate human rights law? As a preliminary matter, the responsibility that I outline is responsibility for the creation of vulnerability through action: the state is responsible because it creates vulnerability while the authorities 'know or ought to have known' that exploitation systematically occurs in the private sphere. The 'know or ought to have known' formulation has been developed by the Strasbourg Court to assign responsibility to the state for wrongs in the private sphere.[7] In the issues that I examine, the authorities may claim that they did not exploit or intend to create vulnerability to exploitation and that they had a legitimate aim when enacting the laws in question. However, malicious intention is not required: what is required is to identify the rules that create vulnerability, to show that there are patterns of injustice that are connected to this vulnerability, and that the state did not consider sufficiently the effects when designing and implementing the rules in question. It is important to highlight that we are primarily looking at state action rather than omission to act, because the ECtHR and other monitoring bodies may recognise discretion for the authorities when assessing responsibility for omissions.[8] The Inter-American Court of Human Rights has articulated clearly the obligation of states to eliminate 'any norms and practices that in any way violate the guarantees provided under the Convention'.[9]

In many of the examples that I discuss we can identify an interference with provisions of human rights law, as we will see, but finding an interference is not sufficient for a violation to be established. State action that interferes with rights can sometimes be justified if it promotes a legitimate aim and if the restriction of the rights is proportionate to the aim pursued. Rights that typically permit limitations include the right to private life and freedom of association. As we saw in earlier chapters, the authorities put forward a justification for

6 For detailed accounts of employment law and human rights in Europe, see eg Filip Dorssemont, Klaus Lorcher, and Isabelle Schomann (eds), *The European Convention on Human Rights and the Employment Relation* (Hart 2014); Niklas Bruun and others (eds), *The European Social Charter and the Employment Relation* (Hart 2019); Filip Dorssemont and others (eds), *The Charter of Fundamental Rights of the European Union and the Employment Relation* (Hart 2019); Steve Peers and others (eds), *The EU Charter of Fundamental Rights—A Commentary* (2nd edn, Hart 2021); Dean Spielmann, 'Companies in the Strasbourg Courtroom' (2016) 5 Cambridge Journal of International and Comparative Law 404.

7 See eg the reasoning of the Court in *DP and JC v UK* App no 38719/97 (Judgment, 10 October 2002) paras 111–12. Sometimes it involves natural disasters: *Özel v Turkey* App nos 14350/05, 15245/05, and 16051/05 (Judgment, 17 November 2015).

8 *Abdulaziz, Cabales and Balkandali v UK* App nos 9214/80, 9473/81, and 9474/81 (Judgment, 28 May 1985) para 67.

9 *Castillo Petruzzi v Peru* (IACtHR, Judgment, 30 May 1999) para 207.

schemes that restrict these rights, such as the control of immigration, reasons of public safety, or economic efficiency. However, monitoring bodies should scrutinise the compatibility of these rules with human rights law particularly closely when assessing the proportionality of restrictions. The fact that there are patterns of exploitation may reflect neglect or contempt of the authorities for groups of workers who are often already disadvantaged, which is incompatible with human rights values of equality and dignity. Moreover, there are certain human rights where this balancing of interests is not permitted: this is the case with the prohibition of slavery, servitude, forced and compulsory labour, for instance, which covers an exceedingly broad range of exploitative practices.

A second issue to consider is whether human rights law is an effective tool to address aspects of the structures of exploitation that are the subject of this book. Some of the monitoring mechanisms that I discuss, such as the ECtHR, involve individual applications primarily, and the decisions of courts and other monitoring bodies address these individual cases. Are these mechanisms suitable and can they lead to broader change? It is of course very challenging to make general empirical assessments about whether human rights law is effective in practice as this involves a variety of factors (different actors of the state, non-state actors, differences from one field of activity to another, as well as differences between countries and regions of the world).[10] The answer to this question will vary from one legal order to another but some general remarks can be made. In relation to the ECHR, when there is a ruling that finds a violation, respondent states do not only comply by offering an individual remedy. The effects of judgments can be broader, and may include changes in laws that were at stake in the judgment, changes in state policy and practice, as well as broader cultural change. Strategic litigation can have a particularly important role to play when individuals and organisations collaborate to challenge laws that impact many.[11] Legal reform can be an important step towards structural change. In addition to removing legal barriers from access to rights, it can also

[10] See eg the following books: Kathryn Sikkink, *Evidence for Hope—Making Human Rights Work in the 21st Century* (Princeton University Press 2018); Gráinne de Búrca, *Reframing Human Rights in a Turbulent Era* (OUP 2021). In the specific areas that interest me in this book, see eg Noel Whitty, 'Human Rights at Risk: UK Prisons and the Management of Risk and Rights' (2011) 13 Punishment and Society 123; Phillippa Kaufmann and Tim Owen, 'The Price of Dignity and Liberty: Legal Aid for Prisoners' (2013) 5 European Human Rights Law Review 482.

[11] On the effects of strategic human rights litigation, see Helen Duffy, *Strategic Human Rights Litigation—Understanding and Maximising Impact* (Hart 2018) ch 4. An excellent example of strategic litigation for workers' rights is *R (UNISON) v Lord Chancellor (Equality and Human Rights Commission Intervening)* [2017] UKSC 51. For analysis, see Alan Bogg, 'The Common Law Constitution at Work: *R (on the Application of UNISON) v Lord Chancellor*' (2018) 81 Modern Law Review 509 and Michael Ford, 'Employment Tribunal Fees and the Rule of Law: *R (UNISON) v Lord Chancellor in the Supreme Court*' (2018) 47 Industrial Law Journal 1.

inspire debate, raise awareness, and motivate other actors to engage with problems that lie in the roots of the injustice.[12] By way of an example, in relation to prisons in the United Kingdom, which is one of the fields that I examine, it has been argued that human rights law plays a significant role affecting prison authorities' approach to prison conditions because of 'the capacity of human rights activism to propel an issue to centre stage, damaging an organisation's operations and reputation, irrespective of actual legal liability'.[13] Decisions or reports of other monitoring bodies may not lead to immediate legal change, and levels of compliance may be low. However, they are often used by civil society organisations campaigning for legal change, by national human rights institutions, or by courts interpreting legal documents.[14] They can therefore feed into reform processes in these and many other ways.

As to courts' competence to adjudicate on these matters, when they decide that there is a violation of human rights law, the reform that is required will involve changes in labour law, immigration law, and other relevant rules, in a way that will remove the provisions that create vulnerability. However, the role of courts when assessing compatibility with human rights law is not to prescribe exactly how these rules should change but to ground an urgent legal requirement for change when there is a human rights violation. As West put it, rights 'are a list of morally grounded imperatives, not a list of suggestions for good governance. It is a language that requires lawmakers to think in terms of what we morally ought to do and be.'[15] It is for lawmakers to legislate in a manner that is compliant with human rights obligations, and when there is a violation, it is for lawmakers to decide how to legislate in order to comply with these norms. My argument is not that labour law as a whole should be re-imagined as a subfield of human rights law.[16] The point is that human rights law has the potential to contribute to our thinking, understanding, and requiring legal change in order to protect workers' rights. This will have an impact on some of the most disadvantaged workers who are often under-represented in politics.

[12] See the discussion in Sally Haslanger, 'Culture and Critique' (2017) 91 Aristotelian Society Supplementary Volume 149.

[13] Whitty (n 10) 124.

[14] See Virginia Mantouvalou, 'Labour Rights in the European Convention on Human Rights: An Intellectual Justification for an Integrated Approach to Interpretation' (2013) 13 Human Rights Law Review 529; Keith Ewing and John Hendy, 'The Dramatic Implications of *Demir and Baykara*' (2010) 39 Industrial Law Journal 2; Tzehainesh Teklè, 'The Contribution of the ILO's International Labour Standards System to the European Court of Human Rights' Jurisprudence in the Field of Non-Discrimination' (2020) 49 Industrial Law Journal 86.

[15] Robin West, *Reimagining Justice—Progressive Interpretations of Formal Equality, Rights, and the Rule of Law* (Ashgate 2003) 88.

[16] On this, see Harry Arthurs, 'Labour Law After Labour' in Brian Langille and Guy Davidov (eds), *The Idea of Labour Law* (OUP 2011) 13, 23–24.

Other Agents with Political Responsibility

Structures that disadvantage social groups involve several factors such as race, gender, immigration status, and poverty, as it also emerged from earlier chapters. It is not only the law that is responsible for these, and changes in the law alone do not necessarily mean that the structures of exploitation will cease to exist from one day to the next. The patterns in question are deeply entrenched, and it takes work from several actors to dismantle them. These actors have forward-looking political responsibility of the kind envisaged by Young to act to both change these laws and achieve structural change.

Given that my focus is on workers' rights, it is crucial to underscore that key agents to support their improvement are workers' organisations, primarily trade unions and other civil society groups specialising in the field. In addition to their more traditional activities, these groups are often involved both in human rights campaigning and advocacy at domestic and international level, and in human rights adjudication.[17] Human rights law, in turn, generally protects the right to associate, including the right to form and join a trade union, as well as other union activities, such as rights to collective bargaining and strike.[18] The role of these organisations can be multifaceted. Non-governmental organisations, trade unions, and other activists participate in the human rights regime in many ways both at national and supranational level, including by being applicants in legal proceedings on behalf of their members, supporting 'test cases', creating synergies, and lobbying for change in political and legal fora. The existence of strong civil society organisations and trade unions is a significant factor that can drive and improve compliance with human rights obligations.[19] The point that I want to highlight here is that these organisations also have a political obligation to press for change in the areas I have examined. Similarly, on the basis of Young's account, workers themselves may have

[17] On the role of activists and civil society organisations alongside human rights institutions in the development of human rights law, see de Búrca (n 10) 30ff. See also Loveday Hodson, *NGOs and the Struggle for Human Rights in Europe* (Hart 2011).

[18] See Ewing and Hendy (n 14); Alan Bogg and Keith Ewing, 'The Implications of the *RMT* Case' (2014) 43 Industrial Law Journal 221; Kalina Arabadjieva, 'Worker Empowerment, Collective Labour Rights and Article 11 of the European Convention on Human Rights' (2022) 22 Human Rights Law Review; Virginia Mantouvalou, 'Is There a Human Right not to be a Trade Union Member?' in Tonia Novitz and Colin Fenwick (eds), *Human Rights at Work* (Hart 2010) 439.

[19] Kevin L Cope, Cosette D Creamer, and Mila Versteeg, 'Empirical Studies of Human Rights Law' (2019) 15 *Annual Review of Law and Social Science* 155, 171.

political responsibility to mobilise and organise in order to challenge and subvert the unjust structures.[20]

Recognising the role of legal rules as a major factor that creates vulnerability to exploitation, a factor that contributes to the clustering of disadvantage,[21] challenging it and changing it, is a vital step. Identifying an agent that is responsible for an injustice (the state in this context that has backward-looking responsibility) places responsibility on that agent to change its conduct that is linked to the structures in question, but recognising the broader structural problem also places obligations, akin to Young's political, forward-looking responsibility, on other agents to play their role in bringing about structural change.

Human Rights Law and State-Mediated Structures of Exploitation

In many of the structures of injustice that I discussed in earlier chapters, through rules regulating labour that have an appearance of legitimacy, the state creates vulnerability of which employers take advantage. It threatens with and imposes sanctions, including deportation, incarceration, withdrawal of welfare support, and destitution. In this way people are forced, and often even trapped, into exploitative work as they have no rights or opportunities to exit this situation for fear of sanctions. Despite being presented as legitimate, the rules in question may indeed violate human rights obligations. In the remainder of this chapter, I look at human rights violations that may stem from rules affecting migrant workers and captive workers. In Chapter 8, I turn to human rights violations affecting those under welfare conditionality programmes and those in precarious work.

Migrant Workers

Rules on admission to a country are generally viewed as a legitimate exercise of state sovereignty. The International Convention on the Protection of the Rights of All Migrant Workers and Members of their Families of the United

[20] On the responsibility of the victims of structural injustice, see Tamara Jugov and Lea Ypi, 'Structural Injustice, Epistemic Opacity, and the Responsibilities of the Oppressed' (2019) 50 Journal of Political Philosophy 7.

[21] Jonathan Wolff and Avner de-Shalit, *Disadvantage* (OUP 2007).

Nations states: 'Nothing in the present Convention shall affect the right of each State Party to establish the criteria governing admission of migrant workers and members of their families.'[22] However, other human rights documents and monitoring bodies have imposed limitations on this power of the authorities in order to protect migrant workers. I begin by looking at the prohibition of slavery, servitude, and forced or compulsory labour in relation to the rights of these workers.

Forced labour

The ECtHR requires a strong element of coercion when examining whether there is a violation of Article 4 that contains this prohibition but has ruled on several occasions that migrant workers face such coercion.[23]

The first judgment that examined the treatment of a migrant worker under Article 4 was *Siliadin v France*,[24] which involved a migrant domestic worker who was brought to France from Togo at the age of fifteen years and seven months and was even more vulnerable because of her age. She had been promised that she would be able to work, be sent to school, and that her immigration status would be regularised, but was instead kept as a domestic worker for many years and was never sent to school. She worked for fifteen hours a day with no pay and no day off, she slept on the floor in the children's room, and her passport was withheld. Her immigration status was never regularised. The Court recognised that the vulnerability of the applicant was partly due to her immigration status[25] and imposed a duty on the authorities to legislate in order to criminalise this treatment by the employers. This case has been followed by a line of applications which involved serious abuse and exploitation of migrant domestic workers. In *CN v UK*,[26] for instance, the Court explained specifically that 'domestic servitude [...] involves a complex set of dynamics, involving both overt and more subtle forms of coercion, to force compliance',

[22] Art 79 of the International Convention on the Protection of the Rights of All Migrant Workers and Members of their Families, General Assembly Resolution 45/158, 18 December 1990. It continues: 'Concerning other matters related to their legal situation and treatment as migrant workers and members of their families, States Parties shall be subject to the limitations set forth in the present Convention.'

[23] For a detailed account of the development of the case law under art 4, see Vladislava Stoyanova, *Human Trafficking and Slavery Reconsidered* (CUP 2017). For a thorough analysis of the concept of exploitation in the context of art 4, see Marija Jovanovic, 'The Essence of Slavery: Exploitation in Human Rights Law' (2020) 20 Human Rights Law Review 674. See also Marija Jovanovic, *State Responsibility for 'Modern Slavery' in Human Rights Law: A Right Not to Be Trafficked?* (OUP 2023) (forthcoming).

[24] *Siliadin v France* App no 73316/01 (Judgment, 26 July 2005).

[25] ibid para 126.

[26] *CN v UK* App no 4239/08 (Judgment, 13 November 2012).

which requires 'an understanding of the many subtle ways an individual can fall under the control of another'.[27]

These cases underline the point that serious labour exploitation falls within the scope of Article 4 of the ECHR and that migrant workers are prone to it. They have led to an assessment of the legal framework in many legal orders and also, crucially, increased the visibility of a work sector that is traditionally undervalued and invisible. The legal obligation on which the Court was asked to focus, though, was the obligation to criminalise employers' conduct, rather than immigration or labour laws that increase vulnerability to exploitation. Similarly, case law that followed placed attention on investigations and enforcement of criminal law.[28] Monitoring of workers' living and working conditions is crucial in the context of a well-functioning labour inspection system. The imposition of an obligation on states to criminalise and prosecute alone, though, centres on individual responsibility of unscrupulous employers, and not on factors that create vulnerability of workers to such treatment. If investigations are solely tied to the criminal justice system, it is hard to see how they can lead to structural change or address the systemic problems that concern me in this study.

Immigration status as a factor of vulnerability to exploitation was also at stake in *Chowdury v Greece*.[29] The applicants were undocumented workers who were seriously exploited by their employer. Even though they were promised 22 euros for seven hours of work and three euros for each hour of overtime, they ended up working for twelve hours a day, with armed guards supervising them, and were told that they would only be paid if they continued working for their employer. When the applicants claimed unpaid wages, they were shot by armed guards. The situation of systematic exploitation in the region of Manolada, Greece, was widely known. It had been covered in the national press and by the Ombudsman who had reported extensively on the issue. In this case the Court clarified that immigration law itself should be scrutinised and that 'it must respond to concerns regarding the incitement or aiding and abetting of human trafficking or tolerance towards it'.[30]

Examining the question of whether these workers had freely agreed to work, or whether they had been coerced, the Court said that when an employer takes advantage of workers' vulnerability, they do not offer their labour voluntarily even if they initially consented, explaining that this question involves

[27] ibid para 80.
[28] For detailed analysis of this kind of obligations, see Marija Jovanovic's monograph (n 23).
[29] *Chowdury v Greece* App no 21884/15 (Judgment, 30 March 2017). I discuss this also in Chapter 3.
[30] ibid para 87.

the assessment of a range of facts.[31] In examining whether labour is 'forced', the Court did not only assess physical coercion and violence; it said that any penalty imposed 'can also take subtler forms, of a psychological nature, such as threats to denounce victims to the police or immigration authorities when their employment status is illegal'.[32] In *Chowdury*, the ECtHR questioned whether the workers had consented to their working conditions, and placed special attention on the fact that when they agreed to do the work, they were in a situation of vulnerability as irregular migrants without resources and at risk of being arrested, detained, and deported. They were aware that if they stopped working, they would never receive their unpaid wages that were overdue, the amount of which was constantly increasing.[33] On this basis, the Court classified their treatment as forced labour, having explained that undocumented workers are in a particularly vulnerable position.

The Court also recognised that very restrictive visa schemes create vulnerability to exploitation in *Rantsev v Cyprus and Russia*,[34] its first case on trafficking for sexual exploitation. This involved a woman from Russia who arrived in Cyprus under an 'artiste visa'. An 'artiste' was defined in the legislation as 'any alien who wishes to enter Cyprus in order to work in a cabaret, musical-dancing place or other night entertainment place and has attained the age of 18 years'.[35] There was significant evidence that this visa scheme was connected to sex trafficking.[36] Under the scheme, Ms Rantseva received a temporary work and residence permit. Having worked at a cabaret for three days, she escaped, only to be captured soon after and taken to the police. Since her immigration status was not irregular, the police returned her to her employer. Later that night she was found dead on the street below the flat where she was staying. The case was taken to the ECtHR by the victim's father, who claimed that Russia and Cyprus had breached Article 4 of the Convention (among other provisions). Cyprus produced a unilateral declaration requesting that the case be not further examined, but the Court rejected it because of the seriousness of the issues raised.

In relation to the immigration rules, of particular concern was the fact that cabaret managers made an application for an entry permit for the artiste in a way that rendered the worker dependent on the employer or agent and in this way vulnerable to human trafficking.[37] The Court found that the obligation of

[31] ibid para 96.
[32] See also *Zoletic v Azerbaijan* App no 20116/12 (Judgment, 7 October 2021) para 151.
[33] *Chowdury* (n 29) para 95.
[34] *Rantsev v Cyprus and Russia* App no 25965/04 (Judgment, 7 January 2010).
[35] ibid para 113.
[36] ibid para 80ff.
[37] ibid paras 89, 91, 94, 100.

the employers to inform the authorities if an artiste leaves their employment is a legitimate means to the end of monitoring compliance with immigration law. However, it is only the authorities that should take steps for non-compliance. Monitoring compliance cannot be the duty of the manager. This is why the Court was particularly troubled by the practice of asking cabaret owners and managers to lodge a bank guarantee covering artistes that they employed. This gave cabaret owners and managers a significant power to control cabaret dancers by encouraging them to track down artistes who are missing or otherwise take personal responsibility for them.

Relying on comments of a non-judicial body, the Council of Europe Commissioner for Human Rights, the Court emphasised that the authorities knew or ought to have known that the visa was problematic. The Commissioner had criticised the aspect of the scheme, whereby cabaret managers had to apply for the artiste, for making the artiste dependent on her employer or agent and increasing the risk of exploitation. The Commissioner had also remarked that the visa made it very challenging for law enforcement authorities to tackle trafficking, and explained that it could be viewed as contradicting anti-trafficking measures.[38] In light of this, the Court ruled that Cyprus had violated the Convention.[39]

Looking at a national legal order where a court has assessed the compatibility of very restrictive visa rules with human rights law, we can examine a legal challenge of a visa scheme that affected migrant workers in Israel.[40] Under the scheme in question, the visa stated the worker's length of stay and the name of the employer. The worker only had the right to work for the specific employer and for the period stated on the visa, while the employer was also in charge of the worker's departure from Israel upon expiry of the visa. The government claimed that the aim of the scheme was legitimate, as its purpose was the control of immigration. However, the visa was linked to structures of exploitation and was challenged before the Israeli Constitutional Court. The Court ruled that the visa scheme violates human dignity and breaches the Constitution by

[38] ibid para 291.

[39] The Court also ruled that Russia violated the ECHR with respect to its procedural obligations under art 4. Other case law that has followed has paid further attention to obligations of member states to investigate effectively cases of human trafficking. See the Grand Chamber case of *SM v Croatia* App no 60561/14 (Judgment, 25 June 2020).

[40] *Kav-Laoved v Government of Israel*, HCJ 4542/02, 2006, [2006] (1) IsrLR 260. See the discussion in Einat Albin, 'The Sectoral Regulatory Regime: Where Work Migration Controls and the Sectorally Differentiated Labour Market Meet' in Cathryn Costello and Mark Freedland (eds), *Migrants at Work* (OUP 2014). For more recent case law that accepted exceptions to the ban of tied visas, see Maayan Niezna, 'Paper Chains: Tied Visas, Migration Policies, and Legal Coercion' (2022) 49 Journal of Law and Society 362, 374.

creating a situation that was described as foreign to labour law principles and to the contract of employment. The Vice-President of the Court said:

> [W]e cannot avoid the conclusion—a painful and shameful conclusion—that the foreign worker has become his employer's serf, that the restrictive arrangement with all its implications has hedged the foreign worker in from every side and that the restrictive arrangement has created a modern form of slavery.[41]

The UK Overseas Domestic Worker visa, which places severe restrictions on the right to change employer,[42] was discussed in a report by GRETA, the specialist body of the Council of Europe monitoring the implementation of the Convention on Action Against Trafficking in Human Beings.[43] The GRETA Report explained that this visa is problematic and underlined the necessity for labour inspections in private households, which is a topic that the ECSR has also examined in this context.[44] It also asked the authorities to implement the recommendations of an independent report on the visa commissioned by the UK government, which proposed that domestic workers have an unconditional right to change employer, inter alia.[45] If we compare the UK visa to the Cypriot visa scheme in *Rantsev*, the latter was more restrictive, as the cabaret manager and artistic agent also had to pay a bank guarantee for the worker to cover possible future costs of the worker.[46] However, the vulnerability for the workers created by the UK Overseas Domestic Worker visa is very significant and the fact that they work in private households is also crucial, for the reason that they are invisible to the authorities. The scheme traps them in employment relations that violate their rights, both while employed by the person to whom the visa ties them and if they escape, as they then become undocumented and trapped in ongoing cycles of exploitation. The GRETA Report and materials of other human rights organisations that have criticised the UK visa scheme,[47]

[41] *Kav-Laoved* (n 40) 313–14.

[42] See the discussion in Chapter 3; see also Virginia Mantouvalou, '"Am I Free Now?" Overseas Domestic Workers in Slavery' (2015) 42 Journal of Law and Society 329.

[43] Council of Europe Convention on Action against Trafficking in Human Beings (ETS No 197), adopted on 15 May 2005, entered into force on 1 February 2008. Evaluation Report, United Kingdom, GRETA (2021) 12, 20 October 2021 <https://rm.coe.int/greta-third-evalution-report-on-the-united-kingdom/1680a43b36> accessed 1 June 2022.

[44] Conclusions XXII-1, United Kingdom, art 1-2, 29 January 2021.

[45] James Ewins, 'Independent Review of the Overseas Domestic Worker Visa' (16 December 2015) para 118.2.

[46] The Court described this as particularly troubling, *Rantsev* (n 34) para 292.

[47] See eg the communication sent to the government by the Special Rapporteur on Contemporary Forms of Slavery; the Special Rapporteur on the Human Rights of Migrants; and the Special Rapporteur

together with evidence on the working conditions of these workers, can provide a basis for courts to rule that it violates principles of the ECHR under Article 4 as well as other provisions.

Similar issues are raised by other visa schemes that effectively bind workers to an employer, such as those introduced in the United Kingdom in the context of Brexit for agricultural workers. In particular, given that when assessing state-mediated structures of injustice we examine how the law operates and what patterns it creates, it is important to assess the legal rights of these workers not only in theory but also in their effectiveness. This is in line with the principle of interpretation developed by the ECtHR that rights have to be 'practical and effective' rather than 'theoretical and illusory'.[48] In Chapter 3, we saw that agricultural workers who arrive in the United Kingdom under a pilot seasonal worker visa have a right to change employer 'where possible'.[49] This is not unconditional and there is evidence that the operators that run the schemes restrict it, making it ineffective.[50] Issues such as these signify that the visa may violate the United Kingdom's obligations under Article 4.

The impossibility of leaving the employer has been viewed by the ILO as a key ingredient of forced labour.[51] The right to leave the employer must be unconditional, for otherwise it will not be effective, as we saw in the case of the UK Overseas Domestic Worker visa in Chapter 3. Moreover, visa conditions that require workers to live in the employer's premises can also restrict their freedom significantly and should be viewed as a factor that creates vulnerability to forced labour.[52] A requirement to live in the employer's premises may also engage the right to private life, to which I now turn.

Private life, labour inspections, and health and safety

A requirement to live in the employer's premises, as well as workers' living and working conditions more generally, may give rise to violations of provisions, such as the right to private life and the right to health and safety at work. The right to private life is protected in several human rights documents.[53] Article

on Trafficking in Persons, Especially Women and Children (27 May 2021) <https://spcommreports.ohchr.org/TMResultsBase/DownLoadPublicCommunicationFile?gId=26423> accessed 1 June 2022.

[48] *Airey v Ireland* App no 6289/73 (Judgment, 9 October 1979) para 24.

[49] See 'Workers and Temporary Workers: guidance for sponsors' (April 2022) s 3.8.

[50] See Focus on Labour Exploitation and Fife Migrants Forum, 'Assessment of the Risks of Human Trafficking for Forced Labour on the UK Seasonal Workers Pilot' (2021) 59.

[51] See ILO Special Action Programme to Combat Forced Labour (SAP-FL) International Programme on the Elimination of Child Labour (IPEC), 'Hard to See, Harder to Count—Survey Guidelines to Estimate Forced Labour of Adults and Children' (2011) 25.

[52] ibid 24.

[53] See eg art 8 of the ECHR and art 11 of the ICCPR.

8(1) of the ECHR provides that '[e]veryone has the right to respect for his private and family life, his home and his correspondence'. The second paragraph permits restrictions in so far as there is a legitimate aim and the restriction is proportionate to the aim pursued.[54] In relation to migrant workers who are already isolated and have very few networks of support in the host state, there can be an interference with the right when immigration rules require them to live in the employer's premises, as this limits greatly their opportunities to have a private life. A further challenge is posed by the fact that in some legal orders the law excludes private households from labour inspections in order to protect the employer's privacy.[55] Migrant domestic workers who accompany their employer under a visa that ties them to the employer or a visa that obligates them to live in the employer's home are known to live and work in poor conditions, with no private space and with very limited opportunities to have a private life or contact with the outside world.[56] The exclusion of their workplace from labour inspections is problematic.

These restrictions on the private life of domestic workers may be presented as legitimate because of the nature of their job, as they may be expected to be constantly available to provide round-the-clock services to the employer,[57] and because their workplace is the employer's private home. Even if the aims of these rules were viewed as legitimate, the extensive intrusions with their humiliating effects, as well as the resulting invisibility of domestic workers to the authorities, should be found to be disproportionate to the aim pursued.[58] This is supported by the fact that the ECSR and GRETA have insisted on the importance of labour inspections in private households in order to examine the working conditions of domestic workers, notwithstanding that such inspections can interfere with the employer's private life.[59]

[54] Para 8(2) states:

> There shall be no interference by a public authority with the exercise of this right except such as is in accordance with the law and is necessary in a democratic society in the interests of national security, public safety or the economic well-being of the country, for the prevention of disorder or crime, for the protection of health or morals, or for the protection of the rights and freedoms of others.

[55] See eg UK Health and Safety at Work Act 1974, s 51.

[56] See eg *Siliadin v France* App no 73316/01 (Judgment, 26 July 2005); *CN v UK* App no 4239/08 (Judgment, 13 November 2012); Mantouvalou (n 42); Natalie Sedacca, 'Migrant Domestic Workers and the Right to Private and Family Life' (2019) 37 Netherlands Quarterly of Human Rights 288.

[57] See ILO Report, 'Domestic Workers Across the World: Global and Regional Statistics and the Extent of Legal Protection' (2013) 59.

[58] For analysis of how the test of proportionality operates in qualified rights under the ECHR, see George Letsas, 'Rescuing Proportionality' in Rowan Cruft, S Matthew Liao, and Massimo Renzo (eds), *Philosophical Foundations of Human Rights* (OUP 2015) 316, 337–38.

[59] GRETA, Second Report on Spain (2018) para 90; ECSR, 2020 Conclusions on Albania. The living conditions of domestic workers when in a situation of servitude have also been presented as giving rise to a violation of the right to housing. See Jessie Hohmann, 'Conceptualising Domestic Servitude

Similarly, seasonal workers in agriculture sometimes live in appalling conditions, as we saw in the example of *Chowdury* that involved undocumented workers who lived in makeshift cardboard, nylon, and bamboo shacks, lacking even the most basic conditions of hygiene.[60] In cases where their living conditions are particularly poor (for instance when they are overcrowded and unsanitary), a claim can be made that they are not compatible with the workers' right to private life.[61] Any visa requirement or the real need to live in the employer's premises in humiliating conditions with no inspection when the authorities know or ought to know of these conditions may give rise to state obligations under human rights law.[62] There may be a legitimate reason why the workers' accommodation is on site, which is the lack of other accommodation in proximity to the workplace. Yet the lack of inspections of poor living conditions of agricultural workers cannot have a legitimate aim, so the inactivity of the authorities when they know or ought to know of this situation may give rise to a violation of the right to private life.

Lack of inspections of working conditions may also be incompatible with the right to health and safety at work, which has been one of the ILO Fundamental Principles and Rights at Work since 2022, and is further protected in other human rights documents, such as Article 31(1) of the EUCFR and Article 3 of the ESC. Article 3 of the ESC contains an obligation to enact health and safety regulations, supervise their enforcement, and consult workers' and employers' organisations on matters of health and safety. In this context, the ECSR has observed that migrant workers are affected by workplace accidents more than non-migrant workers, which may be because they are employed in more hazardous and precarious jobs.[63] The ECtHR has examined questions of health and safety at work in its case law too. For instance, in the case *Mazukna v Lithuania*,[64] where the applicant had a serious and permanent injury as a result of a workplace accident, the Court found that the accident was not properly investigated by the authorities, and ruled that this constituted a violation of procedural obligations to investigate under the prohibition of inhuman and degrading treatment in Article 3 of the ECHR.[65] In *Brincat v*

as a Violation of the Human Right to Housing and Reframing Australian Policy Responses' (2022) 31 Griffith Law Review 98.

[60] On migrant workers' living conditions, see also *Zoletic* (n 32).

[61] In extreme situations, this may also violate art 3 of the ECHR, which I discuss below.

[62] *Moldovan v Romania (No 2)* App nos 41138/98 and 64320/01 (Judgment, 12 July 2005) para 110.

[63] Conclusions XX-2, Greece, 2013.

[64] *Mazukna v Lithuania* App no 72092/12 (Judgment, 11 April 2017).

[65] Art 3 of the ECHR provides as follows: 'No one shall be subjected to torture or to inhuman or degrading treatment or punishment.'

Malta,[66] it concluded that the lack of legislation or other measures to protect workers from asbestos that had serious health effects and in some cases led to death violated the right to life and the right to private life. Similar findings on human rights obligations stemming from health and safety for workers in a high-risk profession, deep-sea diving, were at stake in *Vilnes v Norway*,[67] where the Court ruled that state authorities violated Article 8 of the ECHR on the right to private life for not taking certain necessary measures to protect workers' health and safety.

This line of cases and other materials of monitoring bodies show that poor working conditions and ineffective investigations of workplace accidents can fall short of human rights standards. Particularly when Article 3 of the ECHR is invoked, involving inhuman and degrading treatment, a level of severity has to be reached, but this is indeed sometimes reached when assessing the living and working conditions of migrant workers.[68] At the same time, in provisions that permit limitations subject to a legitimate aim and a test of proportionality, it will have to be shown by the workers that the restrictions in question are excessive. Both empirical research and materials of the ILO, the ECSR, and other bodies that consider working conditions of migrant workers in precarious sectors like agriculture and domestic work can provide support for the position that restrictions on workers' rights to private life and health and safety at work may be of such gravity that a violation of human rights law can be substantiated. The specific examples from the ECHR case law that I discussed in *Mazukna*, *Brincat*, and *Vilnes* did not involve migrant workers, but human rights law does not distinguish between a state's nationals and migrant workers in relation to workers' rights once people are employed, as I explain below.

Equality, human rights, and immigration

The Inter-American Court of Human Rights in its landmark Advisory Opinion on Juridical Status and Rights of the Undocumented Migrants examined extensively the working conditions of undocumented migrant workers.[69] The request for this Opinion was submitted by the government of Mexico, following a case of the US Supreme Court that examined whether the dismissal of an

[66] *Brincat v Malta* App nos 60908/11, 62110/11, 62129/11, 62312/11, and 62338/11 (Judgment, 24 July 2014).

[67] *Vilnes v Norway* App nos 52806/09 and 22703/10 (Judgment, 5 December 2013).

[68] See the description of the living and working conditions in *Chowdury* (n 29) paras 7 and 94.

[69] *Juridical Condition and Rights of the Undocumented Migrants*, Advisory Opinion OC-18/03 (17 September 2003), IACtHR (2003) Series A no 18 (hereafter cited as Advisory Opinion). Noted by Sarah Cleveland, 'Legal Status and Rights of Undocumented Workers' (2005) 99 American Journal of International Law 460.

undocumented worker with no back pay, for the reason that he was involved in trade union activities, was compatible with the US Constitution.[70] The Opinion explored more broadly the exclusion from labour rights of undocumented workers, and its compatibility with human rights law.

The Inter-American Court explained that equality and non-discrimination are peremptory rules of international law, widely recognised in legal documents,[71] and that migrant workers cannot be excluded from these because of their immigration status.[72] It accepted that it is legitimate for states to have rules regulating matters such as entry and right to work requirements.[73] Immigration rules that regulate these are (at least *prima facie*) justified in line with this thinking.[74] However, the Court also explained that once an employment relationship is established, it is discriminatory to exclude undocumented migrants from labour rights, including fair wages, reasonable working hours, safe and healthy working conditions, and social security. These and other labour rights were described by the Court as inalienable.[75]

The Court considered in detail the structural aspect of the vulnerability of undocumented workers and the role of the law, and the Opinion articulated important principles on state-mediated structures of exploitation affecting undocumented workers. This was in line with an amicus brief included in the Opinion, which underlined that undocumented migrants are in a subordinate position to nationals of a country for reasons such as the fact that they are away from networks of support, but also because of the role that the state plays in their condition:

> The position of subordination imposed on aliens/migrants is something that the recipient State 'confirms.' Here, the vulnerability is potentially supplemented by the role of the State, either by act or omission, but always in the context of this differential treatment that the recipient State grants to nationals compared to aliens.[76]

The Court explained that states have an obligation to protect the rights of undocumented migrant workers in their jurisdiction from private employers and made specific reference to state responsibility arising 'for the acts of third

[70] *Hoffman Plastic Compounds, Inc v National Labor Relations Board*, 535 US 137 (2002).
[71] ibid 86 and 101.
[72] ibid 106.
[73] ibid 119, 169.
[74] However, we have seen that other cases, such as *Rantsev*, have recognised limitations to this power.
[75] Advisory Opinion (n 69) 157–58.
[76] ibid, Jorge Bustamante, amicus intervention, para 47.

parties who act with its tolerance, acquiescence or negligence, or with the support of some State policy or directive that encourages the creation or maintenance of situations of discrimination'.[77] Discussing specifically immigration laws as a factor that creates vulnerability of undocumented workers to exploitation and the role of the state, the Court addressed the heart of the issue:

> [I]t is not admissible for a State of employment to protect its national production, in one or several sectors by encouraging or tolerating the employment of undocumented migrant workers in order to exploit them, taking advantage of their condition of vulnerability in relation to the employer in the State or considering them an offer of cheaper labor, either by paying them lower wages, denying or limiting their enjoyment or exercise of one or more of their labor rights, or denying them the possibility of filing a complaint about the violation of their rights before the competent authority.[78]

On the basis of this Opinion, the prohibition of discrimination applies to a number of labour rights, such as the prohibition of forced labour and child labour, the rights to organise and collective bargaining, fair wages, reasonable working hours, safe and healthy working conditions, social security, a right to rest and compensation, protection for women workers, as well as judicial and administrative guarantees. They do not depend on immigration status but on the principle of human dignity that is embodied in Article 1 of the Universal Declaration of Human Rights.[79] The exclusion of undocumented migrant workers from rights that other workers enjoy is not compatible with these provisions.

Wages and social security

The prohibition of discrimination together with the right to property can also serve to address the exploitation of migrant workers who may be excluded from minimum wage or social security rights, or undocumented workers who may not be entitled to pay for work that they performed because they did not have a valid contract. In the European human rights system, we find the prohibition of discrimination in Article 14, which says:

[77] ibid 152.
[78] ibid para 170.
[79] ibid para 157.

> The enjoyment of the rights and freedoms set forth in this Convention shall be secured without discrimination on any ground such as sex, race, colour, language, religion, political or other opinion, national or social origin, association with a national minority, property, birth or other status.

The right to property is protected in Article 1 of Protocol 1 of the ECHR,[80] which states that '[e]very natural or legal person is entitled to the peaceful enjoyment of his possessions'. The ECtHR has frequently ruled that salaries can be protected under this provision.[81]

The right to property covers not only 'existing possessions' but also 'legitimate expectations' of obtaining effective enjoyment of property rights.[82] It is important to appreciate that property is an 'autonomous concept'[83] for the purposes of the Convention, which is independent from the classification in domestic law. It is not necessary for national law to recognise the interest at stake as a property right. In *Belane Nagy v Hungary*,[84] the Court said that 'a legitimate expectation must be of a nature more concrete than a mere hope and be based on a legal provision or a legal act such as a judicial decision'.[85] If national law excludes migrant workers from labour rights that are enjoyed by those who are citizens of the host state, the right to property can be implicated. An exclusion from the minimum wage may not be a violation of the provision but, when examined together with Article 14, the Court simply needs to rule that the claim falls within the ambit of the right to property.[86] It is not necessary to find a violation of the latter provision.

Against this background, it is particularly hard to see how the confiscation of wages of undocumented workers as proceeds of crime under section 34 of the UK Immigration Act 2016 can be compatible with the right to property. This issue was examined in the case of *Paulet v UK*,[87] where the Court ruled that the confiscation of wages of a worker who was undocumented constituted a violation of the provision. In that case, the Court focused on the standard of review applied by national courts, and found that this was lower than the requirements

[80] For an overview of the issues, see Petra Herzfeld Olsson, 'Every Natural or Legal Person is Entitled to the Peaceful Enjoyment of His or Her Possessions: Article 1, Protocol 1 to the European Convention on Human Rights' in Dorssemont, Lorcher, and Schomann (n 6) 381.

[81] See eg *Savickas v Lithuania* App no 66365/09 (Decision, 15 October 2013).

[82] *Presos Compania Naviera SA v Belgium* App no 17849/91 (Judgment, 20 November 1995).

[83] *Oneryildiz v Turkey* App no 48939/99 (Judgment, 30 November 2004).

[84] Belane Nagy v Hungary App no 5380/13 (Judgment, 13 December 2016).

[85] ibid para 75.

[86] See *Abdulaziz, Cabales and Bankadali v UK* App nos 9214/80, 9473/81, and 9474/81 (Judgment, 28 May 1985). I return to this issue in Chapter 8.

[87] *Paulet v UK* App no 6219/08 (Judgment, 13 May 2014).

of Article 1 of Protocol 1 of the Convention. Yet the principle that confiscation of wages falls with the scope of the right to property was set out clearly by the ECtHR.[88] The second paragraph of Article 1 of Protocol 1 allows the authorities to control the use of property to secure the payment of penalties. Here the Court explained that there must 'exist a reasonable relationship of proportionality between the means employed and the aim sought to be realised'.[89] The aim of the confiscation of wages of undocumented workers could be presented as legitimate, given that working without legal documents is a criminal offence in the United Kingdom.[90] However, the fact that the measure is taken in the context of 'hostile environment' policies[91] that aim to marginalise migrants should make the Court question its legitimacy and scrutinise closely its proportionality, as its effect is that people lose all their pay for work that they have done.

Inequality in social security rights faced by migrant workers may also be covered by the right to property together with the prohibition of discrimination.[92] Immigration status in particular was examined in *Gaygusuz v Austria*,[93] where the applicant was a Turkish national lawfully resident and working in Austria, who had paid contributions to an unemployment insurance fund in the same way as Austrian nationals. The authorities refused to pay an advance on his pension as an emergency payment under Austrian legislation for the sole reason that he did not have Austrian nationality. He claimed that this treatment was discriminatory, and hence contrary to Article 14 of the Convention in conjunction with Article 1 of Protocol 1. The ECtHR held that the benefit that the applicant claimed could be classified as 'possessions', so that his situation was within the ambit of Article 1 of Additional Protocol 1. Turning to Article 14, the Court considered whether the difference of treatment between the applicant, on the one hand, and Austrian nationals, on the other, was justified, and ruled that it was not based on an 'objective and reasonable justification'. The Court referred to the possibility of granting state authorities some discretion in the area of the social rights of migrants, by mentioning its margin of appreciation doctrine,[94] but stressed that 'very weighty reasons would have to be put forward before the Court could regard a difference of treatment based

[88] ibid para 64.
[89] ibid.
[90] See UK Immigration Act 2016, s 34.
[91] For discussion of the policies, see Melanie Griffiths and Colin Yeo, 'The UK's Hostile Environment: Deputising Immigration Control' (2021) 41 Critical Social Policy 521.
[92] *Stec v UK* App nos 65731/01 and 65900/01 (Judgment, 12 April 2006) para 53.
[93] *Gaygusuz v Austria* App no 17371/90 (Judgment, 16 September 1996).
[94] On the margin of appreciation, see George Letsas, 'Two Concepts of the Margin of Appreciation' (2006) 26 Oxford Journal of Legal Studies 705; Dean Spielmann, 'Whither the Margin of Appreciation?' (2014) 67 Current Legal Problems 49.

exclusively on the ground of nationality as compatible with the Convention'.[95] There was therefore a violation of the prohibition of discrimination in conjunction with the right to property.[96]

It emerges here that wages and social security rights of migrant workers are potentially protected in human rights provisions regarding property and possessions, and the prohibition of discrimination means that immigration status should be scrutinised very carefully when used as a justification for different treatment of migrant workers. Arbitrary exclusions and disproportionate measures affecting their wages and social security rights may be incompatible with human rights law.

Captive Workers

In Chapter 4, I discussed structures of exploitation that affect captive workers, focusing on legal rules excluding working prisoners, offenders doing unpaid work and those working in immigration detention from protective laws, while employers and the authorities benefit from this situation. Are these exclusions and the resulting structures of exploitation compatible with human rights law? Captive workers are required to work with minimal or no pay, under the threat of punishment, such as solitary confinement, removal of rights to have visits in prison, or incarceration for those doing unpaid work as a sentence. Immigration detainees are not punished if they do not work, so their work could be viewed as voluntary. However, they face serious psychological pressure because of the length of their detention, and have needs to cover while detained, as work is the only way in which many can afford phone credit, for instance, in order to contact their lawyers or relatives and for other related purposes,[97] as I explain further in what follows. On the basis of principles that I discussed earlier on migrant workers who are subject to forced labour, we should question whether their work is a matter of choice or a result of coercion. Not only do they have to work under the threat of punishment but they are also

[95] *Gaygusuz* (n 93) para 42.

[96] A similar finding was also made in a case where the authorities refused a non-contributory disability benefit to the applicant who was a documented migrant in *Koua Poirrez v France* App no 40892/98 (Judgment, 30 September 2003). The same principle was endorsed in cases on maternity and child benefits of foreign nationals with limited residence rights in *Niedzwiecki v Germany* App no 58453/00 (Judgment, 25 October 2005), or those that have the status of a refugee *Fawsie v Greece* App no 40080/07 (Judgment, 28 October 2010).

[97] See Report of the Jesuit Refugee Service, 'Detained and Dehumanised—The Impact of Immigration Detention' (27 June 2020).

trapped into this work as they have no opportunities other than those offered to them while in captivity.

The authorities put forward a justification for the exclusions from labour rights of working prisoners, offenders doing community service, and immigration detainees. The typical response is that those deprived of their freedom need to contribute to the costs of the running of the facilities and that for those in unpaid work as a community sentence, working without pay is their sentence. In addition, it is typically said that work is for them part of the process of rehabilitation, which the ECtHR has ruled to be a crucial factor in the design of penal policies. The Court has recognised that 'the emphasis on rehabilitation and reintegration has become a "mandatory factor" that member states need to take into account when designing their penal policies'.[98]

If work can indeed promote offenders' rehabilitation, it is possible to argue that the state has obligations to promote work opportunities in so far as possible. Yet work must be of such quality as to meet this aim, rather than having schemes that create structures of exploitation, making offenders feel that it is part of their punishment and that the authorities treat them with contempt. What we observe is that the states create a vulnerable workforce that is systematically exploited by the authorities, private employers, or other private entities that run prisons and immigration detention centres or that deliver probation services. This reality has also been described as part of the phenomenon of the 'carceral state', an element of which is that the state manages people by forcing them into precarious work.[99]

Working prisoners

When looking at work in prison, a first hurdle is that international human rights and constitutional rights documents explicitly exclude it from the prohibition of forced labour. Article 4 of the ECHR states: 'For the purpose of this Article the term "forced or compulsory labour" shall not include […] any work required to be done in the ordinary course of detention imposed according to the provisions of Article 5 of this Convention or during release from such detention.'[100] A similar exception is found in the Thirteenth Amendment of the US Constitution that provides that '[n]either slavery nor involuntary

[98] *Khoroshenko v Russia* App no 41418/04 (Judgment, 30 June 2015) para 121. See Sonja Meinjer, 'Rehabilitation as a Positive Obligation' (2017) 25 European Journal of Crime, Criminal Law and Criminal Justice 145.

[99] Noah Zatz, 'The Carceral State at Work—Exclusion, Coercion and Subordinated Inclusion' in Alan Bogg and others (eds), *Criminality at Work* (OUP 2020) 496. See further the discussion in Chapter 4.

[100] ILO Forced Labour Convention 1930 (No 29) art 4, para 3(a).

servitude, except as punishment for crime whereof the party shall have been duly convicted, shall exist within the United States, or any place subject to their jurisdiction'. The ILO draws a distinction between private and public prisons in the Forced Labour Convention No 29, and imposes specific requirements regarding the regulation of private use of prisoners' labour.[101] Article 2(1) of the Convention says that 'forced or compulsory labour shall mean all work or service which is exacted from any person under the menace of any penalty and for which the said person has not offered himself voluntarily'. Article 2(2) contains exceptions, with the relevant one for present purposes being the following:

> (c) any work or service exacted from any person as a consequence of a conviction in a court of law, provided that the said work or service is carried out under the supervision and control of a public authority and that the said person is not hired to or placed at the disposal of private individuals, companies or associations.

These exclusions of working prisoners may have been deemed acceptable in the past,[102] but they are no longer acceptable. The ILO examined in 2007 whether prison labour for private employers complies with Convention No 29 and developed principles in the area.[103] In order for prison work for private employers to comply with the Forced Labour Convention, what is needed is the formal written consent of the prisoner and working conditions similar to a free labour relationship (in relation to wage levels, social security, and occupational safety and health). These would indicate that labour is voluntary.[104] The ECSR also considered prison labour in the context of Article 1 paragraph 2 of the ESC, which protects the right to work in an occupation freely entered upon. It reached similar findings to the ILO, namely that working conditions in prison have to be regulated strictly, and that when employed by private employers, prisoners have to be employed with their consent and in conditions as similar as possible to working conditions outside prison.[105] The Committee also said that the prohibition of discrimination concerns their pay, working hours, and other working conditions, as well as social security rights.[106]

[101] See Colin Fenwick, 'Private Use of Prisoners' Labor: Paradoxes of International Human Rights Law' (2005) 27 Human Rights Quarterly 249, 273; Faina Milman-Sivan, 'Prisoners for Hire: Towards a Normative Justification of the ILO's Prohibition of Private Forced Prisoner Labor' (2013) 36 Fordham International Law Journal 1619.

[102] See eg *Van Droogenbroeck v Belgium* App no 7906/77 (Judgment, 24 June 1982).

[103] ILO Report of the Committee of Experts for the Application of Conventions and Recommendations, 'Eradication of Forced Labour' (International Labour Office 2007).

[104] ibid paras 59–60 and 114 ff.

[105] Conclusions XVI-1, Germany.

[106] Conclusions 2012, General Introduction, Statement of Interpretation of Article 1 para 2.

The Grand Chamber of the ECtHR examined prison labour in *Stummer v Austria*,[107] which involved affiliation of working prisoners with an old age pension system. Here the applicant was not entitled to old age pension despite having worked for lengthy periods of time in the prison kitchen and bakery, because he had not accumulated the required minimum of contributions in order to have this entitlement. Even though the majority of the Court recognised that prisoners should enjoy all rights except their physical liberty while incarcerated, they did not find that the applicant's rights were violated. The majority explained that Article 1 of Protocol 1 does not create a right to acquire property. The authorities are free to decide whether to have a social security system and its details. However, it clarified that as soon as a state has a system in place, the law generates a proprietary interest that falls within the ambit of the right to property. Nevertheless, they said that Stummer's exclusion from social security rights did not violate his right to property (even though pension rights qualify as property rights) together with the prohibition of discrimination or forced labour contrary to Article 4 of the Convention. The Court recognised that the 2006 European Prison Rules require that work be as normal as possible for those in prison, but the majority were reluctant to apply this principle to the old age pension.[108]

However, there were powerful dissenting opinions in *Stummer* on the human rights of working prisoners. Dissenting Judges Tulkens, Kovler, Gyulumyan, Spielmann, Popovic, Malinverni, and Pardalos emphasised that the reason why the applicant was unable to pay his contributions was because of deliberate state policy that withheld 75 per cent of his pay. Because of this large percentage, as they explained, he was deprived of social security rights that constitute 'an integral part of human dignity'.[109] They maintained that the right to property together with the prohibition of discrimination were violated and in doing so they placed special attention on the fact that the ECHR is a living instrument that must be interpreted in light of present-day conditions, and not in light of the drafters' intentions. At the same time, the rights of the ECHR must be practical and effective, as Judge Tulkens particularly highlighted in her further dissent on Article 4:

> [C]an it really still be maintained in 2011, in the light of current standards in the field of social security, that prison work without affiliation to the old-age

[107] *Stummer v Austria* App no 37452/02 (Judgment, 7 July 2011).
[108] European Prison Rules, rule 26.17.
[109] *Stummer* (n 107) dissenting opinion, para 10.

> pension system constitutes work that a person in detention may *normally* be required to do? I do not think so. This, in my view, is the fundamental point. Nowadays, work without adequate social cover can no longer be regarded as normal work. It follows that the exception provided for in Article 4 § 3 (a) of the Convention is not applicable in the present case. *Even a prisoner cannot be forced to do work that is abnormal.*

The line of thinking of the dissenting judges in *Stummer* was not followed through in a more recent case on working prisoners.[110] In addition to exclusions from minimum wage and social security rights, working prisoners in some legal orders are not permitted to organise or engage in union activities.[111] The right to form and join a trade union is explicitly protected in many human rights treaties, and can be particularly important for those in prison as they are faced with serious restrictions of their physical freedom.[112] Article 11 of the ECHR guarantees freedom of association, including the right to form and join trade unions. The Court has ruled several times that the provision has been breached when trade union rights were restricted.[113] Article 11(2) also permits some limitations on the right for reasons of public safety, for the prevention of disorder, for the protection of health, and other such things. It specifically mentions certain groups whose right to organise may be subject to limitations (armed forces, police, and administration of the state) that do not include working prisoners. It might be said that the exclusion or restriction of trade union or other organisational rights of working prisoners is necessary in order to promote one of the legitimate aims in the second paragraph of the provision, such as the prevention of disorder. This may have an appearance of legitimacy but should be rejected decisively.

The ECtHR missed the opportunity to address the problem of the blanket banning of working prisoners from trade union activities in *Yakut Republican Trade-Union Federation v Russia*.[114] It involved a union set up by prisoners to challenge their poor working conditions. The majority of the Court recognised that prisoners in principle continue to have all rights other than the right to liberty, that the ECHR is a living instrument, and that in the future working

[110] *Yakut Republican Trade-Union Federation v Russia* App no 29582/09 (Judgment, 7 December 2021).

[111] See Chapter 4.

[112] See the discussion in Gerard de Jonge, 'Still "Slaves of the State": Prison Labour and International Law' in Dirk Van Zyl Smit and Frieder Dunkel (eds), *Prison Labour: Salvation or Slavery?* (Routledge 1999) 313.

[113] See eg Ewing and Hendy (n 14).

[114] See n 110.

prisoners may have a right to organise. However, in a brief paragraph they explained that there is no sufficient consensus in Europe on this matter, and that the authorities have a margin of appreciation.

By contrast, dissenting Judges Lemmens and Serghides provided a thoughtful and considered analysis of the question of whether working prisoners should have trade union rights. They criticised the reasoning of the majority for being grounded on policy rather than legal considerations, and explained that a total ban on union activities in this context is incompatible with the Convention. A general reference to the prevention of disorder and crime as a reason for restrictions of trade union rights should not have been viewed as sufficient, on the view of the dissenting judges. 'Where a law, a practice or a decision is not compatible with the Convention, or where the Government do not at least provide the necessary justification, it is for the Court to assume its responsibilities and to rule to that effect',[115] they explained. They highlighted that the lack of consensus in Europe should not have impeded this, and concluded that Article 11 was violated in this case.

Incarcerated workers must have a right to organise and engage in union activity, including a right to strike, against exploitative practices by private entities and by the state, as they are faced with a number of exclusions and challenges that make them more vulnerable than other workers.[116] There are particularly strong reasons for this group to have a voice and collective rights, given the restrictions of their physical freedom and choice of work from which they have no right to exit without punishment.[117] As the UK Supreme Court emphasised in *Cox*,[118] the relationship between the prison authorities and working prisoners is even closer than an employment relation because they are compelled to work. This should make us question strongly whether it is legitimate to exclude them from basic labour protections.

The ECtHR has repeatedly recognised that prisoners are a vulnerable group,[119] and this should support the position that their labour and social security rights must be robustly protected in line with the requirements of the

[115] ibid dissenting opinion, para 10.

[116] See Incarcerated Lawyers' Organising Committee, 'Incarcerated Workers: One Big Union Inside and Out' (2019) 82 Socialist Lawyer 26; Keith Armstrong, '"You May Be Down and Out, But You Ain't Beaten": Collective Bargaining for Incarcerated Workers' (2020) 110 Journal of Criminal Law and Criminology 593.

[117] See eg John Washington, 'This Week May See the Largest Prison Strike in US History' *The Nation* (7 September 2016).

[118] *Cox v Ministry of Justice* [2016] UKSC 10. This is discussed in Chapter 4.

[119] See eg *Algür v Turkey* App no 32574/96 (Judgment, 22 October 2002) para 44; *Mikadze v Russia* App no 52687/99 (Judgment, 7 June 2007) para 109; *Aliev v Georgia* App no 522/04 (Judgment, 13 January 2009) para 97.

ILO, the ECSR, and the European Prison Rules. The dissenting opinions in *Stummer* and *Yakut Republican Trade-Union Federation* should form the basis for the development of the law in the future.

The Howard League for Penal Reform, the oldest penal reform charity in the United Kingdom, advocates 'real' work for prisoners, replicating working conditions outside prison in so far as possible and being paid at least the national minimum wage.[120] The Committee of Experts of the ILO also said in a report: 'where private enterprises are permitted to pay prisoners wages that are less than the minimum wage, their relationship cannot be considered comparable to a free employment relationship.'[121] It should not be assumed that working for the state while in prison is less exploitative either. For reasons such as these, compelling people to work while also excluding them from labour rights is unjustified and has to be viewed as incompatible with human rights law.

Unpaid work as a community sentence

The treatment of offenders who do unpaid work may also violate human rights law. The ECHR has been described as 'a largely untapped resource' on community sanctions.[122] Unpaid work requirements may appear to be less restrictive than prison labour because people doing the work are not in prison. However, refusal to do the work may have imprisonment as a consequence. It is a requirement to 'get to work or go to jail', as Zatz put it.[123] These sentences can be viewed in this respect as a continuum with prison labour, rather than an improvement: they are part of the same structure of exploitation, whereby the law creates vulnerability of offenders by excluding them from workers' rights, while private entities and the state take advantage of this situation and make profit. Given that these can be viewed as being on a continuum with prison labour, the principles of the ECHR developed above are also applicable to unpaid work as a community sentence.

Elements of community sentences can be particularly humiliating. It has therefore been suggested that community sentences that employ public shaming may violate the prohibition of inhuman and degrading treatment

[120] Howard League for Penal Reform, 'Business Behind Bars—Making Real Work in Prison Work' (2011).

[121] ILO Report of the Committee of Experts on the Application of Conventions and Recommendations, International Labour Conference (ILO 1990) 90.

[122] See Dirk van Zyl Smit, 'Community Sanctions and European Human Rights Law' in Lucia Zedner and Julian V Roberts (eds), *Principles and Values in Criminal Law and Criminal Justice—Essays in Honour of Andrew Ashworth* (OUP 2012) 191, 203–04.

[123] Noah Zatz, 'Get to Work or Got to Jail: State Violence and the Racialized Production of Precarious Work' (2020) 45 Law and Social Inquiry 304.

under the Convention.[124] This may arise when those sentenced to unpaid work are required to wear high visibility jackets that can only serve the purpose of humiliating offenders. Even though being sentenced for an offence necessarily contains an element of humiliation, the treatment of offenders should respect their dignity and should not deliberately increase public humiliation.[125]

Unpaid work as a community sentence has not been examined by the ECtHR to date, but the UK unpaid work requirements scheme was the subject of a representation to the ILO Committee of Experts on the Application of Conventions and Recommendations, submitted by major UK trade unions.[126] As mentioned earlier, the ILO Forced Labour Convention that prohibits forced labour excludes from its remit any work that follows a conviction by court.[127]

There is no question that the work that offenders do as a community sentence is forced labour: they do not offer themselves voluntarily, they are not asked to consent to performing it, and are not paid; if they do not do it, other criminal sanctions follow. If they are asked to consent to it, their consent would be of limited value given that the alternative would be incarceration. In response to the complaint before the ILO Committee of Experts that unpaid work requirements constitute forced labour, the UK government claimed that the scheme is entirely different to treatment prohibited under the Convention, and that it is legitimate. It posited:

> As an alternative to imprisonment, unpaid work requirement is a less expensive penalty that is more effective in rehabilitating the offender and reducing offending behaviours by instilling a work ethic, providing work experience and skills, and enabling the offender to repay the community the harm caused by his or her criminal conduct.[128]

Is this scheme covered by the exceptions of the Forced Labour Convention, namely that there should be supervision or control by a public authority and that the person should not work for private entities? The ILO typically says that the two conditions have to apply cumulatively.[129] However, as in some

[124] Van Zyl Smit (n 122) 204.

[125] See eg *Pilcic v Croatia* App no 33138/06 (Judgment, 17 January 2008) para 36.

[126] See Report of the Director-General, Eighth Supplementary Report of the Committee set up to examine the representation alleging non-observance by the United Kingdom of the Forced Labour Convention, 1930 (No 29), made under article 24 of the ILO Constitution by the trade unions UNISON, GMB and Napo, 29 October–12 November 2015.

[127] ILO Forced Labour Convention, art 2(2)(c).

[128] ibid para 30.

[129] See eg the Observation of the Committee of Experts on the Application of Conventions on Australia, published on the 104th ILC session (2015) <www.ilo.org/dyn/normlex/en/f?p=NORMLEXPUB:13100:0::NO::P13100_COMMENT_ID:3184674> accessed 15 October 2022.

countries there are privatised prisons, it has also developed further safeguards to protect prisoners in these situations. For instance, the ILO 2007 General Survey on the Eradication of Forced Labour said that in privately run prisons, the question of whether working for a private entity is acceptable involves the degree to which supervision and control is actually exercised by public authorities. It continued:

> Though no general prescription may be laid down which would cover all the possible arrangements for this, the Committee has considered that, if the supervision and control are restricted to a public authority to inspect the premises periodically, this by itself would not appear to meet the requirements of the Convention for supervision and control. As regards a sentence of community work, it is usually carried out under the supervision and control of public officials responsible for the execution of this kind of sentence, such as probation officers.[130]

According to the agreements on unpaid work requirements in the United Kingdom that the ILO Committee of Experts examined, there was no direct public supervision: the work was controlled and supervised by a private body. However, there were certain safeguards in place in relation to the role and functions of the private providers, and the ILO Committee explained in this respect that effective public control and supervision is essential in the delivery of unpaid work requirements.[131] In addition to that, and according to the agreement between the authorities and the private company, the latter could place offenders 'at the disposal of private individuals, companies or associations', and there was no guarantee that the scheme would involve work that is of general interest. In this respect, the ILO Committee emphasised that safeguards should be in place to ensure that the work which offenders are required to do is in the general interest,[132] that providers should not benefit from the unpaid work of the offenders,[133] and that the scheme should 'not result in the private provider placing offenders in compulsory work for profit-making entities for economic gain'.[134]

The principles developed by the ILO on unpaid work as a community sentence should inform the analysis on the compatibility of the schemes with

[130] ILO Report (n 103) para 53.
[131] ibid para 46.
[132] ibid para 49.
[133] ibid para 50.
[134] ibid para 51.

human rights law. Being required to work with no pay or other labour and social security rights, at the same time as private actors or state authorities systematically benefit from this situation, should not be acceptable. People doing community work are forced to work in employment that is not of their choice as a form of payback to the community. This constitutes their punishment. Their exclusion from other labour rights is neither necessary nor justified because it creates vulnerability to exploitation and structures of exploitation. It is important to assess unpaid work requirements as a community sentence carefully, consider their purpose and the means by which it is achieved, and interrogate how private actors as well as the state itself benefit from this situation.

Working immigration detainees

In Chapter 4, we also spoke about work in immigration detention. Immigration detainees are not held because of a crime that they committed. Work in detention centres does not aim to support their rehabilitation. They sometimes spend months (or years) in detention, so work meets a basic human need to make themselves feel useful rather than spending their life idle in uncertainty as to the duration of detention and the outcome of any legal processes. Work generally, and work in immigration detention too, can give people's life a purpose and meaning. This function of work is particularly important in immigration removal centres where very high suicide rates have been documented.[135] In addition, through work they gain some income as the only income that detainees have while in detention in the United Kingdom is an allowance of £5 per week. Exploitative work does not give meaning to people's lives, nor does it help them meet their basic needs.

The exclusion from labour rights of immigration detainees is as problematic as the exclusion of working prisoners, so similar principles should apply here.[136] If we compare working immigration detainees and prisoners, the element of compulsion to work is similar. Both those working in prison and those working in immigration detention perform the work while they are deprived of their physical liberty. Their freedom of movement and freedom to choose work are curtailed. Even though people in immigration detention may seem to have a choice whether to work or not while in detention, the pressure they face makes the freedom of this choice very questionable. The aims of work

[135] Diane Taylor, Peter Walker, and Jamie Grierson, 'Revealed: Two Suicide Attempts Every Day in UK Deportation Centres' *The Guardian* (11 October 2018).

[136] On the separate question of whether immigration detention is compatible with human rights law, see Cathryn Costello, 'Immigration Detention: The Grounds Beneath Our Feet' (2015) 68 Current Legal Problems 143.

in immigration detention and prison may be different to a certain degree (rehabilitation being a central aim of prison work). However, they are not entirely different, given that in both instances work helps those who are deprived of their freedom to alleviate boredom and spend time meaningfully, while being excluded from labour rights. The pressure to cover basic needs, support dependents, and maintain their mental health should be viewed as sufficient at least for the work regime to fall within the ambit of Article 4 of the ECHR.[137]

This matter was examined by the UK Court of Appeal for its compatibility with Article 4 of the ECHR among other provisions. The Court surprisingly said that the work regime is 'entirely voluntary',[138] which is very questionable in relation to work performed by people whose freedom of movement and freedom to do the work of their choice are entirely curtailed, who may at times be threatened by guards in this context, and who may be disciplined if they do not perform the work that they are assigned to a satisfactory standard.[139]

Examining work by immigration detainees in private detention centres in the United States, the American Civil Liberties Union (ACLU) stated that '[e]ven though the programme is supposed to be voluntary, detainees' experiences are illustrative of its coercive nature'.[140] Two reasons support this statement: first, the income earned is used to cover fundamental necessities, and secondly, those refusing to work face retaliation.[141] There have been a number of cases challenging the lawfulness of the practice through which private entities make important profits. In relation to the question of whether this is forced labour, an argument proposed was that it is covered by the 'civic duty exemption' of the Thirteenth Amendment. However, it was ruled that the exemption is not applicable to cases of work in privately run immigration detention centres.[142] Against this background, some legal claims have been successful. For instance, a federal jury in Washington determined that the exclusion of

[137] For an illustration, see 'Working for a Pound an Hour: An Immigration Detainee's Perspective' (*Futures of Work Blog*, 20 September 2019), which I discuss in Chapter 4.

[138] *Badmus, R (On the Application of) v Secretary of State for the Home Department* [2020] EWCA Civ 657 (20 May 2020). See Virginia Mantouvalou, 'Labour Exploitation in Immigration Detention' (*UK Labour Law Blog*, 1 June 2020) <https://uklabourlawblog.com/2020/06/01/labour-exploitation-in-immigration-detention-by-virginia-mantouvalou/> accessed 15 December 2022.

[139] Katie Bales and Lucy Mayblin, 'Unfree Labour in Immigration Detention: Exploitation and Coercion of a Captive Immigrant Workforce' (2018) 47 Economy and Society 191, 193, 198.

[140] ACLU, 'Prisoners of Profit' 57 quoted in Anita Sinha, 'Slavery by Another Name: "Voluntary" Immigrant Detainee Labor and the Thirteenth Amendment' (2015) XI Stanford Journal of Civil Rights and Civil Liberties 1, 35.

[141] See further Jonathon Booth, 'Ending Forced Labor in ICE Detention Centers: A New Approach' (2020) 34 Georgetown Immigration Law Journal 573, 591.

[142] *Menocal v GEO Group*, 113 F Supp 3d at 1133.

immigration detainees from the minimum wage for work they performed to maintain the facilities of the centre violated minimum wage laws.[143]

The working conditions of those working in immigration detention are not widely known but researchers have found that work is strictly structured and supervised, and workers can be sanctioned by being removed if their performance does not meet the necessary standards.[144] Immigration detainees who need to work cannot perform the job of their choice and cannot freely exit the work relation. Immigration detention centres, in turn, take advantage of workers' vulnerability that is created through law and make significant profits from this situation. In a manner similar to working offenders, their exclusion from labour rights is problematic and incompatible with human rights principles, including those developed under Article 4 (the prohibition of forced labour), Article 11 (the right to form and join a trade union), and Article 1 of Protocol 1 (the right to property) of the ECHR.

Conclusion

We saw in this chapter that human rights law can help focus on the responsibility of the state for the structures of exploitation that I described in Chapters 3 and 4. Migrant workers are vulnerable for many reasons, including the fact that they may be isolated, have limited support networks, and may be unaware of their rights and how to claim them. Captive workers are also vulnerable because they are often forced to work under the threat of sanctions and while their freedom of movement is curtailed. That legal rules increase their vulnerability is unacceptable for it creates structures of injustice whereby some people systematically benefit while others are systematically exploited. These laws may not be compatible with human rights law, such as the prohibition of forced labour, the right to property, the right to private life, and the right to equality. Monitoring bodies that assess compliance with workers' rights have a duty to examine this situation closely, scrutinise carefully any justification that the authorities propose, and the proportionality of the restrictions of workers' rights with the aim pursued. In the chapter that follows, I turn to welfare conditionality and precarious work to examine the compatibility of the laws in question with human rights obligations.

143 Washington State Office of the Attorney General, 'Jury Find GEO, for Profit Operator of Tacoma ICE Detention Centre, Must Pay Detainee Workers Minimum Wage' (27 October 2021).

144 See Bales and Mayblin (n 139).

8
Human Rights II

Welfare conditionality schemes with harsh sanctions increase the vulnerability to exploitation of the unemployed poor and turn them into working and exploited poor, as we saw in Chapter 5. Is this structure compatible with human rights law? In this chapter I consider this question in light of provisions such as the prohibition of forced labour, the right to private life, the right to social assistance, and the right to a subsistence minimum. I also assess precarious working conditions separately from coercive conditionality, and explain that legal rules that constitute these structures may also at times violate human rights law, including trade union rights and the prohibition of discrimination. I do not argue that all injustices that arise from welfare conditionality or precarious work can be addressed through human rights law. However, human rights law can challenge aspects of these legal rules and thus destabilise the unjust structures that affect disadvantaged workers.

Working and Exploited Poor

The idea behind welfare-to-work is that the more people are in employment, the better it is, for work is presented as the best route out of poverty.[1] Yet, we observed that schemes with strict conditionality turn the unemployed poor into working and exploited poor. The legal structure that forces and traps people like Toni and Marcell into exploitative work may be incompatible with human rights law.[2]

The severity of the human rights issues that arise from the UK system was highlighted by the UN Special Rapporteur on Extreme Poverty and Human Rights, Philip Alston, following a visit to the United Kingdom in 2018 that focused on the problems of Universal Credit and in-work poverty.[3] The role of

[1] See Chapter 5.

[2] Toni's fictional story is in Chapter 1 and Marcell's real story is in Chapter 2.

[3] Report of the UN Special Rapporteur on Extreme Poverty and Human Rights, Visit to the UK and Northern Ireland, A/HRC/41/39/Add.1, 23 April 2019 (hereafter Alston Report).

Structural Injustice and Workers' Rights. Virginia Mantouvalou, Oxford University Press. © Virginia Mantouvalou 2023.
DOI: 10.1093/oso/9780192857156.003.0008

the Special Rapporteur is to examine and report on the rights of those living in extreme poverty. In this capacity, Alston reviewed extensive evidence on the UK scheme and said that 'the philosophy underpinning the British welfare system has changed radically since 2010'.[4] He emphasised that in the United Kingdom there are 14 million people in poverty, that 60 per cent of those who are in poverty are in families where someone works, and 2.8 million people in poverty are in families where all adults work full-time.[5] The Special Rapporteur also explained that, even if both parents in a family work full-time and earn the national minimum wage, they are still 11 per cent short of the income that is needed in order to raise one child.[6] Alston relied on evidence produced by scholars and organisations, including the Joseph Rowntree Foundation (JRF) which specialises in issues of poverty in the United Kingdom and has repeatedly highlighted in recent years the problem of in-work poverty. The JRF Report of 2018 found that there were 4 million workers in poverty, a rise of half a million in comparison to five years before.[7] Since 2004–05, the number of those in in-work poverty has been rising faster than the total number of people in employment.[8]

The Special Rapporteur noted that the denial of benefits has pushed certain categories of claimants into unsuitable work[9] and explained that people want to work, but are compelled to take work that is badly paid and precarious in order to meet their basic needs.[10] Having spoken with Universal Credit claimants, he said that not only did they have to 'fill out pointless job applications for positions that did not match their qualifications', but that they also had to 'take inappropriate temporary work just to avoid debilitating sanctions'.[11] Alston's report attracted significant media attention and scrutiny of the scheme, and is a powerful example of the role that human rights institutions outside the standard individual or collective complaints processes can play in raising awareness and instigating structural processes to support change.[12]

[4] ibid [95].
[5] ibid [28].
[6] ibid [35].
[7] Helen Barnard and others, Joseph Rowntree Foundation Report, *UK Poverty 2018* <https://www.jrf.org.uk/report/uk-poverty-2018> accessed 15 December 2022.
[8] ibid. In 2011–12, for the first time on record, it was documented that of those who live in poverty, the majority are in in-work poverty. See Tom MacInnes and others, *Monitoring Poverty and Social Exclusion* (Joseph Rowntree Foundation 2013).
[9] Alston makes this point in relation to people with disabilities, eg in [4] of the Alston Report (n 3).
[10] ibid [8].
[11] ibid [57].
[12] For a discussion of the visit and its effects, see Philip Alston, Bassam Khawaja, and Rebecca Riddell, 'Much Ado About Poverty: The Role of a UN Special Rapporteur' (2019) 27 Journal of Poverty and Social Justice 423.

Forced Labour

Courts and other human rights monitoring bodies have also considered the question of whether welfare-to-work schemes violate human rights. A problem with the provision that prohibits slavery, servitude, and forced or compulsory labour in the European Convention for the Protection of Human Rights and Fundamental Freedoms (ECHR) (as well as in other human rights documents) is that it incorporates exceptions, which include 'any work or service which forms part of civic obligations'.[13]

In the case law on welfare-to-work, the European Court of Human Rights (ECtHR) has not ruled that there has been a violation of the Convention thus far. However, it has not examined cases of very harsh sanctions and their implications, such as the ones that we find in empirical research on Universal Credit. By way of an example, in the case of *Schuitemaker v The Netherlands*,[14] the applicant was a philosopher by profession, and was asked to take 'generally accepted' work (rather than work that was 'deemed suitable' for her). If she did not comply with the condition, her benefits would be reduced. She claimed that this was contrary to Article 4. The Court said that:

> it must in general be accepted that where a State has introduced a system of social security, it is fully entitled to lay down conditions which have to be met for a person to be eligible for benefits pursuant to that system. In particular a condition to the effect that a person must make demonstrable efforts in order to obtain and take up generally accepted employment cannot be considered unreasonable in this respect. This is the more so given that Dutch legislation provides that recipients of benefits pursuant to the Work and Social Assistance Act are not required to seek and take up employment which is not generally socially accepted or in respect of which they have conscientious objections.

In this particular case, the condition was not viewed as compelling her to perform forced or compulsory labour. The earlier case of *Talmon v Netherlands*,[15] where the applicant claimed that the only work suitable for him was as an

[13] Art 4(3) of the ECHR. For a detailed overview of the case law, see Elise Dermine, 'Activation Policies for the Unemployed and the International Human Rights Case Law on the Prohibition of Forced Labour' in Elise Dermine and Daniel Dumont (eds), *Activation Policies for the Unemployed, the Right to Work and the Duty to Work* (Peter Lang 2014) 103.

[14] *Schuitemaker v The Netherlands* App no 15906/08 (Admissibility Decision, 4 May 2010).

[15] *Talmon v The Netherlands* App no 30300/96 (Commission Decision, 26 February 1997).

'independent scientist and social critic' as he had serious conscientious objections against any other work, was also deemed inadmissible. None of the welfare conditionality cases examined thus far by the ECtHR and Commission reached the level required for Article 4 to apply.

However, the structure created by the UK system is harsher than these examples in that it both imposes very severe sanctions and forces people into precarious work in the context of a particularly deregulated labour market. There is evidence that some Universal Credit claimants become destitute because of the scheme, while others are employed in very insecure work, with limited labour protections and through which they cannot meet their basic needs.[16]

The UN Human Rights Committee (HRC), monitoring compliance with the International Covenant on Civil and Political Rights (ICCPR), has also examined related complaints. Article 8 of the ICCPR contains a prohibition of slavery, servitude, and forced or compulsory labour, the formulation of which is similar to Article 4 of the ECHR. In *Faure v Australia*,[17] the claimant argued that the requirement to work under the Australian Work for Dole programme constituted forced labour under the ICCPR. The Committee turned down this part of her claim. However, it considered the exemption of normal civic obligations from the prohibition of forced labour and said:

> [T]o so qualify as a normal civil obligation, the labour in question must, at a minimum, not be an exceptional measure; it must not possess a punitive purpose or effect; and it must be provided for by law in order to serve a legitimate purpose under the Covenant. In the light of these considerations, the Committee is of the view that the material before it, including the absence of a degrading or dehumanizing aspect of the specific labour performed, does not show that the labour in question comes within the scope of the proscriptions set out in Article 8.

The HRC accepted that people may have a duty to work as part of their normal civic obligations. When looking at Universal Credit, though, it is highly questionable whether working on zero-hours contracts for a private employer, in conditions such as the ones described in Chapter 5, can be viewed as constituting a normal civic obligation. It may therefore violate the prohibition of forced labour under the ICCPR.

[16] See Human Rights Watch, 'Nothing Left in the Cupboards—Austerity, Welfare Cuts, and the Right to Food in the UK', 20 May 2019. See also Suzanne Fitzpatrick and others, 'Destitution in the UK', Joseph Rowntree Foundation, 2018 52, and the Alston Report (n 3).

[17] *Faure v Australia*, Comm 1036/2001, UN Doc A/61/40, Vol II, 97 (HRC 2005).

The UK Supreme Court examined welfare-to-work in *Reilly*, a 2013 judicial review case.[18] One of the questions for the Court was whether a jobseeker's allowance that made a benefit conditional on her working for Poundland, in a position that would not advance her employment prospects, was contrary to Article 4. The argument presented was that the requirement that Ms Reilly work for Poundland as a condition for claiming her benefit constituted forced or compulsory labour in contravention of Article 4(2). This was because the work at Poundland 'was exacted … under menace of [a] penalty'.[19] The Supreme Court ruled:

> The provision of a conditional benefit of that kind comes nowhere close to the type of exploitative conduct at which Article 4 is aimed. Nor is it to the point that according to Ms Reilly the work which she did for Poundland was unlikely in fact to advance her employment prospects. Whether the imposition of a work requirement as a condition of a benefit amounts to exacting forced labour within the meaning of Article 4 cannot depend on the degree of likelihood of the condition achieving its purpose.[20]

The threshold set by the UK Supreme Court, the HRC, and the ECtHR is high.[21] Even if the Supreme Court was correct that Ms Reilly did not suffer a violation of her Convention rights, the treatment of several Universal Credit claimants who in recent years have been forced into work that they do not want to take precisely because of its precarious nature, with the menace of sanctions that may leave them destitute, may reach the level of exploitation required for a violation of Article 4.[22]

In *Reilly*, the Court referred to earlier Strasbourg case law, and highlighted that for Article 4 to be violated, 'the obligation to work, or its performance, must be "unjust", "oppressive", "an avoidable hardship", "needlessly distressing" or "somewhat harassing"'.[23] It explained that these expressions serve to define the concept of exploitation in Article 4.[24] This is in line with the position

[18] *Reilly, R (on the application of) v Secretary of State for Work and Pensions* [2013] UKSC 68 (hereafter cited as *Reilly*). There have already been successful instances of judicial review on the calculation of Universal Credit Regulations 2013 (SI 2013/976). See *R (on the application of Johnson) v Secretary of State For Work and Pensions* [2019] EWHC 23 (Admin).

[19] *Reilly* (n 18) [80].

[20] ibid [83].

[21] See further Elise Dermine, 'Limitation of Welfare to Work: The Prohibition of Forced Labour and the Right to Freely Chosen Work' in Anja Eleveld, Thomas Kampen, and Josien Arts (eds), *Welfare to Work in Contemporary European Welfare States* (Policy Press 2020) 67.

[22] See eg the following discussion that reveals a change in policy in more recent years: Rowena Mason, 'Jobseekers Being Forced Into Zero-Hours Jobs' *The Guardian* (5 May 2014).

[23] *Reilly* (n 18) [89].

[24] ibid.

of the ILO on welfare-to-work. The ILO Global Survey on the Eradication of Forced Labour, for instance, explained that the requirement to work could be contrary to the forced labour prohibition if work is used as a penalty and there are no safeguards that will guarantee that the work is compatible with the 1930 Forced Labour Convention (No 29) and the 1952 Social Security Convention (No 102), particularly with respect to its suitability.[25] As I mentioned in Chapter 7, the approach of the ILO is often taken into account by other bodies that monitor compliance with workers' human rights, and can also help elucidate the meaning of forced labour in this context.[26]

The structures created through welfare-to-work with strict conditionality, which force and trap large numbers of people in zero-hours work for private employers, normalise 'all but the most extreme forms of abusive employment arrangements, leaving a rapidly increasing number of workers without recourse to employment protective norms', as Adams, Freedland, and Prassl put it.[27] This situation should make us reopen the question of whether welfare conditionality schemes that are particularly punitive while requiring people to accept precarious work, such as the UK scheme, are compatible with the prohibition of forced or compulsory labour.

Right to Work

Aspects of welfare-to-work schemes may also violate elements of the right to work, which we find in the UN International Covenant on Economic, Social and Cultural Rights (ICESCR), the EU Charter of Fundamental Rights, and the ESC.[28] The ICESCR, for example, states that the right 'includes the right of

[25] International Labour Conference, *Global Survey on the Eradication of Forced Labour, 2007*, para 205.

[26] See Virginia Mantouvalou, 'Labour Rights in the European Convention on Human Rights: An Intellectual Justification for an Integrated Approach to Interpretation' (2013) 13 Human Rights Law Review 529; Keith Ewing and John Hendy, 'The Dramatic Implications of *Demir and Baykara*' (2010) 39 Industrial Law Journal 2; Tzehainesh Teklè, 'The Contribution of the ILO's International Labour Standards System to the European Court of Human Rights' Jurisprudence in the Field of Non-Discrimination' (2020) 49 Industrial Law Journal 86.

[27] Abi Adams, Mark Freedland, and Jeremias Prassl, 'The "Zero-Hours Contract": Regulating Casual Work or Legitimating Precarity?' (2015) Oxford Legal Studies Research Paper 11/2015, 3.

[28] See art 6 of the ICESCR, art 15(1) of the EUCFR, and art 1(2) of the ESC. See also the discussion on the right to work and the duty to work in Amir Paz-Fuchs, 'The Right to Work and the Duty to Work' in Virginia Mantouvalou (ed), *The Right to Work: Legal and Philosophical Perspectives* (Hart 2015) 177. On working conditions and the right to work see Virginia Mantouvalou, 'The Right to Non-Exploitative Work', in the same volume, 39. For a detailed overview of the principles, see Elise Dermine, 'Activation Policies for the Unemployed and the International Human Rights Case Law on the Right to Freely Chosen Work' in Elise Dermine and Daniel Dumont (eds), *Activation Policies for the Unemployed, the Right to Work and the Duty to Work* (Peter Lang 2014) 139. On the right to work in international

everyone to the opportunity to gain his living by work which he freely chooses or accepts', and requires that the authorities 'take appropriate steps to safeguard this right'.[29] In the process of specifying the content of the right to work, the Committee on Economic, Social and Cultural Rights (CESCR), which monitors compliance with the ICESCR, issued General Comment 18 that provided an authoritative interpretation of the Covenant.

On the basis of Article 6 and General Comment 18, the right to work guarantees both a right not to be forced to work and a right to decent work. The negative, immediate duties imposed by the right to work suggest that the authorities cannot compel people to work. In other words, individuals should be able to control their labour, and this can also be viewed as an instantiation of their right to lead their life autonomously.[30] General Comment 18 refers to the quality of work, stating that work has to be decent in order to be compatible with the right to work. As was explained in Chapter 6, though, zero-hours and agency work can be exploitative. Forcing people into this kind of work under the threat of serious sanctions and destitution can therefore be viewed as a violation of the right to work.

A very strict welfare-to-work scheme may also give rise to issues under the right to work in Article 1(2) of the European Social Charter (ESC), which provides that '[w]ith a view to ensuring the effective exercise of the right to work, the Parties undertake [to] protect effectively the right of the worker to earn his living in an occupation freely entered upon'. The European Committee of Social Rights (ECSR) has found in this context that contracting parties may violate the provision when they have schemes with excessive conditionality. As discussed earlier, there are different types of activation policies and different kinds of welfare conditionality schemes, some of which are stricter than others. According to the ECSR, welfare-to-work may be incompatible with Article 1(2), when work is inconsistent with human dignity or more generally when it is exploitative.[31]

The Committee has explained that activation policies violate the right to freely chosen work if they require claimants to accept work that is not suitable.

human rights law, see Colm O'Cinneide, 'The Right to Work in International Human Rights Law' in Mantouvalou (ed), *The Right to Work* (n 28).

[29] ICESCR, art 6.

[30] Richard Lippke, 'Prison Labor: Its Control, Facilitation, and Terms' (1998) 17 Law and Philosophy 533.

[31] See ECSR Conclusions 2012, Statement of Interpretation, art 1(2). See further the discussion by Simon Deakin, 'Article 1—The Right to Work' in Niklas Bruun and others (eds), *The European Social Charter and the Employment Relation* (Hart 2017) 147, 159. See also Adams, Freedland, and Prassl (n 27).

Criteria on the meaning of 'suitable employment' are found in a Guide drafted in 2010 by the Committee of Experts on Social Security, in charge of the promotion of the Council of Europe European Social Security Code (1968). Do zero-hours contracts constitute suitable employment? The answer to this question will often be in the negative because the concept of suitable employment is defined by reference to a decent wage.[32] For this reason, the UK system of strict conditionality that forces people into zero-hours work may be viewed as incompatible with the ESC.

Prohibition of Inhuman and Degrading Treatment

In addition, the imposition of very harsh sanctions on welfare claimants who fail to comply with welfare conditionality requirements by not accepting precarious work may be contrary to the prohibition of inhuman and degrading treatment under Article 3 of the ECHR. There is evidence that some Universal Credit claimants become destitute because of the scheme.[33] This may be due to either the cruelty of sanctions, or because of the way that the Universal Credit payments are made: for instance, the first payment of benefits takes five weeks, which forces people to take on loans to cover their basic needs. This pushes them into debt.[34] Michael Adler put forward the argument that sanctions may lead to a violation of Article 3 of the Convention in his study on welfare conditionality in the United Kingdom.[35]

According to well-established case law of the Court, for Article 3 to be breached, the conduct in question has to reach a 'minimum level of severity'.[36] In order to assess this threshold, the Court takes into account factors such as the duration and physical or mental effects of the treatment, as well as the sex, age, and health of the victim.[37] The ECtHR has not had to examine the compatibility of benefit sanctions with Article 3 to date. However, it has examined

[32] On this see Elise Dermine, 'Activation Policies for the Unemployed and the International Human Rights Case Law on the Right to Freely Chosen Work' in Dermine and Dumont (n 28) 166ff.

[33] See n 16.

[34] See Trussell Trust, 'Five Things You Should Know about Universal Credit' <www.trusselltrust.org/2022/04/05/5-things-you-should-know-about-universal-credit/> accessed 1 July 2022.

[35] Michael Adler, *Cruel, Inhuman or Degrading Treatment? Benefit Sanctions in the UK* (Palgrave Macmillan 2018) ch 1. See also Mark Simpson, '"Designed to Reduce People ... to Complete Destitution": Human Dignity in the Active Welfare State' (2015) European Human Rights Law Review 66, 71.

[36] *Ireland v UK* App no 5310/71 (Judgment, 18 January 1978) para 162.

[37] ibid.

the question of whether destitution may in certain conditions violate it.[38] In *Larioshina v Russia*,[39] it said that 'a complaint about a wholly insufficient amount of pension and other social benefits may, in principle, raise an issue under Article 3 of the Convention which prohibits inhuman and degrading treatment'.[40] In *MSS v Belgium and Greece*,[41] the Grand Chamber of the Court ruled that leaving asylum seekers in conditions of destitution and homelessness constituted a violation of Article 3, while the UK House of Lords reached a similar conclusion in *Limbuela, Tesema and Adam*.[42] According to *Limbuela*, there has to be deliberate state action that denies the satisfaction of basic needs, such as shelter or food, and this has to be of such severity as to have seriously detrimental effects or cause serious suffering.[43]

Can the threshold of severity under Article 3 be reached in instances of sanctions imposed on benefit claimants? The answer to this question has to be positive in some situations. This is because the effects of the imposition of sanctions sometimes lead to the inability of claimants to meet their basic needs and thus to destitution. Non-compliance with Universal Credit requirements incurs the second-harshest sanctions in the world.[44] It has been established that people on Universal Credit have to resort to food banks in order to satisfy their basic needs.[45] For instance, someone using a food bank said:

> The only time I come [to the food bank] is if my benefits have been stopped or cut. I had a sanction once because I was overpaid child tax credit, so they stopped the payment completely. It's not a nice way of living, literally living day by day ... We're lucky the food bank is here but there should be a system to catch us before we fall through the net.[46]

This reality can be viewed as deliberate state action, even if welfare-to-work schemes are supposed to have a legitimate aim, because the imposition of these

[38] See eg Colm O'Cinneide, 'A Modest Proposal: Destitution, State Responsibility and the European Convention on Human Rights' (2008) European Human Rights Law Review 583.

[39] *Larioshina v Russia* App no 56869/00 (Decision, 23 April 2002).

[40] ibid, under 'The Law', para 3.

[41] *MSS v Belgium and Greece* App no 30696/09 (Grand Chamber Judgment, 21 January 2011).

[42] *R v Secretary of State for the Home Department (Appellant), ex p Adam (FC) (Respondent); R v Secretary of State for the Home Department (Appellant), ex p Limbuela (FC) (Respondent); R v Secretary of State for the Home Department (Appellant), ex p Tesema (FC) (Respondent) (Conjoined Appeals)* [2006] 1 AC 396.

[43] ibid [7]–[8], per Lord Bingham.

[44] See Herwig Immervoll and Carlo Knotz, 'How Demanding Are Activation Requirements for Jobseekers?' (2018) OECD Social, Employment and Migration Working Papers No 215, 12 July, 47. See further discussion in Chapter 5.

[45] See Trussell Trust, 'Early Warnings: Universal Credit and Foodbanks' (2017).

[46] Human Rights Watch (n 16).

sanctions is deliberate state policy and the authorities know or ought to know of the effects of this policy on people's lives.[47] These effects include shock and confusion (because they thought that they had complied with the conditions), economic hardship, deep poverty, debt, eviction threats, homelessness, food bank use, and ill-health.[48] It is therefore possible to envisage individual cases where the deprivation is so extreme that it can ground the responsibility of the state for violations of Article 3.

Universal Credit claimants under zero-hours contracts in the United Kingdom face additional problems to those of other claimants. This is because the benefit is paid in arrears on the basis of earnings for the previous month, on the assumption that in the following month a claimant will make the same earnings. As this is not the case for many on zero-hours contracts, they regularly receive payments that are not correctly calculated, and do not cover their basic needs.[49] It is not only the sanctions that may reach the level of severity of Article 3, in other words, but also the effects of the design of payments. The argument that harsh sanctions may violate Article 3 of the ECHR finds further support in a judgment of the German Constitutional Court and findings of the ECSR, which I discuss in the section that follows.

The Right to a Subsistence Minimum and the Right to Social Assistance

A good example of how the questions that arise regarding human rights compatibility should be addressed when harsh sanctions are in place was provided by a national court. The German Constitutional Court examined whether welfare conditionality complies with the fundamental right to the guarantee of an existential minimum in accordance with human dignity (Article 1(1) in conjunction with Article 20(1) of the Basic Law).[50] Even though the Court

47 The 'know or ought to know' formulation is regularly used by the ECtHR to establish positive obligations of state authorities for human rights violations. See eg *Osman v UK* App no 23452/94 (Judgment, 28 October 1998) para 116.

48 Beth Watts and Suzanne Fitzpatrick, *Welfare Conditionality* (Routledge 2018); Fitzpatrick and others (n 16); Ciara Fitzpatrick, Graine McKeever, and Mark Simpson, 'Conditionality, Discretion and TH Marshall's "Right to Welfare"' (2019) 41 Journal of Social Welfare and Family Law 445; Sharon Wright and Alasdair Stewart, 'First Wave Findings: Jobseekers' (May 2016) <www.welfareconditionality.ac.uk/wp-content/uploads/2016/05/WelCond-findings-jobseekers-May16.pdf> accessed 15 October 2022; Adler (n 35) ch 6.

49 See the submissions of the Welfare Conditionality Project to the UN Special Rapporteur on Extreme Poverty and Human Rights, 6 <www.ohchr.org/Documents/Issues/EPoverty/UnitedKingdom/2018/NGOS/Welfare_Conditionality_Sanctions_SupportandBehaviourChange.pdf> accessed 15 October 2022.

50 BVerfG 1 BvL 7/16 (05.11.2019).

accepted that welfare benefits can be conditional and limited to those who are in true need, it also explained that any sanctions imposed have such an effect on human dignity that they should be subject to a strict test of proportionality (meaning that they should be suitable, necessary, and reasonable).

The Court considered the effects of benefit sanctions extensively and highlighted that they can include 'social withdrawal, isolation, homelessness, severe psychosomatic disorders and crime to access alternative sources of income',[51] because people cannot meet even their most basic needs such as paying for their rent and electricity. In addition to the fundamental right to the guarantee of an existential minimum in accordance with human dignity, the Court explained that it pays attention to other rights that are affected, such as protection of family, occupational freedom, or health, which are all included in the Basic Law.[52] It ruled that while the provisions on welfare conditionality appear legitimate on their face, they fail the strict proportionality test that the Court applied.[53] It accepted that the authorities have a margin of appreciation on these matters, but that in this case they had not engaged in an assessment of the effects of the sanctions on claimants. The Court therefore found that the sanctions failed to satisfy the test of proportionality where they result in a withdrawal of 60 per cent and 100 per cent of benefits from sanctioned individuals. In addition, the Court was concerned that the rigidity of the scheme did not permit discretion on whether sanctions will be imposed, even if it is counterproductive for the social inclusion of the claimant. The reasoning of the German Constitutional Court underlines the cruel effects of harsh sanctions and the importance of assessing the impact of these sanctions on people's lives. It provides support for the position that harsh sanctions may violate Article 3 of the ECHR, when the effects of the withdrawal of benefits are such that claimants cannot meet their basic needs.

Further support for the argument that harsh sanctions fall short of human rights standards is found in Article 13 of the ESC that provides for a right to social assistance, which guarantees state support for those who cannot meet their basic needs.[54] In this context, the ECSR has maintained that

[51] ibid para 65.
[52] ibid para 135.
[53] ibid para 136.
[54] For a detailed overview, see Anja Eleveld, 'The Sanctions Mitigation Paradox in Welfare to Work Benefit Schemes' (2018) 39 Comparative Labour Law & Policy Journal 449. For discussion of other related provisions in international human rights law, see Valery Gantchev, 'Welfare Sanctions and the Right to a Subsistence Minimum: A Troubled Marriage' (2020) 22 European Journal of Social Security 257, 265ff.

> [t]he establishment of a link between social assistance and a willingness to seek employment or to receive vocational training is in keeping with the Charter, in so far as such conditions are reasonable and consistent with the aim pursued, that is to say to find a lasting solution to the individual's difficulties.[55]

It has said, though, that '[r]educing or suspending social assistance benefits can only be in conformity with the Charter if it does not deprive the person concerned of his/her means of subsistence'.[56] In relation to the UK scheme, the ECSR raised questions about its compatibility with the right to social assistance, particularly with respect to the severe sanctions that can be imposed on claimants.[57]

The Right to Private Life

Aspects of welfare-to-work structures may also give rise to violations of the right to private life under Article 8 of the ECHR. The Court interprets Article 8 broadly so as to cover activities that take place not only in one's home or other private space, but also in an individual's personal and social life: 'the guarantee afforded by Article 8 of the Convention is primarily intended to ensure the development, without outside interference, of the personality of each individual in his relations with other human beings',[58] as the Court puts it.

The digitalisation of the UK scheme entails very close monitoring of claimants' everyday lives, which may violate Article 8. Aspects of the system, such as the Claimant Commitment, have been described as an authoritarian approach towards the unemployed.[59] Social policy scholars have suggested that there is 'large-scale surveillance of detailed back-to-work plans, involving variable coercion, since claimants can be sanctioned for non-compliance with any item written in the document'.[60] Claimants have to show that they look for work for

[55] ECSR, Conclusions (2013), Norway, Article 13-1.

[56] ibid.

[57] ECSR, Conclusions XXI-2 (2017), United Kingdom. See Mark Simpson, 'Assessing the Compliance of the United Kingdom's Social Security System with its Obligations under the European Social Charter' (2018) 18 Human Rights Law Review 745, 759.

[58] *Von Hannover v Germany (No 2)* App nos 40660/08 and 60641/08 (Judgment, 7 February 2012) para 95. Other examples that illustrate the broad coverage of art 8 include *Niemietz v Germany* App no 13710/88 (Judgment, 16 December 1992) and *Sidabras and Dziautas v Lithuania* App nos 55480/00 and 59330/00 (Judgment, 27 July 2004).

[59] Del Roy Fletcher and Sharon Wright, 'A Hand Up or a Slap Down? Criminalising Benefit Claimants in Britain Via Strategies of Surveillance, Sanctions and Deterrence' (2018) 38 Critical Social Policy323.

[60] ibid 330.

at least thirty-five hours a week, and the main system to monitor this is an online electronic search engine for jobs. This electronic system has been characterised by Fletcher and Wright as a 'digital panopticon', and criticised for being 'laced with compulsion and intrusive surveillance'.[61] People's work coaches can see their daily online activity, such as the jobs for which they have applied, and use the information in order to impose sanctions on them. The extensive monitoring of how they spend their life, and the fact that the participants feel that they are always being checked on, bring their experience within the scope of the right to private life under Article 8 of the ECHR.

When there is an interference with Article 8, the Court applies a test of proportionality under the second paragraph of the provision in order to assess whether the interference is justified or whether it violates the right to private life: it first assesses whether the interference has a legitimate aim, and then whether the means employed by the authorities are proportionate to the aim pursued. The aim of the welfare conditionality scheme may be presented as legitimate for it seeks to help people get into work, and the UK government would argue that the surveillance is justified as a proportionate restriction of the right to private life. However, it should be viewed as only *prima facie* legitimate for, if we observe the overall structure created by it, it will be obvious that 'the balance between sanction and support has tipped firmly in favour of the former'.[62] This calls into question whether the aim is really to support the poor or whether it is to sanction and manage them, as Adler argued.[63] Even if the aim were viewed as legitimate, the extensive intrusion in private life through close monitoring and surveillance of claimants can be viewed as disproportionate to the aim pursued.[64] This may be the case, for instance, when monitoring is employed in a way that is particularly intrusive, oppressive, and humiliating towards the welfare claimant.[65]

The sanctions that are imposed on claimants and the quality of the work that they are required to undertake can also bring their experience within the scope of the right to private life, if viewed as particularly punitive and similar to criminal sanctions in their harshness.[66] The principle in the case of *Lacatus*

[61] ibid 332.
[62] Fletcher and Wright (n 59) 330.
[63] Adler (n 35).
[64] On the test of proportionality in qualified rights, see George Letsas, 'Rescuing Proportionality' in Rowan Cruft, S. Matthew Liao, and Massimo Renzo (eds), *Philosophical Foundations of Human Rights* (OUP 2015) 316, 337–38.
[65] On the humiliation experienced by welfare claimants, see Sharon Wright, Del Roy Fletcher, and Alasdair BR Stewart, 'Punitive Benefit Sanctions, Welfare Conditionality, and the Social Abuse of Unemployed People in Britain: Transforming Claimants into Offenders?' (2020) 54 Social Policy and Administration 278, 284.
[66] Adler has compared benefit sanctions to criminal sanctions, see n 35.

v Switzerland[67] supports the point that the ECtHR is open to accepting that criminalising certain activities that are linked to poverty is not compatible with the right to private life. *Lacatus* did not involve welfare conditionality. It examined the criminalisation of begging. It was brought by an applicant who came from a background of poverty, did not work or receive social support, and had to beg in order to meet her basic needs. The Court ruled that the imposition of a penalty on her, and her detention for five days because she did not pay her fine struck at the heart of human dignity. It explained that human dignity is seriously compromised if someone cannot meet their basic needs[68] and emphasized the particular vulnerability of the applicant who was destitute, illiterate, and unemployed.[69] It found that the criminalisation of begging violated her right to private life under Article 8 because it was through begging that she could secure income to meet her basic needs. The principle that punishing the poor and rendering them in this way destitute is incompatible with the right to private life has implications for schemes where people who are in economic need are forced and trapped into exploitative work through harsh sanctions, in a manner that punishes them, instead of promoting their social inclusion.

We have seen that it is arguable that several aspects of welfare-to-work schemes interfere with the right to private life, and may even violate it when the monitoring of claimants is particularly intrusive or the sanctions imposed on them are particularly punitive. Even if there is no violation of this provision alone, namely if the Court rules that the test of proportionality is met, Article 8 may be violated in conjunction with the prohibition of discrimination, which I discuss below.

Non-Discrimination

Is the treatment of welfare claimants in the instances that I discuss compatible with principles of equality and non-discrimination that we find in human rights law? Article 14 of the ECHR prohibits discrimination, but this is not a general, free-standing equality provision.[70] It prohibits discrimination in the

[67] *Lacatus v Switzerland* App no 14065/15 (Judgment, 19 January 2021) (in French). I discuss further the criminalisation of begging in Virginia Mantouvalou, 'Structural Injustice and Human Rights: The Case of Begging' in Virginia Mantouvalou and Jonathan Wolff (eds), *Structural Injustice and the Law* (forthcoming).

[68] *Lacatus*, para 56.

[69] ibid para 58.

[70] Protocol 12 of the ECHR contains a free-standing equality provision but it has not been ratified widely.

enjoyment of the rights of the Convention, which means that it needs to be invoked together with another ECHR right. The Article is not exhaustive in enumerating the prohibited grounds of discrimination but is open-ended.[71] In this context, Judge Tulkens has argued that the ECtHR has interpreted it in a manner that is particularly sensitive to structurally vulnerable groups.[72]

The examples that I have identified in several chapters of this book, including welfare-to-work and precarious work, may ground racial discrimination,[73] which has been described by the Court as 'a particularly invidious kind of discrimination and, in view of its perilous consequences, [one which] requires from the authorities special vigilance and a vigorous reaction'.[74] It can be seen that many of the laws at stake have a disproportionate adverse effect on minority racial and ethnic groups, if compared to white people in a similar position.[75] This is not direct discrimination, in other words, but indirect discrimination. In this regard, the ECtHR has ruled that 'a general policy or measure that has disproportionately prejudicial effects on a particular group may be considered discriminatory notwithstanding that it is not specifically aimed at that group'.[76]

In assessing whether indirect discrimination constitutes a violation of the Convention, there is scope for justification through a test of proportionality, which tends to be often less strict than the scrutiny of direct discrimination. However, instances of indirect discrimination, such as the ones that I examine here, may be as morally troubling as instances of direct discrimination.[77] As Moreau argued, indirect discrimination may instantiate negligence on the part of the moral agent—the state authorities in our case—in failing to take seriously into account the interests of disadvantaged groups when designing the rules in question.[78] For this reason, the test of proportionality should assess closely whether the state examined the effects of the rules on the most disadvantaged groups when designing and implementing them.

[71] See generally Sandra Fredman, 'Emerging from the Shadows: Substantive Equality and Article 14 of the European Convention on Human Rights' (2016) 16 Human Rights Law Review 273.

[72] Françoise Tulkens, 'The Contribution of the European Convention on Human Rights to the Poverty Issue in Times of Crisis' (European Court of Human Rights—European Judicial Training Network Seminar, Strasbourg, 8 July 2015) 14.

[73] Aspects of the welfare benefits system in the United Kingdom have also been said to constitute discrimination on the basis of gender. See the discussion in Megan Campbell, 'The Austerity of Lone Motherhood: Discrimination Law and Benefit Reform' (2021) 41 Oxford Journal of Legal Studies 1197.

[74] *DH v Czech Republic* App no 57325/00 (Grand Chamber, 13 November 2007) para 176.

[75] On indirect discrimination under the Convention, see *DH* (n 74).

[76] ibid para 175.

[77] Sophia Moreau, 'The Moral Seriousness of Indirect Discrimination' in Hugh Collins and Tarun Khaitan (eds), *Foundations of Indirect Discrimination Law* (Hart 2018) 123, 143.

[78] ibid 144.

For instance, looking at Universal Credit in the United Kingdom, there is evidence that black and Asian people are disproportionately represented in households that are found in poverty and unemployment, and are therefore in need of welfare support.[79] To the extent then that these groups have been forced into this situation through strict conditionality and harsh sanctions, an argument can be made that the policy is indirectly discriminatory.[80] In cases of destitution or labour exploitation of workers under these schemes, it can be argued that there is a violation of Article 14 together with Article 4 (prohibition of forced and compulsory labour), Article 3 (prohibition of inhuman and degrading treatment), or Article 8 (the right to private life) of the ECHR. These provisions do not have to be breached when invoked in conjunction with Article 14. The action in question simply has to 'fall within their ambit'.[81] The ground of discrimination would be race, and the test of proportionality in the context of Article 14 has to assess closely the effects of the policies on the racial groups that are affected most and examine whether the authorities considered these effects when designing and implementing the rules.

The issue of indirect discrimination in state-mediated structures of injustice affecting precarious workers was tackled by the Court of Justice of the European Union (CJEU), following a request for a preliminary ruling on the exclusion of domestic workers from social security legislation in Spain.[82] The question for the CJEU was whether Spanish legislation that excluded domestic workers from access to social security benefits violated EU Directive 79/7 on equal treatment in matters of social security.[83] The Court observed that the overwhelming majority of domestic workers are women,[84] and that the Spanish legislation at issue places female workers in a particular disadvantage in comparison to male workers, which makes it indirectly discriminatory. Turning to the question of whether this treatment can be justified, the Court found that the proposed justification by the Spanish government is legitimate

[79] UNITE, 'Universal Credit: Not Fit for Purpose' (September 2019) available at <https://unitetheunion.org/media/2631/8869_universal-credit-report_a4_finaldigital.pdf>.

[80] For an example of a successful case of indirect discrimination on the basis of race for people in precarious work, see the employment tribunal Royal Parks decision 2202211/2020, 2204440/2020, and 2205570/2020.

[81] See eg *Thlimmenos v Greece* App no 34369/97 (Grand Chamber, 6 April 2000).

[82] Case C–389/20 *CJ v Tesorería General de la Seguridad Social (TGSS)* 24 February 2022. Noted by Elisa Chieregato, 'The First CJEU Decision on Domestic Workers: The Role of EU Equality Law in Challenging Unjustified Exclusions from Labour Rights and Social Protections' (*European Law Blog*, 8 March 2022) https://europeanlawblog.eu/2022/03/08/the-first-cjeu-decision-on-domestic-workers-the-role-of-eu-equality-law-in-challenging-unjustified-exclusions-from-labour-rights-and-social-protections/ accessed 15 December 2022.

[83] Council Directive 79/7/EEC on the progressive implementation of the principle of equal treatment for men and women on matters of social security OJ L6/24.

[84] ibid para 45.

(having aims such as the encouragement of recruitment), but that the exclusion of this group of workers from social security rights was not suitable as a means to pursue these aims, and was therefore incompatible with the principle of equal treatment in the Directive.[85] This kind of analysis that assesses the effects of seemingly legitimate rules and identifies that these rules may place groups with protected characteristics at a particular disadvantage can play an important role in addressing state-mediated structures of exploitation.

Moreover, it can be said that human rights law may be developing the view that poverty is a prohibited ground of discrimination.[86] On this basis, welfare conditionality schemes that treat people living in poverty with disrespect may be viewed as discriminatory. Poverty is not generally explicitly mentioned in human rights law as a prohibited ground of discrimination and the ECtHR has not yet examined the question directly in its majority rulings, but in some legal orders issues of poverty fit within concepts such as 'social origin' or 'social status',[87] which are prohibited grounds of discrimination. The issue of discrimination on the basis of poverty was discussed in a dissenting opinion in the case of *Wallova and Walla v Czech Republic*.[88] The applicants and their children were separated following court orders, because they could not afford housing that would be spacious enough for the whole family. As the sole reason for the separation was the applicants' material deprivation and inadequate housing, and not their relationship with their children, the action of the authorities was viewed as disproportionate to the aim pursued. The Court explained that:

> in order to comply with the proportionality requirement in this case, the Czech authorities should have considered other measures, less radical than the placement of the children. Indeed, the Court considers that the role of the social welfare authorities is precisely to help people in difficulty who do not have the necessary knowledge of the system, to guide them in their efforts and

[85] ibid art 4(1).

[86] For examples from several jurisdictions, see Olivier de Schutter, 'A Human Rights-Based Approach to Measuring Poverty' in Martha Davis, Morten Kjaerum, and Amanda Lyons (eds), *Research Handbook on Human Rights and Poverty* (Edward Elgar 2021) 2, 5ff; Sarah Ganty, 'Poverty as Misrecognition—What Role for Antidiscrimination Law in Europe' (2021) 21 Human Rights Law Review 962; Shreya Atrey, 'The Intersectional Case of Poverty in Discrimination Law' (2018) 18 Human Rights Law Review 411; Sandra Fredman, 'Redistribution and Recognition: Reconciling Inequalities' (2007) 23 South African Journal on Human Rights 214; Tulkens (n 72).

[87] eg art 26 of the ICCPR; art 2(2) of the ICESCR; art 1 of the ACHR; art 1(1) of the ILO Convention concerning Discrimination in Respect of Employment and Occupation; the UN Educational, Scientific and Cultural Organization Convention against Discrimination in Education; or art 14 of the ECHR and art 1 of Protocol No 12 of the same Convention.

[88] *Wallova and Walla v Czech Republic* App no 23848/04 (Judgment, 26 October 2006).

to advise them, among other things, on the different types of social benefits, the possibilities of obtaining social housing or other means of overcoming their difficulties.[89]

However, the ECtHR ruled that only the right to private life was violated, and in light of this it did not consider whether there was a breach of Article 14.

The issue of poverty as a prohibited ground of discrimination also arose in *Garib v The Netherlands*,[90] which involved the right to choose one's residence under Article 2 of Protocol 4 of the ECHR on freedom of movement. The majority of the Court did not examine the role of poverty as a prohibited ground of discrimination (which was not invoked by the applicant). However, Judge Pinto de Albuquerque, joined by Judge Vehabovic, was critical of this aspect of the majority ruling, and discussed it extensively. He said that poverty 'contains within it a highly destructive potential as it jeopardises the fulfilment of many fundamental freedoms',[91] and explained that many international and national human rights documents prohibit discrimination on the basis of 'economic condition or status' or 'social origin'.[92] He also highlighted that the Inter-American Court of Human Rights has explicitly ruled that poverty is a ground of discrimination.[93] In light of the international and regional approaches to poverty in this context, the dissenting opinion suggested that the ECHR should also be interpreted as prohibiting discrimination on the grounds of poverty.

Structures of injustice that affect workers under welfare conditionality schemes and other precarious workers may in certain circumstances constitute discrimination on grounds of race, gender, or poverty. They can also be examined as instances of intersectional discrimination, as I explain below.

Intersectional discrimination

State-mediated structures of exploitation affecting those employed in precarious work can also be challenged on the basis of intersectional discrimination, which is a category of claims that has emerged more recently in the case law of courts and other monitoring bodies.[94] The concept refers to treatment

[89] ibid, para 74.
[90] *Garib v The Netherlands* App no 43494/09 (Grand Chamber Judgment, 6 November 2017).
[91] ibid para 25.
[92] ibid para 26.
[93] See *Gonzales Lluy et al v Ecuador* Inter-American Court of Human Rights, Series C No 102/13, 1 September 2015.
[94] The term was coined by Kimberlé Crenshaw, 'Demarginalizing the Intersection of Race and Sex: A Black Feminist Critique of Antidiscrimination Doctrine, Feminist Theory and Antiracist Politics' (1989) 1(8) University of Chicago Legal Forum 139. For a thorough analysis of the term in human rights and discrimination law, see Shreya Atrey, *Intersectional Discrimination* (OUP 2019).

of groups that is discriminatory because of a number of protected characteristics. The idea of intersectional discrimination is pertinent in assessing state-mediated structures of exploitation as it focuses on the role of the law in compounding the vulnerability of disadvantaged groups. Equality provisions in human rights law, such as Article 14 of the ECHR, can serve to address this kind of discrimination, and the ECtHR acknowledged this in *BS v Spain*,[95] where it said that 'the decisions made by the domestic courts failed to take account of the applicant's particular vulnerability inherent in her position as an African woman working as a prostitute'.[96] In *Garib*, the Court did not take the opportunity to address intersectional discrimination but was criticised for this reason in the dissenting opinion by Judge Pinto de Albuquerque, joined by Judge Vehabovic, who analysed the concept and explained:

> [T]he applicant's intersectional situation, being both a woman and impoverished, considerably exacerbated her vulnerability *vis-à-vis* the Dutch housing policy in question. In order to assess the effects of the interference with her right to freely choose her residence, the authorities and—all the more so—the Court, should have taken into consideration this particular vulnerability resulting from the combination of a number of factors of discrimination.[97]

A case of the Constitutional Court of South Africa, *Mahlangu v Minister for Labour*,[98] provides an excellent illustration of how human rights law can address intersectional discrimination affecting precarious workers. The Court examined a claim involving rights to social security of domestic workers. It addressed the exclusion of these workers' families from a benefit paid to other workers following injury or death in the workplace, holding it to be in violation of rights to social security, equality, and human dignity. Such exclusions of

[95] *BS v Spain* App no 47159/08 (Judgment, 24 July 2012).

[96] ibid para 62.

[97] *Garib* (n 90) para 39.

[98] *Mahlangu v Minister of Labour* (CCT306/19) [2020] ZACC 24. For a general discussion of equality in this context, see Catherine Albertyn, '(In)equality and the South African Constitution' (2019) 36 Development Southern Africa 751. On *Mahlangu*, see the analysis in Shreya Atrey, 'Beyond Discrimination: Mahlangu and the Use of Intersectionality as a General Theory of Constitutional Interpretation' (2021) 21 International Journal of Discrimination and the Law 168; see also Virginia Mantouvalou and Natalie Sedacca, 'The Human Rights of Domestic Workers: *Mahlangu v Ministry of Labour* and the Transformative Nature of the South African Constitution' (*UK Labour Law Blog*, 11 December 2020) <https://uklabourlawblog.com/2020/12/11/the-human-rights-of-domestic-workers-mahlungu-v-ministry-of-labour-and-the-transformative-nature-of-the-south-african-constitution-by-virginia-mantouvalou-and-natalie-sedacca/> accessed 15 December 2022.

domestic workers from protective labour and social legislation are common in many legal orders.[99] *Mahlangu* marked a decisive step towards addressing the legal rules that exclude this group of precarious workers from protections that other workers enjoy as a matter of intersectional discrimination.

The Court recognised the vulnerability of these workers, placing attention on several factors that cause structural injustice and how these interact. It looked at 'the intersection of compounded vulnerabilities due to intersecting oppression based on race, sex, gender, class and other grounds'.[100] Having acknowledged these factors, the Court examined the exclusion of domestic workers from social security rights and explained that '[t]o allow this form of state-sanctioned inequity goes against the values of our newly constituted society namely human dignity, the achievement of equality and ubuntu'.[101]

The Court emphasised the importance of adopting an intersectional approach to the interpretation of the Constitution in order

> to consider the social structures that shape the experience of marginalised people. It also reveals how individual experiences vary according to multiple combinations of privilege, power, and vulnerability as structural elements of discrimination. An intersectional approach is the kind of interpretative approach which will achieve 'the progressive realisation of our transformative constitutionalism'.[102]

It highlighted that 'the Constitution enjoins us to dismantle [several levels and forms of social differentiation and systematic under-privilege] and to prevent the creation of new patterns of disadvantage', and explained that courts have to examine carefully the situation of claimants, whether they are vulnerable and subject to injustice historically, along with other factors.

Mahlangu illustrates how constitutional human rights can address the exclusion of precarious workers from protective laws on the basis of equality principles. It also exemplifies how trade unions and other actors that participated in the case and continued putting pressure on the government in its aftermath can be involved in claiming the rights of workers in courts and pressurising for impactful legal reform.

[99] See Chapter 2 and the CJEU decision on Spanish legislation (n 82).
[100] *Mahlangu* (n 98) [65].
[101] ibid.
[102] ibid [79].

Organising

The treatment of precarious workers may also violate trade union rights that are protected in several human rights documents.[103] A striking example of exclusions from trade union rights of precarious workers emerged in Chapter 6 when assessing the practice of blacklisting of workers because of their trade union membership or activities.[104] In *Smith v Carillion*, it was ruled that a construction worker could not claim his legal rights because he worked through an agency. Blacklisting of workers because of their trade union activities is known to have had devastating effects on their lives because they were excluded from work with further implications for their income, self-esteem, and personal life.[105] Blacklisting can ground violations of the right to private life and other provisions.[106] However, this is not my primary focus here. Blacklisting is an illegal activity in which some employers engage secretly. If state authorities support it or engage in it, this constitutes direct action with intention to harm, with no legitimate justification in human rights law. In that sense it differs from the state-mediated structures of injustice that I discuss.

My focus instead is on the fact that legal rules on precarious work with an appearance of legitimacy exclude agency workers altogether from protection of their trade union rights. In *Smith*, we saw that the blacklisted worker could not turn against the entity that provided information on his union activities for the purposes of blacklisting, because of his status as an agency worker and the resulting lack of a contractual relationship between him and the entity for which he worked. As a result, he was deprived of the most basic protection of trade union rights: the right to be a member of a trade union without suffering devastating consequences. The claim went up to the ECtHR but the case of *Smith v UK*[107] was declared inadmissible. As Mr Smith was awarded some compensation at domestic level, the Court ruled that he had not met the admissibility criterion of the ECHR according to which a victim has to suffer 'significant disadvantage'.[108] It is unfortunate that the Court did not examine

[103] See eg art 11 of the ECHR; arts 5 and 6 of the European Social Charter; art 22 of the ICCPR; art 8 ICESCR; freedom of association is also included in the ILO Declaration of Fundamental Principles and Rights at Work, adopted in 1998 and amended in 2022. For further discussion of this issue, see Valerio De Stefano, 'Non-Standard Work and Limits on Freedom of Association: A Human Rights-Based Approach' (2017) 46 Industrial Law Journal 185.

[104] *Smith v Carillion* [2015] EWCA Civ 209, [2015] IRLR 467. See discussion in Chapter 6.

[105] This has been documented extensively in publications of the Institute of Employment Rights. The first publication was by Keith Ewing, *Ruined Lives—Blacklisting in the UK Construction Industry* (IER 2009).

[106] See Virginia Mantouvalou, 'Human Rights, Labour Rights and Criminal Wrongs' in Alan Bogg and others (eds), *Criminality at Work* (OUP 2019) 210.

[107] *Smith v UK* App no 54357/15 (Admissibility Decision, 28 March 2017).

[108] See art 35(3)(b) of the ECHR.

the merits, despite the gravity of the issue. Had the Court assessed its merits, it is hard to see how blacklisting workers because of their union membership with no remedy to challenge this because of legal rules on the regulation of agency work in the United Kingdom could be ruled to be compatible with the Convention.[109]

Conclusion

The aim of these last two chapters was to argue that human rights law can help focus on the role of the state in producing the wrongs in question, offer a route to challenge some of the injustices, and hold the authorities accountable for exacerbating workers' vulnerability to exploitation. When legal rules set up the background conditions for workers to be exploited, human rights law can be employed to challenge the lawfulness of some of these rules and help destabilise the unjust structures in question. My objective was not to provide a comprehensive account of human rights violations that arise in state-mediated structures of injustice, but to offer a critical overview of central provisions and highlight possibilities for presenting the argument on the basis of human rights law. It is important to be reminded here that for structural change to occur, a number of actors need to engage and a variety of strategies need to be employed. Workers and their organisations should consider carefully which avenues for structural reform are promising in each instance, and use different methods to bring it about. In this context, with the involvement of several actors, I argued that human rights law can provide useful and powerful tools to achieve legal, cultural, and broader structural change.

[109] *Wilson, National Union of Journalists v UK* App nos 30668/96, 30671/96, and 30678/96 (Judgment, 2 July 2002).

9
Epilogue

The law should not be exacerbating and entrenching the vulnerability of the most disadvantaged and marginalised workers. That identifiable legal rules with an appearance of legitimacy, which regulate labour, play this role is wrong. In this book I explained this legal and social problem. I sought to expose the reality that sometimes people who are disadvantaged are not in this position simply because of unscrupulous employers, general market relations, or other background factors, but because of legislation. On the basis of legal rules, large numbers of people are exploited, while many others benefit from this situation. A typical policy response to labour exploitation in recent years is to criminalise employers and others who engage in its most serious forms.[1] This is at best inadequate, and at worst distracting. Punishing isolated employers who engage in serious abuse cannot be a sufficient response when we are dealing with a systemic problem, consisting in patterns of exploitation that affect large numbers of people. We need to look at the bigger picture and question the rationale and effectiveness of this response. If we shift attention away from criminal responsibility for severe labour exploitation, it may seem impossible to identify moral agents who play a major role in this structural problem. Yet, I explained that sometimes when we are faced with workers' exploitation that appears to be structural, we should examine the role of the law more closely, for it may be that legal rules are partly to blame for this problem.

To illustrate my point, I discussed legal rules that affect different categories of disadvantaged workers. I examined the position of migrant workers who are employed under restrictive visas, who will become undocumented if they escape abusive employers, as well as undocumented workers, underpaid or unpaid, who are often excluded from the labour rights that other workers have. I then turned to captive workers: those who work when in prison or immigration detention, as well as other offenders who are required to work while being excluded from labour rights, such as a minimum wage, trade union

[1] I referred to this in Chapter 1 when I referred to the UK Modern Slavery Act 2015 and in Chapter 3 where I discussed the treatment of migrant domestic workers in the United Kingdom. See further Virginia Mantouvalou, 'The Modern Slavery Act Three Years On' (2018) 81 Modern Law Review 1017.

Structural Injustice and Workers' Rights. Virginia Mantouvalou, Oxford University Press. © Virginia Mantouvalou 2023.
DOI: 10.1093/oso/9780192857156.003.0009

rights, and social security rights. In that context we saw that criminal offenders and immigration detainees are faced with a continuum of exploitation. Very often coming from backgrounds with limited opportunities, they work for the state or private entities, with hardly any pay or other labour rights, and frequently under the threat of sanctions, including criminal sanctions. Instead of being supported and rehabilitated, they find themselves caught in cycles of exploitation. Immigration detainees who have been victims of trafficking are held and exploited in immigration detention, deported, and placed at risk of re-trafficking.

I also examined welfare conditionality schemes, and particularly the most punitive schemes of strict conditionality that require benefit claimants to accept insecure work, and impose harsh sanctions on them if they do not comply with the requirements placed upon them. I explained that these may force people into precarious work that they do not want to do for otherwise they may be faced with destitution. Even though there is a promise that work is the best route out of poverty, we observed that the unemployed poor become working and exploited poor. Finally, I examined certain instances of precarious work, particularly zero-hours contracts and agency work, to show how the law sometimes excludes these workers from important protections that others enjoy. These areas were just some examples where we identify the problem, and the list is not exhaustive. Similar issues emerge in other fields, such as working conditions in global supply chains and the regulation of non-standard work more broadly.[2] In trying to understand these laws, I also looked at empirical evidence in the work of academic scholars, non-governmental organisations, journalists, trade unions, and think tanks that specialise in each of the fields. Given the fact that the laws in question have an appearance of legitimacy, and that many of these workers are already marginalised, stigmatised, underunionised, underrepresented in politics, and fearful of the authorities, the evidence that shows the effects of the law on them was of vital importance.

I placed all this against a novel theoretical framework of state-mediated structures of injustice at work. This helped maintain awareness of the broader structural factors that create vulnerability, while also gaining a better understanding of the role of the law in compounding unjust structures. Clear patterns of legal rules that exclude disadvantaged workers from important protections

[2] See Maeve McKeown, 'The Law's Contribution to Deliberate Structural Injustice' in Virginia Mantouvalou and Jonathan Wolff (eds), *Structural Injustice and the Law* (forthcoming); Hugh Collins, 'Segmented Labour Markets, Structural Injustice and Legal Remedies' in the same volume. The contributions in the volume explore several instances of structural injustice and the role of the law therein.

are discernible from the above discussion, and empirical evidence also shows that these patterns multiply and detrimentally impact workers' lives.

In her theory of structural injustice, Young explained that no-one is responsible for the injustice that Sandy suffered, but everyone has forward-looking, political responsibility to address it. While Young was right that everyone has political responsibility to address structures of injustice, it is important to underline that the state may have special political responsibility to address the injustice because it has contributed to it.[3]

I could have ended this inquiry here. The point could be that legal rules with an appearance of legitimacy are responsible for increasing vulnerability to exploitation and structures of exploitation and that the authorities have a political obligation to change these rules to make them more just. People are vulnerable and disadvantaged for many reasons, including race, gender, migration, and poverty, and the role of the law must be to support them and address the power imbalance at work. Instead, we saw that certain legal rules compound disadvantage and set up the conditions for people to fail. This realisation is disturbing. These legal rules have no place in a fair legal system, and the state has responsibility to change them.

However, if we identify legal rules that are to blame for a social problem, we may also be able to challenge some of these rules through law. The law is a powerful institution. It can misallocate power but it can also help challenge unjust structures in society and the economy, and reallocate power more fairly. I therefore argued that, in addition to constituting a moral wrong, aspects of this situation may constitute a legal wrong that the authorities have a responsibility to address. This responsibility can be grounded in human rights law. To this end, I considered how human rights law can hold the authorities accountable for these state-mediated structures of injustice at work.

Human rights typically have higher status that other legislation in many legal orders. They have increased legal force, so to speak. Courts and other monitoring bodies assess compliance of state conduct with them. When they rule that state conduct, including legislation, executive action, or lower courts' decisions, violates human rights, they can declare it incompatible with human rights law, order remedies, and require that the law changes. Many of the human rights cases that I discussed were from the European human

[3] Powers and Faden also assign responsibility to the state to secure structural justice because of their role in distributing power and the normative position of state authorities. See Madison Powers and Ruth Faden, *Structural Injustice—Power, Advantage and Human Rights* (OUP 2019). See particularly 114–15, and their ch 6.

rights system, and mostly from the ECtHR that has a long, developed, and influential jurisprudence. I also referred to rulings of other national courts and international bodies that have examined some of the issues that I addressed.

In some of these instances, court decisions and other monitoring bodies' findings have maintained that legal rules that regulate labour increase vulnerability to exploitation and violate human rights law, including the prohibition of slavery, servitude, and forced or compulsory labour, the right to private life, the right to work, the right to property, the right to social security, and the prohibition of discrimination. A judicial finding that there is a violation of human rights law can be a significant step. In order to comply with judgments, there is often legislative change. This can be crucial. To give one example, a change in a visa scheme that ties migrant workers to an employer, or the recognition that they have a right to be paid for their work despite the fact that they are undocumented cannot address all the structural problems that affect migrant workers. However, a change in the visa recognising an unconditional right to change employer, as well as labour rights when they are employed, can help them exit work with less fear of destitution and deportation, challenge the employer in court, and look for a new job while having secure legal status. Prison labour can be important for the rehabilitation of prisoners, yet not when they are seriously underpaid or when they are excluded from labour rights, such as trade union organising and activity. Welfare conditionality schemes can support people to not live in poverty, but not when they are forced into precarious work under the threat of destitution. Work can be a key source of income and self-realisation, but exploitative work does not meet these ends. It also breaches human rights provisions. On this basis, changes of legal rules that are a source of state-mediated structures of injustice will recognise that these disadvantaged workers have rights like all other workers.

The legal rules that I discussed in Chapters 3 to 6 have to change, and it is not my purpose (or the role and purpose of courts and other monitoring bodies) to make detailed legislative and policy proposals. These will vary from one country to another. It is for legislatures and policymakers to consider how they will reform the legislation in order to make it compliant with human rights standards, as well as to develop detailed plans on its enforcement. The general direction is clear. Legal rules should not increase vulnerability, compound disadvantage, and entrench structures of exploitation that disadvantage large numbers of people while others benefit from this situation. Migrant workers should not be tied to an employer, and visas must provide a route to settlement and citizenship in the country where they work because the fear of deportation if they escape exploitative employers undermines all their rights. They should also not be required to live in the employer's premises unless it is truly essential for their job. When it is, their living and working conditions have to be humane and to comply with the requirements of the right to private life and to health and safety at work. Undocumented workers must not be excluded from the protection of labour rights that all other workers enjoy.

Workers in prison, immigration detention, and offenders sentenced to community service must not be excluded from protection of their labour rights. Work is not meant to be their punishment. They therefore have to enjoy rights to a minimum wage and working time, rights to organise and make demands regarding their working conditions, as well as rights to social security. Those in need of welfare benefits must not be forced into insecure and exploitative work through which they cannot make a living. Work is not punishment for this group of workers either: it is supposed to support them to leave poverty. Workers in the most precarious arrangements, including those on zero-hours contracts and agency workers, have to be entitled to workers' rights, like everyone else, and to be able to turn against the employer with whom they work to claim these rights. Not only should the legal rules change, but also, when they are amended, their possible effects have to be carefully considered, and the new protective rules should be effectively enforced.

Courts are often powerful actors that can take decisions which lead to legal change, as mentioned earlier. However, because of the nature of these claims, and particularly the fact that they involve issues of labour and social rights, they may at times be reluctant to interfere with the unjust structures in question. They should not be. The increase of vulnerability through law in a way that compounds disadvantage can be viewed (and has been viewed in several of the examples that I discussed in Chapters 7 and 8) as a legal wrong on the basis of existing human rights commitments at national and supranational level.

In this process, courts face significant pressures from other powerful actors, such as branches of government that may threaten non-compliance if they are dissatisfied with their rulings. The balancing exercise is challenging but courts should resist these pressures. Several agents need to engage with both the legal and political process, in order to implement the rulings and remove the rules that violate workers' rights, to bring about change in the culture as well as broader structural change. Civil society organisations, including trade unions, are often involved in litigation, and particularly strategic litigation, supporting claimants and bringing test cases which may lead to outcomes beneficial for a large number of people who are not represented directly in court. They can also press for cultural and structural change in different aspects of the political process, by lobbying the government, raising awareness of the social problems, organising workers, and taking collective action against exploitative working arrangements. All these actors have political responsibility of the kind that Young developed to act against these unjust structures which violate human rights, as well as broader principles of equality and justice.

Compliance with findings of monitoring bodies that do not have the status of a court, such as the European Committee of Social Rights (ECSR) or UN Special Rapporteurs, is far from perfect of course. This is a problem but no one strategy for change is perfect. When there is reluctance to comply, their materials that provide reasons explaining why there is a violation of human rights can play a valuable role in raising awareness, enriching debates, exerting political pressure, and can also be used in litigation to help with the interpretation of justiciable norms. Even if, say, a report of the UN Special Rapporteur on Extreme Poverty and Human Rights or the International Labour Organization does not bring about immediate legislative change, it can set in motion social processes that can lead to change in the longer term. It can raise awareness, serve as evidence in litigation, attract media attention, inspire academic debate, and provide support to efforts of civil society groups. Structural change is not a quick or easy process, and it has to be pursued in different ways. Legal change is crucial, but it also has to be accompanied by change in people's culture. Human rights law, with its moral force, can help support this cultural change by engaging and changing minds, and providing powerful tools to activists who campaign for political change.

Moreover, human rights law cannot address all structures of injustice and is also not the only way in which unjust structures can be challenged. Social justice and redistribution for a fairer workplace and society are broader projects that involve many actors. My purpose was neither to provide a comprehensive theory of justice at work nor full strategic and detailed policy proposals. My aim was to diagnose concrete wrongs affecting vulnerable and marginalised groups, where legal rules with an appearance of legitimacy have a significant role to play, and examine how the law can also be used to bring about change. The steps to be taken in response are urgent and can have broad impact, as

I explained earlier. Moreover, workplace exploitation and poverty are not the only structures of injustice that are connected to precarious work. Influential studies analysing the social determinants of health that are associated with health inequality, including lower life expectancy, identified precarious work arrangements as a central factor of ill-health.[4] Change in the legal rules that I examined is an urgent legal, political, and moral duty, and can contribute to the improvement of many aspects of workers' lives.

[4] See Michael Marmot and others, *Health Equity in England: The Marmot Review Ten Years On* (Institute of Health Equity 2020).

Index

For the benefit of digital users, indexed terms that span two pages (e.g., 52–53) may, on occasion, appear on only one of those pages.